170

27

Canadian Values in the World Community

Building Trust
Balancing Global Power

Canadian Values
in the World Community
Building Trust
Balancing Global Power

The Sheldon Chumir Foundation
for Ethics in Leadership

Edited by Marsha P. Hanen
and David W. Cassels

Copyright © 2005 The Sheldon M. Chumir Foundation

Paperback ISBN 0-9730197-2-7

Printed on acid free paper in Canada by Friesens Corporation

Cover design by Sharon Abra Hanen and David Cassels

———————————

Library and Archives Canada Cataloguing in Publication

Canadian values in the world community: building trust, balancing global power / edited by Marsha P. Hanen and David W. Cassels.

Proceedings of a symposium held in Calgary, Alberta, May 14-16, 2004.

1. Canada–Foreign relations–Moral and ethical aspects–Congresses. 2. Canada–Foreign relations–1945-–Congresses. 3. Canada–Moral conditions–Congresses. I. Hanen, Marsha P., 1936- II. Cassels, David W., 1959- III. Sheldon M. Chumir Foundation for Ethics in Leadership

FC242.C455 2005   172'.4'0971   C2005-905351-8

Contents

Acknowledgements

This book grows out of the third public Symposium of the Sheldon Chumir Foundation for Ethics in Leadership,[1] held on the weekend of May 14-16, 2004. Entitled "Canadian Values in the World Community: Building Trust, Balancing Global Power", the Symposium brought together a group of outstanding speakers who spent the weekend engaging in an ongoing dialogue with Symposium participants from Calgary and many parts of Canada.

By the time of publication, it will have been some fifteen months since that Symposium took place and, as we prepared the volume for publication, we have had the benefit of reflection on the topics of the event from a number of our major speakers. There has also been a considerable amount of discussion in the media and in government about Canada's role on the international stage. Much of what is contained in this volume will serve as a useful commentary on that discussion and, we hope, an extension of it.

Naturally, any effort of this sort comes together only as a result of a great deal of work by a great many individuals, and we wish to express our thanks to all of them. As always, our first debt of gratitude is owed to the Symposium presenters whose work is represented here: Andrew Cohen, Jennifer Welsh, David Bercuson, Clifford Krauss, George Russell, Paul Heinbecker, Ahmad Kamal, Arnoldo Listre, Karl Henriques, Michael Byers, Roy Lee, David Wright, Kathleen Mahoney, Madelaine Drohan and Robert Kagan. Joel Bell provided an introduction to the Symposium, reproduced here as the Introduction to the volume, which set the stage and raised the

---

[1]Further information about the Sheldon Chumir Foundation's programs and publications is available on the website at www.chumirethicsfoundation.ca.

questions to be addressed during the succeeding two days. Each of the speakers responded with unfailing enthusiasm to the opportunity to participate in the Symposium, and nearly everyone spent the entire weekend engaging with each other and with the audience in meaningful discussion of the topics at hand. One of the more prolonged and interesting such discussions was transcribed and appears here as the conclusion to Section V. Each participant either provided a text of his or her remarks, or agreed to the editing of a transcript of their actual Symposium talk. For all of this, we express our profound gratitude. Biographies of all authors appear toward the end of the volume.

Joel Bell, David Taras, Marsha Hanen, Michael Keren, Aritha van Herk and Ronald Bond served as chairs or moderators of sessions, and we are grateful to each of them. Paul Heinbecker, in addition to his luncheon address on the first full day of the Symposium, kindly agreed to provide some summary comments at the end of the second day's sessions, to give an impression of the flow of the discussion and some of the themes that emerged. Appendix A is an outline of his synopsis. The audience was unusually engaged throughout the Symposium, contributing insightful questions and comments which helped to advance the discussion along fruitful lines. So we thank each of the participants most warmly.

As well, the program on the last afternoon involved a series of discussion groups devoted to particular aspects of the topics of Canadian values in the world community. Each group had two or more facilitators, who helped to make the discussion stay focused and run smoothly. Those who gave of their time in this way were: Amanda Affonso, Kristen Boon, Suzanne Boss, Bediako Buahene, Alison Dempsey, Bruce Foster, Christian Idicula, Janet Keeping, Cynthia Mackenzie, Michelle McCann, Donna McElligott, Nahid Nenshi, Duyen Nguyen, Chima Nkemdirim, Ruth Shapiro and Elaine Ward. They all did an excellent job and we thank them all. Cynthia Mackenzie played a major role in organizing these groups, briefing the facilitators and generally making sure the sessions proceeded in a way that would be useful to developing the themes of the conference. Colin Jackson was a most able and engaging moderator of the final wrap-up session in which the various reports were presented and discussed; and Michelle McCann carefully crafted the various reports, which were presented orally, together with her own notes into the report which appears here as Appendix B, using as a basis the oral reports and her own notes.

The Symposium itself, and especially the participation of a large number of students, was made possible through the generosity of several sponsors: our partners, the Kahanoff Foundation, who have unfailingly supported our work on a number of occasions; the University of Calgary and Mount Royal College who helped to make it possible for a substantial group of students to participate in the Symposium; our sponsors C.D. O'Brien of Bennett Jones, Barristers and Solicitors, and Mawer Investment Management; and supporters Nexen Inc. Generous support was also extended by James Whitehouse of National Bank Financial, Petro-Canada, CIBC, and Steve Sparks and friends; and The Calgary Herald and Sheraton Suites Eau Claire provided in-kind sponsorship. We extend our thanks to each of these organizations.

CBC IDEAS taped the Symposium sessions and has aired, on several occasions, a program narrated by Paul Kennedy entitled *Values Are Not Enough*[2] using excerpts from a number of the presentations. We are most grateful to Senior Producer Dave Redel for his partnership in this venture and his excellent insights around which to frame the program.

The Honorable Ron Ghitter Q.C., member of the Foundation's Board, once again ably chaired the gala dinner and speech by Robert Kagan, contributing his insights into the events of the weekend. Foundation staff and volunteers Alison Dempsey, Michelle McCann, Linda Van Dyke, Chris & Lydia Wojtkiw, Allison Wojtkiw, and Stacey Benedet contributed greatly to the success of the event; David Cassels took responsibility for audio-visual matters, for much of the technical preparation and for support of our guests; and Elaine Wojtkiw's

---

[2] *Values Are Not Enough* can be ordered on audio CD from www.cbc.ca/ideas/transcripts/index.html or by calling CBC IDEAS in Toronto at (416) 205-6010.

organizational skills were in evidence at every stage and every level of the planning and execution of the event, ensuring that all details were dealt with and that the atmosphere was pleasant and welcoming throughout.

David Cassels has played a major role in the preparation of the manuscript for publication, from transcribing tapes to editing the articles and from ongoing contact with all contributors to producing the manuscript and working with the printers. His careful attention to form and detail as well as his technical and design skills are evident throughout the book. Where we had to work with transcripts of tapes of the sessions, we have attempted to preserve the immediacy and conversational tone of the Symposium presentations while ensuring that the editing would help to make the resulting volume easy to read. The cover, based on a design by Sharon Abra Hanen, was developed by David Cassels and Sharon Abra Hanen. David Cassels, Marsha Hanen, Kelly Hogan and Heather MacIntosh all participated in the proofreading of the manuscript, in hopes of making the final volume as error-free as possible.

Gerhard Aichelberger of Friesens Printing has been most helpful in publication arrangements. The photograph of Sheldon Chumir on the back cover was taken by Brian Harder. The other photos on the cover are, left to right: Madelaine Drohan (by Sebastian Citro), Andrew Cohen (from The *Ottawa Citizen*), Paul Heinbecker (Wilfrid Laurier University Public Affairs), Jennifer Welsh (photographers-workshop.com), and Robert Kagan (by Claudio Vasquez).

Finally, we express our appreciation to the Foundation's Board, Chairman Joel Bell, The Honorable Ron Ghitter, Q.C., Mr. Justice Clifton D. O'Brien and Professor Aritha van Herk for their unfailing support of the publication project and the Symposium from which it resulted. Joel Bell was fully engaged at all stages of the planning of the Symposium, and his involvement had a major influence on its focus and content. Cliff O'Brien provided moral and financial support and Aritha van Herk not only chaired a session but was unfailingly present whenever needed. Ron Ghitter's involvement, as always, encompassed the entire project and his chairing of the gala dinner made it a warm and memorable event.

Preface

Canadians have, for many years, been much exercised by the question of Canada's role in the world and the part that values – specifically Canadian values or more universal ones – should play in defining that role. In 2003, Andrew Cohen's important book, *While Canada Slept: How We Lost Our Place in the World* appeared, to great acclaim and general consternation. Was it really true that our influence in the world was seriously diminished from the days of Prime Minister Lester B. Pearson? And was it the case that our self-image, as the world's peacekeeper and honest broker in international affairs, was seriously at variance with reality? What place should be accorded to more recent manifestations of our foreign policy in the promotion of human security, 'soft' power, anti-landmines activity and an International Criminal Court?

At the same time, the first foreign policy review since 1995 was underway, with nationwide consultations, academic conferences and numerous discussions about the direction we should be taking occupying the policy stage for many months. Meanwhile, a new book by Oxford political scientist and Canadian Jennifer Welsh was much anticipated both in government and in the academy, and some of Dr. Welsh's views formed part of the policy discussion.

This was the context within which we organized the third major Symposium of the Sheldon Chumir Foundation for Ethics in Leadership.[1] This volume presents the proceedings of that Symposium "Canadian Values in the World Community: Building Trust, Balancing Global Power" held on the weekend of May 14th-16th, 2004, in Calgary, Alberta, Canada. The pro-

---

[1] For further information about the Sheldon Chumir Foundation's programs and publications, please see the website at www.chumirethicsfoundation.ca

gram brought together an array of extraordinary speakers to address a variety of critical questions concerning the nature and role of Canadian values in an international context. We wanted to deal with questions of just what values count as Canadian, whether they differ in important respects from the values held by people in other democracies, whether our values are at odds with Canada's economic and political interests in particular situations and, if so, which should prevail.

As part of our series of "flagship" Symposia the program planning, as always, engaged the question of how the Sheldon Chumir Foundation for Ethics in Leadership could, at this time, best fulfill its mandate of supporting the open expression and dissemination of ideas and tolerant discussion, and its commitment to exposing prejudice, by providing a forum for informed dialogue on important public issues that have an ethical dimension. The issue of Canada's role in the world had elicited strong, and frequently conflicting, views. Have we lost our 'moral force' on the international stage, and if so, why? Again, if so, what can be done to regain it? Or is the view that we are less powerful in the world based on a misconception, and even confusion, between power and influence? The context of this discussion included considerable questioning within the Canadian government of Canada's role in the world in the early part of the 21st century. Government was in process of preparing the first new public statement of foreign policy directions and priorities in ten years, and we hoped to be able to contribute to this discussion as it continued, even after the expected release of the foreign policy document.

That is, then, the purpose of this book: to encapsulate in a single volume some of the best concentrated thinking on the nature and role of Canada and Canadian values on a variety of topics ranging from our relations with the U.S. to how we are perceived in other parts of the world and how that should influence our actions; from our involvement in international institutions to how Canadian business might play a positive role in informal foreign policy; and to considering the question of whether we have a part to play in helping to reconcile some of differences between the U.S. and Europe concerning power, influence and leadership in the world. We also wished to model the involvement of younger Canadians in these deliberations, both in their presence and questioning at all sessions of the Symposium, and also in a number of discussion groups held toward the end of the Symposium. Certain important topics touching on Canada's role in the world would be addressed by groups led by two moderators, one of whom was, in each case, a younger person, usually someone involved with the very active organization *Canada 25*.

The way in which the discussion developed through the weekend was fascinating to behold. The questions being addressed were, after all, extremely challenging and difficult, requiring concentrated analysis and attention to detail, and all of our participants rose to the occasion magnificently. Not only did nearly all of the speakers make themselves available for the entire duration of the Symposium, but they did so by engaging the audience and their fellow speakers in an ongoing conversation, visiting and revisiting topics and positions, sharing ideas in a way that was not only valuable in terms of content but also respectful of varying positions and perspectives. The questions and comments from the audience were perhaps the most informed and incisive that we have seen at any of these events, contributing enormously to advancing the discussion as the program went on.

To ensure that our discussion would start on the best possible footing, we selected as our keynote speakers both Andrew Cohen, author of *While Canada Slept: How We Lost our Place in the World* and Jennifer Welsh, whose book *At Home in the World: Canada's Global Vision for the 21st Century* was published some months after the Symposium and was highly influential in shaping Canada's articulation of its foreign policy directions for the future. We were delighted to have their participation, and our keynoters did not disappoint, as you will see from reading their contributions.

We have also included here the introductory remarks to the entire Symposium made by our Board Chair Joel Bell, which were intended to set the stage for the various presentations to follow throughout the weekend, to direct our attention to some of the many questions we wished to address and the interrelationships among them and to provide a framework for thinking about Canadian values and Canada's role in the world.

As another introduction to the Symposium, we asked all participants, both audience and speakers, to think about two main issues:[2] the nature and role of Canadian values in an international context and the relationship between our values and our interests – economic, political, cultural and military. As a multicultural nation and a society with a policy of constructive engagement in North America and the world, Canada appears to be uniquely positioned both to provide leadership in, and to benefit from, globalization. But if we are to benefit from globalization, perhaps we need to do so in a strategic way, concentrating on those areas that fit best with our capabilities and our values, with a keen eye to the role ethics can play in our international leadership.

The question we wished to address was: just what role(s) can and should Canada be playing in the world over the next decade or two? Although not a major power, many have argued that this does not preclude Canada's ability to exercise considerable influence on the world stage. If we wish to exercise such influence, what paths must we follow? What should be our areas of focus in international relations, and how should we go about deciding this? Do we have a role to play in helping to build trust internationally and balance global power? And what does this have to do with Canadian values?

In the contemporary world, both Canada's interests and its values appear to demand strategic and innovative global engagement. We already have many of the tools necessary for this task. Virtually every country, culture, and religion is represented within our borders and, with over a million Canadians living around the world, we are ideally positioned to operate as both conduit and locus for the transnational exchange of ideas, knowledge, and people.

---

[2] Cynthia Mackenzie contributed an early draft of the issues to be discussed.

Knowing of this opportunity, can we make a claim to having 'Canadian values' to guide us in building this trust and international reputation? And if so, what *are* those values?

When we ask what kinds of values Canadians are thought to espouse in relation to our role in the world, we are often said to believe in democracy, freedom, equality, human rights, human security, peacekeeping and peacebuilding, promoting a sustainable environment for all, adequate health care, education and social programs, investment in children, pluralism, fiscal responsibility and accountability, and balancing individual autonomy with collective responsibility. A long list.

Are some of these values "Canadian"? All? any? or others that should be included? Or is the aggregation of them 'uniquely' Canadian? Does it matter that we agree on the details of just which values are Canadian? Or is it more important that we agree that some notion of a national value system exists in Canada, and that we agree that this value system ought to be important in our determination of how we deal with international policy priorities and decisions? Indeed, would it be more fruitful to characterize our values in relation to what we are *not,* so as more clearly to differentiate ourselves from others?

References to Canadian values in the context of foreign policy are sometimes seen as naïve. After all, in the world of realpolitik, the argument goes, we must surely base decisions and actions on Canada's interests in achieving certain ends for the good of the country. But the question arises: to what extent is there a tension between acting on our values and acting out of interests? Do we necessarily sacrifice our best interests if we make ethical, values-based decisions in foreign policy?

A commonly held belief is that Canada (in common with other countries) both should (and necessarily does) act in its own interests. That is, as a nation of middle power with a potentially strong role to play in the international community, we should be acting out of a directive to meet our domestic best interests, irrespective of other competing national or values-based demands. This argument seems to rest on an assumption that in order to meet our national interests,

Canadian values must necessarily come lower down among our considerations and may even, at least much of the time, be at cross-purposes with our interests. Is this in fact the case?

For example, should Canada assist in stabilizing the HIV/Aids crisis in southern Africa because we believe we have a moral responsibility to do so, or should we act in this situation because we understand that a country so destroyed by a major plague – and one which may leave millions of children without an adult presence – is a threat to global security, and ultimately, Canadian security?

In this situation Canada's interests and our values seem to lead us to the same policy and result. The question we need to ask is: is this convergence always, or at least frequently the case, so that attention to our interests and our values typically work in tandem? Is it important that we do the right thing for reasons prompted by our values and morality, or is it enough that we do the right thing, regardless of our motives? And, in cases where our interests may be in conflict with our values, which should prevail? To what extent and where can (and should) we commit to taking the moral high ground, no matter what the consequences?

Perhaps the representation of interests and values as in opposition to one another presents us with a false dichotomy: perhaps a fuller discourse about directions for foreign policy needs to address both Canada's interests and Canadian values, and needs to ask how these approaches can be balanced and reconciled. Perhaps, indeed, interests and values are frequently complementary. Certainly we are hearing more and more, especially from younger voices, that the language of values matters, and must be expressed in discussions of interests-based foreign policy.

In the example of the HIV/AIDS crisis, it is reasonable to point out that Canadian foreign policy, in recognizing that the need to stabilize the political situation in Africa, depends on both moral and interest-based arguments, and that both may have essentially the same ends in view: global security, peace, prosperity, and a key role for Canada in the facilitation of those conditions. We could reasonably argue that Canadian foreign policy must not only engage in international areas of crisis and conflict, but must assist in building the capacity of these states to solve some of the problems that confront them. And this may be an example of a way in which Canada can help to build trust across national boundaries and play a key role as an 'honest broker' in the international community. But we also need to ask whether the "honest broker" role is enough for Canada's sense of its potential contributions in the 21st century.

As Canadians, should we insist that space be made for values-based discussions, even in the midst of tough interests-based international policy? If so, how should this be done? Attention to values in contradistinction to interests is seen as, at best, a distraction by some; but others think the distinction a red herring, in that our values and our interests are, and must be, inextricably intertwined.

In some ways, these questions arise most obviously in our considerations of our relations with the U.S. Indeed, the centrality of that relationship caused us to undertake a prior discussion of exactly these issues at a conference entitled "Redefining U.S.-Canada Relations" and held in New York City on May 7, 2004 – a week before the beginning of our Symposium. That conference, co-presented by The Council for Canadian-American Relations, the Council of the Americas/Americas Society, The Center for Global Finance at Pace University and the Sheldon Chumir Foundation for Ethics in Leadership, provided a concentrated introduction to the topics of one of the key sessions of our Symposium one week later in Calgary.

The program in New York featured Canadian and American speakers on a range of topics, including attitudes and issues between our two countries, and possible approaches to further developing the relationship. The programme was as follows:

Session I: Attitudes and Issues
- **Thomas Axworthy,** Executive Director, The Historica Foundation of Canada, Toronto
- **Karl Meyer,** Editor, *World Policy Journal*, New School University, New York

Moderator/Discussant:
- **Pamela Wallin,** Consul General, Canadian Consulate General, New York

Session II: Possible Approaches to Moving Ahead
- **John Manley,** Former Deputy Prime Minister and Minister of Finance of Canada
- **Tom Niles,** President, U.S. Council for International Business (USCIB), New York
- **John (Rick) MacArthur,** Publisher, *Harper's Magazine,* New York
- **Andrew Coyne,** National Affairs Columnist, Publisher, *The National Post,* Toronto

Moderator/Discussant:
- **Susan Kaufman Purcell,** Vice President, Council of the Americas, New York

Session III: Suggesting a Path Forward
- **Janice Stein,** Director, Centre for International Studies, University of Toronto, Canada

Moderator/Discussant:
- **Joel Bell,** Chair of the Board, Sheldon Chumir Foundation for Ethics in Leadership and of the Council for Canadian-American Relations

Because of the importance and constant presence of the Canada-U.S relationship, we devoted an entire session of the Symposium to this relationship, and you will see that many of the questions we had raised are addressed here by David Bercuson, Clifford Krauss and George Russell. Directly following this session, some of the assumptions and conclusions of the speakers were directly challenged in a luncheon address by Paul Heinbecker, currently Director of the Centre for Global Relations, Governance and Policy at Wilfrid Laurier University, Senior Research Fellow at the Centre for International Governance Innovation, and recently retired from his post as Canadian Ambassador to the United Nations. Ambassador Heinbecker's remarks provide an interesting and important contrast with those of our earlier three speakers, showing that there are many conversations still to be had on this topic.

From the Canada-U.S. relationship we moved to a discussion of some views of Canada's international role from other parts of the world – from former United Nations Ambassadors from Argentina (Arnoldo Listre), Pakistan (Ahmad Kamal), and from a specialist on Europe (Karl Henriques). It was clear from this session and the discussion which followed that Canada is seen not only in a positive light within some international institutions but also as a nation able to make a difference in moving the UN forward.

A discussion of Canada's role in international institutions more broadly conceived was the obvious next step, and we were fortunate to have Michael Byers, Roy Lee, David Wright and Kathleen Mahoney to present their varied views on this topic. The discussion following this session was a model of the kind of engagement we had hoped for and which we, in fact, experienced throughout the weekend. The discussion is reproduced here following the session papers, not only to exhibit the way in which the conversation developed but also to show the committed involvement of our speakers during the entire Symposium.

As an example of another kind of international engagement, Madelaine Drohan provided a practical and balanced look at some of the roles being played by Canadian business in Africa. Her analysis provides ways of looking at what Canada might do in this sort of international context, and how we might proceed in constructive ways.

We asked Ambassador Heinbecker to prepare some summary comments about what he and we had heard during the weekend, and a version of these is reproduced here as Appendix A. Appendix B is a brief digest of the reports offered by the various discussion groups which convened on the final afternoon of the Symposium.

Robert Kagan, our concluding speaker at the gala closing dinner, had recently published an afterword to his very influential book *Of Paradise and Power* (as well as articles in such publications as *Foreign Affairs* and *The New York Times*) in which he raised serious questions about perceptions of American legitimacy in the international community. It was a considerable departure from his position in the first edition of his book, and we asked him to address this issue at the Symposium. He offered an analysis of some of the differences he perceives between the U.S. and Europe, and some suggestions about a way forward not only for the U.S. and Europe, but also for Canada on the international stage.

Clearly, the notion of 'legitimacy' has come to occupy a central place in justificatory discussions in relation, particularly, to intervention in the affairs of sovereign states and to the 'responsibility to protect' or, more recently, the 'responsibility to prevent'. So the question of what brings legitimacy to a nation's actions in the eyes of the world community is an important one which requires attention.

During the course of the Symposium, it became clear that we need also to pay attention to the tension between what has come to be known as 'Realism', especially in debates about foreign policy in the U.S., and a more 'idealistic' vision of the basis for international dealings. Although the world of international relations analysts is neither neatly nor exhaustively divided into 'realists' and 'idealists', these terms do seem to identify contrasting turns of mind which, for better or worse, form one possible framework for current discussions. And it may be helpful, on occasion, to give explicit recognition to this tension as we endeavour to create consensus around particular policies or actions.

As you will read from the many comments of speakers and panellists, and from audience comments where we have included those discussions, this Symposium provided, for those in attendance, a remarkable and sustained focus on some critical issues around the development of Canadian foreign policy in the broadest sense. We hope this volume will bring that discussion to a wider community and that it will be helpful to many groups and individuals, both inside and outside government, as these issues are further debated and refined.

Marsha P. Hanen
September, 2005

Introduction

CANADIAN VALUES IN THE WORLD COMMUNITY: THE ISSUES

Joel Bell

We chose the topic for this weekend's Symposium

CANADIAN VALUES IN THE WORLD COMMUNITY:
BUILDING TRUST, BALANCING GLOBAL POWER

- because there are clearly choices to be made, as to what we do on various international issues, that raise significant values-related questions;
- because we see a challenge now in how a country like Canada – and many others for that matter – can go about making a difference in these matters, given the dominance of one country's views and instruments on many such issues – that is, given the dominance of the U.S.; and
- because, while our core values and fundamental national aspirations endure over time, both the world and we have changed dramatically from the period when our basic international policy precepts and responses were developed – and, even from the time of the most recent foreign policy review – suggesting the appropriateness of a fresh look.

The world is now facing issues such as:
- Iraq, as a manifestation of a new U.S. strategy of "preemptive strikes" to confront foreign governments supporting terrorism or, allegedly, the proliferation of weapons of mass destruction, despite: the misgivings, in some cases, of historic allies; some expressions of concern about a cultural clash with the Islamic world; and, risks of creating an environment in which future situations raising humanitarian or other legitimate grounds for intervention or policy initiatives are approached with excessive hesitancy as a result of failures or problems encountered in what the dissenters regard as this non-essential intervention;

- An increasingly distributed and menacing terrorist environment, demonstrating that our security has come under assault from a new kind of enemy, no longer geographically described or remote. This enemy plays on insidious perversions of religion, ethnicity and inflamed national passions that also test our values domestically on occasion, and capitalizes on modern mobility technology and interdependence to exercise non-governmental power, lashing out close to where we live, even against frustrations existing in locations remote from our lives;

- A world that includes failing and failed states that lack the ability to provide for their populations, are unable, or perhaps unwilling, to prevent terrorist presence, or, worse, that support human atrocities;

- Questions about the willingness and ability of the UN – or other international institutions – to help when called upon, for reasons of the absence of resources, lack of ability to ensure the security of their personnel in inflamed conditions, or because of decision-making impasses, or because of an ignoring of the role or decisions of the institutions;

- A Latin America in which democracies are fragile, governance concerns abound and economic anxieties loom large, and where much touted economic liberalization, democratization and freer trade agreement are stalled and challenged;

- A Middle East that still strains hope for progress toward peace;

- An expanding and changing European Union with a world vision and foreign policy attitude on the part of some of its member states diverging from that of its traditional ally, the U.S., at a time of the latter occupying a position of world predominance that is unique in modern times;

- Asia, where economic tigers have migrated to China and India; regional trade links are expanding with economic and political consequences; and where the world faces rogue state concerns that also produce U.S. rumblings;

- Trade issues that pit consideration of economic efficiency, developing economies, trade opportunities and divergent standards of social policy, safety, environmental management, minimum incomes and possibly minimum human rights standards against one another – and confront politically motivated domestic initiatives in subsidies and trade interferences;

- Increasingly divergent incomes between the "haves" and "have nots", despite targets and promises of shared gains from globalization and from development assistance;
- Africa, a neglected region, lagging in its development and governance and faced with challenges of widespread disease and occasional genocidal outbreaks;
- An absence of agreement or resolve regarding environmental alarms sounded at a global level and coming from some thoughtful sources; and,
- Drug and arms trade that may seem remote, but could be breeding grounds for future problems affecting us closer to home,

all making for a changing world and certainly justifying a revisiting of international policy questions and priorities, as well as posing challenges as to the actions that our values and interests would dictate. It also bears recognition that governments have limited capacities as to the number of issues they can effectively address at any one time, while the agenda is long.

It is only seventy-three years since Canada acquired the legal basis for an independent foreign policy – long enough to give us a history to mine as prologue and to have experienced some glory days, criticisms and self-doubts. But, Canada, along with many other countries, seeks by its policies to advance three principal objectives:

- a healthy and growing economy to generate the resources for good living conditions from which to pursue our social values;
- an ability to formulate policy independently, despite an increasingly interdependent world – or, at least, as independently as possible – pursuing policies based on OUR values, objectives and priorities; and
- security for our people, at home and abroad, as we move about experiencing and transacting internationally, without sacrificing cherished freedoms, civil liberties and social values, including as expressed in immigration policy and refugee treatment.

The pursuit of these goals for each national community is affected by forces and by policies made by others, both beyond our borders and control. This is particularly so for those of us who value open societies for their social and cultural variety, their economic opportunities and their human and social values. U.S. convictions that the world has changed fundamentally since 9/11 – or at least having certain realities made brutally visible by this event – and U.S. actions in response, have heightened the awareness that our world has come to be greatly influenced by a single country, the United States. While that country is happily democratic, essentially non-imperialist and imbued with many attractive values held in common with Canadians, its views, preoccupations and actions heavily condition pursuit of others' national objectives – particularly for Canada, but also for many others – whether dealing with this phenomenon bilaterally, or attempting to condition U.S. actions multilaterally. We do well to remember, however, that the U.S. is a dynamic society, with a multi-centred governmental decision-making structure and is a country with the possibility for policy shifts in light of open debate.

That debate currently, broadly speaking, gravitates around two poles:

-   the one holding that other countries should recognize the predominance of the U.S., the international role into which this casts the country and the national vulnerabilities to which this gives rise (especially currently). The U.S., in this view, legitimately expects support for its initiatives from those who claim to share its goals and seek its friendly attitudes. Further, these goals and U.S. national interests and actions in pursuit of them cannot be expected, in this view, to be subordinated to bilateral or multilateral decision and control – at least not until the U.S. is comfortable that such ceding of decision-making is to a group of like-minded players. In this view, international rules and institutions cannot be relied upon. U.S. power, including military power, must in the end be relied upon; and

- the other view holds that the U.S. should accept that even it is affected by an interdependent world; that it may not be able to control everything it might like unilaterally; and that it should seek – even must secure – legitimacy (currently eroded) for its actions beyond its own borders from significant international consensus, ideally through ceding some decision-making to accepted international procedures and institutions. Doing so would allow the burdens to be shared, the goals to be more readily realized and would permit those institutions designed to promote peace, security and social justice to have their utility preserved – all to better serve the objective of a stable world order. In this view, such an approach should be the essence of U.S. foreign policy even if there are fewer forces constraining the U.S. and select allies in a post Cold War world. The world should, at least, be able to expect a higher threshold of national necessity before the U.S. moves ahead, largely unilaterally, without such support.

This debate in the U.S. is actually often more over whether the techniques for pursuing the U.S. objectives should be by way of diplomacy or by use of military force, rather than over whether the objective itself is appropriate – it being taken for granted by both sides in some U.S. dialogue that the objectives are good and right – although this view is something other countries sometimes want to be able to raise. Perhaps it is that Americans see, and can better afford to see, world affairs through domestic impact eyes and less in terms of their international impacts.

Over the next two days we will explore a range of issues:
1.) In our first session we will look at ourselves here in Canada to start with: what values, objectives and priorities do we claim for our foreign policies? Do our methods and resources address these values and the international issues that we should prioritize today?

Canada, although not alone in doing so, historically lays claim to high moral ground in international affairs, having a history of not exercising colonial power, and one of non-aggression and constructive, honest-broker intervention and high-minded purposes. We have few enemies and a base from which to deal that is relatively strong economically and educationally, respected for its governance practices and its traditions of democracy, pluralism, openness, human rights and willingness to fight for its beliefs. We have been strong supporters of multilateral solutions to international issues. We seem to believe ourselves to remain on such "principled" ground, if the latest international policy review conclusions are read – perhaps evidencing a public willingness to respond to leadership based on such principles. But some, including our first speakers, question whether we measure up as well as we once did. Are we deluding ourselves? Have we consciously, or otherwise, allowed our international influence to diminish unnecessarily – and, perhaps, inconsistently with our objectives and self-image?

Is any diminution of our international influence a result primarily of our policies of economizing on international assets of defense, development and diplomacy, or perhaps in meaningful part a result of a changed environment to a world in which Canada is beyond an immediate post war standing of having been called upon by circumstances to play a disproportionately large wartime role; and, beyond the Cold War, during which the bonds between allies, including middle powers, counted differently than they do currently.

If our admittedly relatively limited spending practices on these internationally-relevant activities – defense, development and diplomacy – is the cause of much loss of international power and influence, is that spending decision evidence of a shift in our values, to domestic social priorities, fiscal repair and enjoyment of a peace dividend? Or have our spending policies not reflected our values and expectations?

If we were to spend more on defense, how would we focus our efforts – what kind of capabilities would best suit our objectives and abilities (e.g. peacekeeping, counter-terrorism, nation building initiatives, versus more traditional military capacity)? What role and influence can and should we expect over North American defense matters, including its new technology frontiers in missile defense?

If we spend more on aid, on what countries and activities and on what pre-conditions would we do so? With what Canadian capacities and characteristics can we make the biggest impact, and where, or by what criteria, should we be most interested in applying them? If we increase resources for foreign affairs generally, where would we concentrate? The U.S. counts greatly to Canada economically, while the world, and many Canadians, might seek a broader and less U.S.-centric input. How can we best manage the desired economic closeness to the U.S. that is widely supported and valuable, alongside policy independence in international matters and in the areas into which heightened U.S. security considerations can be seen to intrude (e.g. immigration, refugee policy and law enforcement methods)? What policy actions might be called for in Canada and in the U.S. in order to use energy supply – much needed in the U.S. and more available in Canada – as a positive instrument? If we push to advance a trade agenda, would we concentrate on the U.S., where we ship 80% of our exports and almost half of our manufactured goods? Or would we try again to diversify our economic links? Would we cultivate a closer relationship with Europe, Asia, Latin America, Scandinavia – for common values or Canadian interests? Where and how can we make a difference in the world and serve our interests by our international initiatives?

Despite the decline in development spending as a percentage of GNP (on which Canada is not alone), and even acknowledging the case for an increase in defense spending and an updating of military capability, (hopefully targeted to serve identified goals and conditions and not just a pro-rata mirroring of U.S. spending priorities), would the world share the conclusion that our influence has diminished? We have played a significant role in the last number of years on international accords such as that on the International Criminal Court and the prosecution of crimes against humanity, on the International Land Mines Treaty, on the Kyoto environmental protocol; on the International Commission on Intervention and State Sovereignty and the recommended 'responsibility to protect'; we have participated in international hotspots, (even if others have increased their roles and relative importance and contributions to such efforts); we have played active roles in the UN, OECD, NATO, IMF, trade liberalization and AIDS assistance and pharmaceuticals.

2.) Following this self-assessment, we will dedicate a session to the ever-present Canadian reality and unavoidable priority of the overwhelming importance to us of our relationship with the U.S.. How well are we managing the balancing of our economic interests and the realities of huge economic interdependence and of trade impacts across this border, with our efforts at independent policy-making and persuasion of the U.S. of the legitimacy of the subjects and scope for us to differ on policy, despite common core values, where these differences are important to us – on social policies and on some international subjects, such as Iraq recently, Cuba for some time and earlier Vietnam and China; and on our view of the role of multilateral institutions, or international consensus in many such decisions? This is our closest and friendliest relationship, but also the one that it is paradoxically most critical to manage for our sense of independence. It is the one that most frequently affects our national policies on economic management, industrial activities, security, continental defense, immigration, refugees, and many social and cultural matters that can give rise to cross-border tensions, including differences arising from the Canadian conviction that its success as a national community often requires more governmental involvement than is the case for our larger neighbour.

The two countries have collaborated closely on security and will continue to do so – Canadians are clearly driven to do so for the free flow of goods and people in trade on which Canada is dependent; but, the U.S. may want to go even beyond these dictates.

We have a history of close cooperation on continental defense, even if we are reluctant in the run-up – and there are issues currently in the continental setting, of U.S. anti-missile initiatives and coastal defense, and more broadly on the ability of Canada to be helpful on a world scale.

We have moved jointly to bring our economies to an interdependent state, with a relatively open border and significant industrial integration, even while working to remove remaining impediments through some greater harmonization of regulations where intentions are very compatible, and through a more rules-based relationship – to reduce trade remedy irritants, provide business predictability and to address sectoral problems in agriculture and occasionally in cultural industries; and we should be continuing to explore an expanded role that Canada could play in providing greater energy security to the U.S..

And, we share many values and international objectives. How significant are the issues on which we seek to differ – how wide are the differences on those issues – and what is the impact of those differences on the relationship? As we often do help in the aftermath of U.S. international initiatives we opposed, might our distinct stance serve both us and the U.S. better in the end, since the contribution we would make by a pro-rata cloned role would be small, and our ability to help in the healing and rebuilding process in trouble spots and internationally is far greater as a result of our earlier differentiation? Does our relationship have the maturity and understanding to effectively manage and even exploit the potential benefits of such disagreements between friends?

3.) We will go from there to discuss the broader context of relations involving many other countries and regions of the world. How does Canada, its unavoidable relationship with the U.S. and its international policy role and its potential roles look to the rest of the world? For what do they look, or hope to look, to Canada? What role has, can and should Canada play on the various fronts, and what opportunities are there for Canada, given the international landscape?

4.) We will look at the role, condition, opportunities, challenges and reform issues facing international institutions in the new world environment; and at how Canada and other countries can best contribute to international well- being.

Canada has been a strong proponent of international rules and multilateral institutions – the UN, IMF, World Bank, WTO, NATO, Asian Development Bank, International Criminal Court and others. How well have these commitments served in our national interests and their declared purposes, since we should not be supporting multilateralism per se, but supporting it because it produces good results for Canada's influence, for sound development objectives and for world security and peace. Where should other countries and these institutions be pressed to do more? How do we address the failings of these institutions when majority decisions of member states – including many new states and failed or rogue states – produce outcomes that fail to meet some minimum standards of liberal democracies, or produce unpalatable outcomes? How do we advance a world of fair laws and reasonable rules if the U.S. is disinclined to follow suit?

5.) We will ask how Canadian international business practices do or should reflect Canadian values and behaviour. What role can business play in Canada's foreign relations? What role can the organizations of civil society play?

The group of speakers we have gathered for these discussions is both informed and diverse. The discussions will attempt to draw out an identification of the values we wish as a country to pursue; the extent to which our policy decisions and actions require distinguishing our interests from our values; and some ideas on what concrete steps we might consider in pursuit of our overall objectives.

We are most grateful to those on the program. Their knowledge and expertise will help shape some constructive thinking on the questions we have raised.

· I ·

CANADIAN VALUES, CANADA'S ROLE: MYTHS AND REALITIES

Andrew Cohen

I never met Sheldon Chumir. I wish I had. By all accounts, he brought great qualities to the practice of politics – intelligence, eloquence, honesty, empathy – and they animated his short, distinguished career. In an age of cynicism, he believed in the idea of public service and he thought politics was an honourable profession, as John F. Kennedy once described it. This foundation is a fitting monument to the man and his memory. We need more Sheldon Chumirs in public life, and we need more organizations of this kind to make us ponder who we are and why we are here, and make those existential questions a part of the discourse in Canada.

I have been asked to talk about values, ethics, myths and realities in Canada's foreign policy. It is an opportunity to consider, in broad terms, the decisions that we make every day as a nation in the world in war and peace, in trade, in diplomacy and in development. It is an opportunity to ask if what we do really reflects, as this Symposium suggests, our "values" as Canadians, or if that is just a grand delusion.

In fact, are we guided by values in the world? If so, what are they? Do they reflect our national character? What are the elements of an ethical foreign policy? Do we have one? Are ethics enough?

That is what I will try to examine in these remarks. I will be followed by my friend, the formidable Jennifer Welsh, who will offer her own perspective. I should say that it is a pleasure to see her, as I have some half-dozen times in the last half year, sharing public platforms in Oxford, Banff, Meech Lake, Ottawa and Toronto. She crosses the Atlantic Ocean as you and I cross the street, which is why I call her a latter-day argonaut. Wherever she goes, she brings a startling originality and thoughtfulness.

We hear more and more today about values in foreign policy, even if we are not always sure what they are. Ten years ago, values assumed a place of prominence when the government published a seminal review of Canada's foreign policy, the most sweeping a government had undertaken since 1970. It called its blueprint "Canada in the World", the kind of title only a bureaucrat could love, but it declared a trinity of principles underlying our international relations: the protection of security, the promotion of prosperity and employment, and the projection of Canadian "values" abroad. These were called the three pillars of Canadian foreign policy. When the government made values the third pillar, it largely meant the promotion of our national culture through our writers, artists, filmmakers, performers and all those who give expression to the impulses of the Canadian identity.

What are those values? It is important to define them. They are a belief in participatory democracy and the rule of law; a belief in free enterprise, which means the free market tempered by a commitment to social justice; a belief in peace, order and good government; a belief in bilingualism, pluralism, and federalism.

More substantively, these values mean a commitment to human rights in all forms, without discrimination on the basis of religion, sex, race or ethnicity; a commitment to compassion and compromise in how we organize our political affairs, with jurisdictional checks and balances; a belief in interventionist government and a belief in the right to own property.

Historically, these essential values have come to mean a commitment to international organizations, especially to the United Nations (but also a host of others), as a forum for debate and the resolution of conflict. It has come to mean membership in the Atlantic community, principally through the North Atlantic Treaty Organization and a web of other security alliances such as the NORAD, as the guarantors of our freedom. It has come to mean a belief in peacekeeping, which made us the world's leading peacekeeper from the 1950s to the 1980s. It has come to mean an aversion to war, but not a fear of it, which is why we fought in three major conflicts in the 20th century and left 100,000 dead in foreign fields. It has meant a belief in open borders, allowing the free movement of people, goods and capital, which is why we support the World Trade Organization and have been party to every major agreement, regional and international, on free trade since the 1930s. It has also come to mean a belief in immigration, producing perhaps the most liberal policy in the world, which is why we admit some 250,000 people every year to Canada. And it has come to mean a respect for the environment, at home and abroad, because we know the wealth of Canada, and the wealth of the world, is its wilderness. Our land is us, a truth that is dramatically apparent in this city in the glorious shadow of the Rocky Mountains.

So, put succinctly, these values have made us who we are in the world, or, who we *were*. To reiterate, it has made us:

- a peacekeeper, keeping peace when we could;
- a soldier, making war when we must;
- a social worker, making us one of the world's leading donor nations;
- a trader, committed to the commerce which generates some 43 per cent of our national wealth;
- a builder, erecting the architecture of the post-war order, such as the United Nations, the World Bank, and the General Agreement on Tariffs and Trade, the North Atlantic Treaty Organization;
- a diplomat, in Korea, in Suez, in Vietnam, the prime mover behind the International Criminal Court and the Anti-Landmines Treaty, the world's honest broker and helpful fixer.

These roles, then, are the personification of those values. Collectively, they are the elements of our identity, and they reflect what it means to be Canadian in the world, yesterday and today. Call them the stuff of international citizenship.

We do not lay sole claim to them. Other nations share our values and beliefs; indeed, most of the civilized world does. We have no monopoly on seeking peace, discouraging war, and urging compromise. They aren't peculiarly Canadian values, as much as observers like Michael Adams, the pollster and author, argues that we are so different from the Americans. Indeed, that is the thesis of his book, *Fire and Ice*. With some differing levels of emphasis, to be sure, I think we share these values with the Americans, as well as the British, the French and others.

At the same time, we Canadians know what we aren't. We don't believe in the command economy or the unitary state; if we did, we wouldn't have capitalism, federalism and three levels of government, not that that is always a blessing. We don't believe in unilateralism or neutrality; if we did, we wouldn't have gone to war abroad, and then always as part of a coalition. We don't believe in monoculturalism or monolingualism; if we did, 46 per cent of the City of Toronto would not have been born somewhere else, and Canada would not be one of the most heterogeneous societies in the world.

In how we present ourselves to the world, we are not dogmatic or doctrinaire. We have no history of colonialism. Until Osama bin Laden, we had no real enemies. By and large, everybody likes us. Our passport is welcome everywhere; the Maple Leaf on the traveller's backpack has become almost a diplomatic letter of passage. And why not? Canadians are moderate, reasonable, polite, deferential. We are, in a phrase only people of a certain age understand (which sadly doesn't include my 20-something students) "the Danny Kaye of Nations." In other words, the world's nice guy. The world's boy scout.

No doubt declaring our open-mindedness and tolerance makes us feel good about ourselves. We are good, some think, therefore we do good. We would like to see ourselves as part of a larger moral realm, as the Governor General once put it. But this culture of contentment has also created a mythology about ourselves which has made us blind to some hard truths.

We think, for example, that we are still peacekeepers because that reflects our Pearsonian tradition. A survey last summer of Canadians under 30 asked what made them proud to be Canadian. They said the size of the country, our mix of nationalities, the Charter of Rights and Freedoms. Seventy-two percent said peacekeeping. The trouble is that we aren't the world's leading peacekeeper anymore. As measured by soldiers under UN command, we are 34th in the world. Nonetheless, as Jews believe in the coming of the Messiah, despite their history of persecution, we believe in peacekeeping, despite our reality. We have made peacekeeping part of our iconography, celebrating it on the back of the five-dollar bill and in a memorial on Sussex Drive in Ottawa.

We think that we are generous. In a survey in 1997, 94 percent of Canadians thought they were "very generous" in offering aid to foreign countries. The trouble is that we aren't any-more. We have fallen into the bottom ranks of the world's benefactors; in 2001, we ranked 19 of the 22 donor countries of the OECD. Nonetheless, we believe in this, too.

We think that we are still a mediator and a broker, which makes us comfortable. But we aren't a leading diplomat any longer either. Our foreign service is in trouble, and our diplomacy is unfocused. Norway is a smaller country doing more than we do. As author and columnist Jeffrey Simpson has written: "Never has the world meant more to Canada; never has Canada meant less to the world."

Mythologies sustain nations, and they sustain us. In thinking that we still matter in the world, we have built a Potemkin village of false beliefs. It's hard to come to terms with our decline because we do have these values and we cling to them, and they are us. And how we like to celebrate them! We love to tell the world how progressive we are, how cosmopolitan and modern, as if we were the world's pacesetters and tastemakers, a new 21st century smart set, because we endorse gay marriage and the de-criminalization of marijuana and stayed out of Iraq.

We are happy to be on the cover of *The Economist*, a moose in sunglasses, under the caption "Cool Canada." Some suggest that our fourth "D" – after defence, diplomacy and development – is identity, a body of values. To them, values are so exemplary, noble and incandescent that they have become our foreign policy. This, in a sense, was the message of human security and soft power in the middle 1990s. Soft power is all about influence through ideas. For us, it was about creating institutions, treaties or protocols. The former Minister of Foreign Affairs, Lloyd Axworthy, was the sultan of soft power. He thought it was the way forward. In some ways it was. But while he was celebrating soft power, his government was starving the military, rationing aid and diluting diplomacy. It had no money, so soft power became a substitute. But soft power doesn't keep the peace, dislodge tyrants, feed, clothe and cure people or rebuild shattered nations.

Indeed, in the absence of hard power, soft power has become the face of Canada abroad. What we do at home becomes who we are abroad. We are an exemplar, and this is good as far as it goes. Much of this is through arts and culture, which is the new vehicle of Canadian values. Today it is all about Shania Twain, Yann Martel, Christopher Plummer, Margaret Atwood and Margaret MacMillan. I was in Berlin earlier this week and in magazines and posters everywhere I saw two familiar faces – Diana Krall and Avril Lavigne. In the expanse of their fame, they are to the world what Lester Pearson and Barbara Anne Scott were in the 1950s, the two most recognized Canadians of their day. Fine. But while I like the sultry Diana Krall as a face of Canada, I recoil at the post-adolescent pout – well, scowl – of Avril Lavigne.

And with great respect to both of them, I look at Diana Krall and Avril Lavigne and ask if we are making too much of them. I wonder if we are relying on the third pillar to hold up the others which we have so sorely neglected. In that white paper on foreign policy ten years ago, it seemed that other values – peacekeeping, diplomacy – suddenly didn't matter. After all, what does it say about our values if we don't fund international aid? Will Diana Krall help there? What good are values if you don't have boots on the ground? Will we dispatch Margaret Atwood? Well, we could send in Avril Lavigne and insurgents everywhere will lay down their arms and come out with their hands up.

In 1984, at the height of the famine in Ethiopia, Canadian musicians produced a popular record called "Tears Are Not Enough." It might be said today that values, at least those values of identity, are not enough, either. You cannot sustain an effective foreign policy, an ethical foreign policy, on soft power alone. You must go out and do things. You must act. In Canada, however, we have moved away from acting.

That white paper of 1995 was about a less idealistic, less engaged, less empathetic foreign policy. As it described it, the new world, post-Cold War, valued a sense of price more than passion. It was no place for dreamers or do-gooders. Much as the world heralded the new internationalism at the end of the 1980s, there was no market anymore for well-meaning, weak-kneed, quaint notions of compassion and solidarity.

In this world, economics mattered more than ethics. Everything was a choice and every choice had a cost, even if it was discounted. It was the 1990s, the decade of debt and deficit and despair. This was the shrinking world of doing more with less or doing nothing at all, of limits rather than opportunities (unless they happened to be free). This was the world of accountants, entrepreneurs, traders and brokers. Foreign policy had become a matter of what Canada could afford, and it couldn't afford to be as generous and involved. In tone, this marked a retreat for Canada, a dilution of the principles that had driven its foreign policy for a half century. It saw the world in starkly economic terms.

For example, foreign aid. Ten years ago, in the review, the purpose of our aid changed. It was now to become a tool of prosperity and employment. No longer was the government talking about aid as a way to alleviate poverty and help the world's poor – a point made repeatedly in earlier policy statements and parliamentary reviews. No longer was there talk of nation-building.

Now, it seemed, the government was enlisting aid in the cause of general foreign and economic policy. The review never made the case for aid, or mourned the disparity between North and South, or restated Canada's commitment to the poorest of the poor. More practically, the government saw aid as an investment "in prosperity and employment" which "connects Canada to some of the world's fastest growing markets" – a phrase ministers of international co-operation much favoured. Of course, these arguments have been used to make the argument for *increasing* aid, but not here, not then.

So, for example, there was no interest in addressing the contentious "tying" of aid and trade, which makes recipients buy food and other services from the donor country, which distorts the market and gives those who need it most a worse deal. The government also stressed "business development".

The emphasis on private sector, trade promotion, and tied aid ten years ago raised critical questions: Whose prosperity? Whose benefit? And most pointedly, whose values? It still does.

We don't often think that underfunding our aid, or tying aid, or using it for other purposes, is also a moral question. Just as we don't think that starving our military, or ignoring our foreign service, are also moral questions. Yet the erosion of the instruments of our internationalism doesn't inhibit us from making pronouncements on other questions – such as how the United States handles its prisoners in Guantanamo Bay, for example – with a certain sense of righteousness. This isn't new; we have always had an element of sententiousness when it comes to the United States. This particularly bothered Dean Acheson, the tall, patrician, moustachioed former Secretary of State of the United States who knew Canada well. He never forgave Lester Pearson for pushing the United States on Korea, and he didn't like it on Vietnam either. He wrote a searing essay on Canada's penchant for moralizing in 1966 which he called – using a line from Wordsworth –"Canada, Stern Daughter of the Voice of God."

He thought we should watch what we say, and consider that our interests were not necessarily as important as those of the United States. "If you think after all the agonies we have gone through here to get an agreement on this matter, we're going to start all over again with our NATO allies, especially you moralistic, interfering Canadians, then you're crazy," he wrote.

Acheson was often wrong, as he was on Vietnam, Korea and Cuba though I think he was on to something with Canada. Still, he listened to us; I don't think he would today. Years ago, when we took ourselves seriously in the world, ideas, envoys, arms and alms gave us the currency to pronounce on these questions. We had a voice, and it was the vehicle of values. We had earned one in war and peace. We had paid our way and carried our weight. If we offered advice or sounded arrogant, it was advice and arrogance with authority.

Today, having eroded our military, slashed our foreign aid and diluted our diplomacy, we have turned to our values, themselves, as our calling card in international affairs. It is our passport. It is our credential. It is enough today to be a progressive nation-state, even if we stay closer to home than we once did. You would be surprised at the number of Canadians who believe that is all we have to do in the world. I like our values, but I wonder if we understand what we have done to ourselves. We have obligations and duties. In withdrawing from the world, however, we have abandoned our moral obligations and betrayed the very values we embrace so proudly at home.

A moral foreign policy, then, begins with honouring our commitments and accepting our obligations, consistent with a country which is the second biggest in the world in physical size, the seventh highest in per capita income and the twelfth in the size of its economy. That suggests responsibilities. It means acting your age.

At the same time, a moral foreign policy means understanding the implications of your actions, and trying not to stray too far from your values, though you sometimes will.

In international relations today, the great battleground for this is foreign trade. It is one of the arms of our internationalism, with defence, diplomacy and development, but unlike them, it is flourishing. Here we have abandoned the moral high ground. Here it is not so much what we are not doing, as in the three D's, but *what* we are doing. Here it is about the perennial struggle for human rights against the demands of economic growth.

This issue is always before us because trade is a part of our international personality, reflecting the enduring tension between commerce and conscience. Here we have not only values, but something else: interests. Interests are not values. They are interests. There is a difference.

Consider, for a moment, the case of China, and the recent visit of the Dalai Lama to Canada, where we saw, in sharp relief, the collision of values and interests.

That China is one of the world's great economies is now one of the world's great clichés. It is the world's factory floor. Its transformation from an agrarian economy to an industrialized one in the space of twenty-five years has been astonishing. In the 1980s, when I began visiting Asia, I remember "the irrational exuberance", to borrow a phrase once used to describe the American stock market, surrounding China. It was the spicebox of hope and opportunity. The Middle Kingdom was full of riches. And they were there for us to reap.

The rhapsody over China hasn't faded. Indeed, it is in full flight. "Enter the Dragon", declared *Maclean's* a month ago. "As the Asia giant opens for business, Canada in particular is feeling the impact." This was followed by the cascade of claims from breathless businessmen and the diplomats. In *Maclean's*, the salesman-in-chief was Canada's Ambassador in Beijing, Joseph Caron, who said: "Every Canadian company, no matter how large, needs to be aware of what's happening in China. And every Canadian citizen needs to be aware of what's happening in China. There's no hiding from China."

And why would we want to hide? Mr. Caron, and the other excited pitchmen in the Department of Foreign Affairs, would tell us that we sold $5 billion in goods to China in 2002, and that's just the beginning. Look East, young man! There's opportunity, stupid! China, they tell us, is the fastest growing country in recorded history. With 1.3 billion people, an economy surging at nine per cent a year, a gross national product at $1.4 trillion, China will become the world's biggest economy by 2040. It is already the largest producer of steel, textiles and clothing. It has the world's biggest telecommunications market, and hey, we make phones, don't we? They need cars, computers, cement, as well as grain, wood and gas and we make them too, don't we? That's why there are 400 Canadian companies in China, double the number there were eight years ago, which has made China our second largest trading partner.

There is another China. It has one of the world's worst records on human rights. Fifteen years ago next month, you will recall, it committed one of the greatest outrages of the last generation. It murdered a thousand, perhaps two or three, of its own people – its own people – who were demonstrating for democracy in Tiananmen Square. For that it never apologized. Unfortunately, Tiananmen was just one in its catalogue of abuses. It intimidates, it imprisons, it tortures, it murders. It does not allow any of the key freedoms. It has been this way for years. Let us speak bluntly: as much as China is affluent, it is still authoritarian (though admittedly less than it was).

We know that, of course. There was a time it bothered us. After Tiananmen, the government of Canada, led by Prime Minister Brian Mulroney, announced economic retaliation in protest. True, the regime of sanctions didn't last long, but at least they said something. Later, the government showed a similar distaste for the massacre by the Indonesians in Dili, in East Timor, in 1991. Once we were bothered by this. No longer.

Indeed, we have lost our capacity for anger. In 1994, Prime Minister Jean Chrétien said: "If I were to say to China, 'We are not dealing with you anymore', they would say, 'fine.' They would not feel threatened by Canada strangling them." He said it would be presumptuous of a country of 28 million, as it then was, to tell a country of 1.2 billion, as it then was, what to do. "I am not allowed to tell the Premier of Saskatchewan or Quebec what to do. Am I supposed to tell the president of China what to do? I'm a big shot here, but there ..." With that, Canada abandoned whatever moral argument it had made for the cause of democracy in China, broke faith with dissidents there, and removed any philosophical impediment to doing more business. It seemed that the Prime Minister never lost a moment's sleep over China, which was all about winning a share of its riches. He was happy to lead Team Canada missions to China and when he did, commerce trumped conscience.

It wasn't just internal repression. We know what China is doing in Hong Kong, where it is now dismantling the institutions it inherited and promised to honour. Quietly, it is undermining democracy there. We know, as well, what it is doing in Taiwan, where it threatens to invade if Taiwan becomes more independent. That only about ten percent of Taiwanese are born on the mainland, that it has an exemplary record on human rights, that it is a democracy, matters little to the Chinese, and, more pointedly, it matters little to us, because we refuse to recognize Taiwan. So does almost everyone else. The reason is that China would punish us, and we cannot afford that. Or, so we think.

But China's greatest sin is Tibet, which it invaded in 1950. It banished the Dalai Lama, closed the monasteries, murdered monks, flooded the country with native Chinese to dilute the power of Buddhism and overwhelm the indigenous culture. If its purpose was to wreck Tibet, it has largely succeeded.

Why do I mention all this? Because this is about values in foreign policy, where our morality meets theirs. Morality comes into sharp focus in China, especially so in Tibet. Indeed, when the Dalai Lama came calling last month, he presented a delicious dilemma for the government of Canada. The Dalai Lama, always looking for legitimacy, wanted desperately to meet the Prime Minister. The government of China, always looking to deny the Dalai Lama legitimacy, warned him not to, and suggested that there would be consequences if we did. The Prime Minister had to choose, or thought he did.

Ultimately, the Prime Minister met the Dalai Lama, promising that he would talk about only spiritual questions, not human rights, because, after all, that would offend the Chinese. That was fine with the Dalai Lama, whom Jean Chrétien had refused to meet; His Holiness was thrilled to be in the same room with the Prime Minister. The Chinese, for their part, were not happy, but if they were to retaliate, it was unclear how.

For this, Mr. Martin was cheered. Perhaps by the standards of the Sino-Canadian relationship, where we dare to say little anymore about human rights and democracy, it was courageous. But you had to wonder about this little affair and where it has left us.

Did we feel better about welcoming the Dalai Lama? Perhaps. Did we serve our interest in seeing him? Probably not, if we define that as trade and investment with China. After all, Tibet is finished. The Friends of Tibet and other supporters of a free Tibet may urge Canada to broker talks between China and Tibet, but realistically, that's hopeless. Tibet is a noble cause but it is a lost one. In the meantime, we have real tangible interests in China which provide work and income for Canadians. You might wonder, then: why are we even bothering to talk to the Dalai Lama? Practically speaking, he is a spent force, a king without a kingdom, dethroned 45 years ago.

The answer is that there is something else at stake here, and it speaks to who we are. There are times to do things because they are right, even if they don't appear to be in the national interest. Nine times out of ten, interests trump values in foreign policy. It is why, essentially, that we chose to say little critical about China because China is critical to us, and we have felt that there is little we can do.

That may or may not be – some argue that a common front on the part of the international community could push China more quickly toward liberalization, but there is no will for that. Everyone is making too much money to make noise.

If you want to try to act morally in an immoral or amoral world, there are times to do things even if they are risky. When our Ambassador to China says "every Canadian needs to be aware of what's happening in China," I think he's right, though I am sure he and I don't mean the same thing. I hope as he celebrates opportunity, he will consider oppression – such as who has been detained, who has been silenced, who has been executed. Then urge us to trade, yes, to make China wealthy, expand its middle class, and China will become democratic, open and western.

When we lend even modest support to Tibet, it is because we think it reflects our deepest values. When we lend support to dissidents in China, or other places, it is the least we can do and still hope to look ourselves in the mirror. There are too many examples of the world not acting, whether it was Rwanda or, in the more distant past, Ethiopia, or Czechoslovakia.

A moral foreign policy need not be a windy, empty foreign policy. It is forever a series of questions, a quotidian conversation, asking ourselves what we can do in the world, for the world. It is an enduring challenge of weighing possibility against practicality, as Franklin D. Roosevelt and Eleanor Roosevelt used to do around the dinner table, she the idealist and he the realist – she arguing what *should* be done, he arguing what *could* be done. It is the unending struggle between poetry and prose.

So the elements of a moral foreign today must mean first equipping yourselves to make a real difference in the world. In our case, I believe, it means reclaiming the elements of hard power: a military which can wage war and keep the peace; an aid program which is focused, concentrated and flush; a diplomacy which is muscular and sets priorities, represented by the best diplomats a country can field.

In other words, it is not enough to be a moral power or a model power distinguished by narcissistic rhetoric, stern admonitions and sorrowful rebukes, forever ready to mobilize the legions of its conscience and send them into battle. That is self-righteous and irritating, and it does us no good. We must be willing to make a difference rather than to make a point.

What is more credible, and more useful to the world, is to become a self-aware country again that decides what it wants to do in the world, finds the tools to do it, and understands that there will be times to take positions which are not always easy. But take them we must because to decide not to is to deny who we are and where we came from, to betray our history, geography and morality, and worst of all, to diminish our humanity.

Jennifer Welsh

I want to thank Marsha and the Sheldon Chumir Foundation for the opportunity to speak at this Symposium. It is bold to take on the topic of ethics, values, and foreign policy in the context of international politics today. As events unfold in Iraq, some would say we are witnessing the very antithesis of ethics and values: a spiral of violence breeding violence.

I want to tackle the challenging topic of ethics in Canadian foreign policy in four steps. I'll begin at a general level, and reflect on whether an ethical foreign policy *is actually possible*. In doing so, I'll draw briefly on Tony Blair's first period of government in the United Kingdom, when New Labour explicitly committed itself to putting human rights and development at the heart of its foreign policy. Second, I'll examine the developing consensus in Canadian foreign policy circles that we need to focus more on interests, and less on values, in our foreign relations, especially if we wish to maintain a constructive relationship with the United States. I want to challenge this argument, and suggest that for Canada interests and values are inextricably linked. Third, I want to analyze – rather than simply re-state – the values that form the basis of Canadian foreign policy. I believe we are entering a phase when these values will be tested as never before, and Canadian policy makers must be ready to defend our particular understanding of them. Finally, I will sketch out my vision of Canada's role in a more complex and dangerous world, using the idea of Canada as a *Model Citizen*.

I. Ethical Foreign Policy?

So, to begin: what do we mean when we use the phrase "ethical foreign policy"? In 1997, soon after the Labour Party's election victory, Britain's new Foreign Secretary, Robin Cook, announced the government's intention to integrate an "ethical dimension" into its foreign policy. As you might expect, this announcement raised some eyebrows among Britain's chattering classes, and particularly its media. Simon Jenkins, a journalist with *The Times*, summed up the reaction. "When foreign ministers turn to philosophy," Jenkins wrote, "decent citizens should run for cover."

Britain's New Labour government made some very important strides toward enacting an ethical foreign policy – most notably through its creation of a new Department for International Development, its decision to write off a substantial portion of third world debt, its creation of an annual report on the Government's human rights record, its support for the International Criminal Court, and its leadership in the Kosovo War to prevent the ethnic cleansing of 1999 and its intervention in Sierra Leone in 2000. However, Blair's government also confronted a series of difficult trade-offs which illustrate the challenges inherent in trying to pursue an ethical foreign policy. One of the most problematic was in the arms trade where, despite efforts to set up an ethical regulatory framework for arms exports, New Labour faced the counter-argument that arms exports are crucial to its prosperity. (Britain is the second largest exporter of arms in the world after the U.S.A.; in 1997, Britain accounted for almost a quarter of the global arms export market, with sales valued at over £5 billion annually.) Its decision not to revoke licences for Hawk jets to Indonesia in 1997 was described by commentators as the darkest hour of New Labour's ethical foreign policy. Not surprisingly, the British media took delight in pillorying the Blair government for its double standards.

Aside from the question of whether New Labour set itself up for failure, there is a more fundamental question to ask: what constitutes ethical behaviour on the international stage? There is a well-established school of thought, commonly known as 'political realism', which questions the very application of the adjective 'ethical' to the notion of foreign policy. There are three reasons for this.[1]

The first, which harks back to the Renaissance and that great political spin-doctor Machiavelli, is that statesmen and diplomats must be given licence to operate according to an exceptional set of rules. Actions of dubious merit are not just accidents in the world of politics: *they are part and parcel of the game.* Machiavelli became famous for insisting that the ethical qualities we admire in private life – honesty and restraint, for example – can be liabilities in the context of public life. To apply these ethical standards to the positions that statesmen have to take – especially in times of great danger – is to condemn one's country to ruin. Therefore, the same political leader who would never use a gun privately must not hesitate to order her army into battle to defend the country from its enemies.

While this is an appealing argument that has stood the test of time, I don't think it holds up. We might say that the ethics that operate in public life are different from those that operate in private life, but that doesn't mean they are absent altogether. So, for example, it is possible to talk of 'just wars' in international relations – judged with criteria that scrutinize the purpose of the military action, the way in which the action is carried out, and the outcomes that are achieved. It is undeniable that state leaders occupy a particular role, which raises new and different moral dilemmas from those that face ordinary individuals. But then let's call it 'political morality'. By dropping any reference to ethics or morality, we prevent ourselves from passing any kind of judgment on it.

The second reason to doubt the possibility of ethical foreign policy – which for lack of a better label I'll call 'Noam Chomsky cynicism' – claims that states *never* act in moral or selfless ways. In short, political action is *always* contaminated. Even if

---

[1] The following discussion draws upon some of my earlier writings. See 'Taking Consequences Seriously: Objections to Humanitarian Intervention', in Jennifer M. Welsh (ed.), *Humanitarian Intervention and International Relations* (Oxford: Oxford University Press, 2004), chapter four.

states claim they are intervening on humanitarian grounds, they are actually attempting to further their own self-interest. In the case of Kosovo, political realists would argue that intervention was really about upholding the credibility of NATO, and therefore not really about upholding human rights.

Again, though this argument has a strong hold on the public imagination – just look at the dominance of Chomsky's books on bestseller lists – there are problems with the logic. In my view, it sets up a 'straw man' by insisting that an ethical action must be driven by pure motives. We know that this is not always the case with respect to individual action, so why do we demand it from nation-states? It is simply an empirical fact that governments use humanitarian rationale for their actions – particularly those involving the use of military force. Undoubtedly there have been mixed motives at work (we would look forever for a pure case of a humanitarian intervention). To me, the real question that political realists are asking is not whether states actually engage in humanitarian intervention, but whether they *should*. Realists, whether they admit it or not, do take an ethical stand on this question.

And this brings me to the third, and I think most interesting argument put forward by political realists. This is the claim that the proper function of the state – and therefore the primary responsibility of the statesman – is to protect and further the national interest. Scratching a bit deeper, one finds that this pursuit of the national interest is also a *moral* enterprise – albeit a different kind of morality from what we are used to. In this view, statesmen are entrusted with a daunting task: they have responsibility for the fate of those who form part of their political community. Their foreign policy actions, therefore, must always be judged in terms of how they affect the well being of their own citizens. Making that judgment, and balancing the conflicting forces, is a profoundly ethical task. To put it in legalistic terms, state leaders have an overriding fiduciary obligation to serve the interests of their own citizens and should use the resources of the state to improve the lot of outsiders.

This version of political realism is extremely powerful, and finds an echo in modern Western democracies, when statesmen are criticized for globe-trotting rather than focusing on domestic policy priorities. But I think it has a particular resonance in the context of the 'war on terrorism', when our governments are facing what is described as the ultimate enemy.

Again, however, I would argue that this position isn't tenable. While I would agree that the *primary* duty of the statesman is to his own citizens, this does not preclude *some* duties to those living outside our borders. We have traditionally characterized these in negative terms: i.e., we have an obligation not to harm the civilians of other states in the course of pursuing our particular foreign policy objectives. But in a world of globalization and increasing interconnections between economies and peoples – not to mention the obligations we have undertaken when we sign onto international human rights treaties – the line between negative and positive duties begins to blur. Furthermore, in a world where the 'CNN effect' has taken hold, we now face the situation where public opinion often calls for foreign policy action to address suffering elsewhere, as it did in the United States during the crisis in Somalia in the early 1990s or more recently, in Haiti.

So to sum up, I see two dimensions to the idea of ethical foreign policy. First, ethical concerns in foreign policy are both 'self' and 'other' regarding: protecting and promoting the well-being of our own citizens is an ethical task, but we also have ethical concerns that extend to outsiders – whether it be to promote human rights or to assist in development. Second, ethical action in foreign policy involves a consideration not only of *ends*, but also of means and consequences. In other words, it is not enough to have good intentions: our leaders must also make ethical calculations about *how* they pursue their objectives, and reject those options that explicitly involve negative outcomes.

II. Pursuing the National Interest

This brings me to my second topic: the challenges facing Canada's leaders and policy makers in the pursuit of foreign policy. Here, as I noted earlier, there seems to be a growing consensus in the foreign policy literature that we have paid too much attention to cosmopolitan values (the 'other') in our foreign policy, and not enough to the 'self', the national interest.

It is true that the word 'interest' doesn't roll off the Canadian tongue very easily.[2] Canadian foreign policy since 1945, particularly during our Middle Power hey-day under Pearson, has often had a whiff of moralism about it: while *other* countries have interests, *we* have values. As Andrew Cohen has shown, Canadian criticism of U.S. foreign policy – which often draws on values-based language – has been a source of irritation in Washington, where our views are dismissed as self-righteous and insufficiently appreciative of the complexities and burdens faced by a great military power.

A number of distinguished commentators on Canadian foreign policy have recently called for an abandonment of this good boy scout mentality. In a recent speech to the Institute for Research on Public Policy, Tom Axworthy argued that Canada is damaging its all-important relationship with the United States through its all-talk-no-action approach to foreign policy. We might feel virtuous, Axworthy claims, but (in a nice twist on Ralph Emerson) "virtue is not reward enough." J.L. Granatstein's line, articulated in his book, *Who Killed the Canadian Military*, is even tougher. According to Granatstein, Canada has grossly under-invested in the real things that serve our national interest. "Moral earnestness and the loud preaching of our values," he laments, "will not suffice to protect us in this new century."

But as tempting as the interests-before-values mantra is, we cannot abandon a values-based agenda. We live in a democratic society, where the values and principles we stand for *must* form a critical part of our activities on the international

---

[2] The following discussion is taken from my book, *At Home in the World: Canada's Global Vision for the 21st Century* (Toronto: HarperCollins, 2004), chapter six. The Sheldon Chumir Foundation wishes to thank HarperCollins Canada for their permission to reprint some of that material.

stage. Such values help to forge cohesion across a huge terri-
torial mass and diverse population, and make collective action
possible. Furthermore, the values we project globally help to
define who we are. Foreign policy is partly an exercise in forg-
ing national identity. Rather than trying to deny or hide this fact,
we should recognize this as part and parcel of our contemporary world. I would go even further, and suggest that we should
stop trying to juxtapose interests and values, as if the former
were selfish and narrow, and the latter ethical and internation-
alist. In reality, values and interests work much more in tandem.

Moreover, this nexus between values and interests is
something that the United States instinctively understands and
employs in its own foreign policy. Despite the widely held view
that President George W. Bush's 2002 National Security
Strategy was a defence of 'realism' and unilateralism, the document actually lacked any careful and coherent articulation of
U.S. national interests. Instead, it is dominated by the notions
of freedom and democracy, and links these historical themes of
U.S. foreign policy with a new willingness to use power to project them. Thus, far from being an irritant to Washington, as
those like Granatstein suggest, values-based perspectives (as
opposed to rhetorical jibes) can make an impact, even in the
Canada-U.S. relationship. During Canada's latest term on the
UN Security Council, in 1999-2000, our representatives pursued policies that were grounded in Canadian values, such as
the creation of the International Criminal Court. While our perspective clashed with that of the U.S., our two governments
'agreed to disagree' and did not allow these differences to over-
shadow the larger set of issues on which Canada and the U.S.
do agree.

A key strength of British Prime Minister Tony Blair's leadership has been his ability to fuse values and interests in foreign
policy making. One of his strategies has been to expand and
deepen the traditional notion of the national interest. For example, during the Kosovo crisis in 1999, British representatives
contended that a response to ethnic cleansing could be com-

patible with the national interest once the notion of "nation" was widened to include the principles that Britain stood for. Britain, as a 'civilized nation', had an obligation to respond and demonstrate horror in the face of 'uncivilized' action. In a similar way, Blair's New Labour Government has argued that changes in the international system, driven by the forces of globalization, have necessitated a wider conception of the national interest. As Prime Minister Blair proclaimed in his speech to the Labour Party Conference in 2001:

> The critics will say: "but how can the world be a community? Nations act in their own self-interest." Of course they do. But what is the lesson of the financial markets, climate change, international terrorism, nuclear proliferation or world trade? It is that our self-interest and our mutual interests are today inextricably woven together.[3]

There are two consequences of this kind of thinking: first, transnational forces (such as crime, the drugs trade, or weapons proliferation) become part of the national security agenda; and second, pursuit of the national interest requires steps to minimize the causes and effects of political and economic instability around the globe. In the end, values and interests start to merge.

The strategy of widening the national interest, however appealing, does have limits. They arise primarily from the need for our government to set priorities in the face of budgetary constraints and competing social objectives. Choices still need to be made as to which problems Canada will seek to solve. Not all relate to the national interest to the same degree – no matter how strong the ethical pull – and not all can be addressed with the current state of our resources. In the end, while we have important obligations to those who live beyond our borders, they are not as strong as the obligations we have to one another as Canadians. And we should never forget the argument of the political realists: promoting the well-being of 30 million Canadians is a noble pursuit.

---

3 British Prime Minister Tony Blair, Speech to the Labour Party Conference, reprinted in *The Guardian*, 3 October 2001.

III. Rethinking Canadian Values

Even if we haven't always been able to articulate our national identity – who we are – we have always prided ourselves on being able to articulate *what we believe in*. One of the most impressive statements can be found in our own Charter of Rights and Freedoms, which establishes the rule of law and enshrines a commitment to human rights and democracy. It's hard to disagree with this list. All three values have sacred status in most of the world's industrialized countries and we all want to be 'for' them. But the real challenge, it seems to me, is to articulate what these notions *actually* mean and require – both at home and abroad – in the 21st century.

Take, for example, democracy. In the days following the toppling of Saddam Hussein's statue in Baghdad, the first post-war administrator of Iraq, retired Lieutenant General Jay Garner, proclaimed that U.S. troops would not stay in that country a moment longer than it would take to get the electricity up and running and to stage free elections. But this minimalist American position was quickly proved wanting. Holding an election – we have come to see – is only part of what is needed to establish an effective democracy.

Democracy, at its simplest, is government by the people. But before any vote by the 'people' can occur, someone has to define who the 'people' actually are and what kind of government they are choosing. This requires a constitution – which as we in Canada know so well, cannot be written overnight. In the case of Iraq, constitutional negotiations since March 2003 have been focused on resolving complex questions about the boundaries of the provinces that will make up a federal Iraq and finding the right form of government to manage the country's distinctive ethno-religious mix. Only when a constitution, complete with elements of federalism, is in place, can an election have any chance of producing a fair outcome. Similarly, without protection for a broad set of human rights, such as free speech, freedom of assembly, and freedom of religion, it is hard to imagine a truly competitive election, where Iraqis are exposed to a broad set of ideas about the future of their country.

An even tougher challenge is to figure out whether and how the values of democracy, rule of law, and human rights fit together. Western countries like Canada seem to place great value on a political system's possession of all three attributes. Yet, as shown by Fareed Zakaria[4] in his influential book, *The Future of Freedom,* democracy and human rights do not always go hand in hand. The most disturbing example is Adolf Hitler, who rose to leadership of the German state via the ballot box. But we can find examples of these *illiberal democracies* in our own twenty first century, as shown in contemporary Russia. George W. Bush might like to count Russia in his list of 120 democracies around the world and staunch ally in the war against global terrorism, but this country can hardly be called a beacon of individual liberty. According to the international observers who monitored the parliamentary elections in December 2003, the extensive use of the state-owned media to support Vladimir Putin's United Russia party created an unequal playing field among the competitors. The result was an election that was technically free, but not necessarily fair.

In reality, the model of government that represents Canadian values is a constitutional democracy – a very particular constellation that combines representative government, an impartial and independent judiciary, and a charter of civil and political rights that are both negative (for example, freedom from cruel treatment) and positive (for example, the right to due process). While this model includes a very strong democratic component (universal suffrage, regular elections, and a representative legislature), it also relies on un-elected experts to resolve important issues of rights and social policy. There are, I might add, very good reasons for this non-majoritarian component. But they cannot obscure the fact that we live under a mixed government, not a purely democratic one, and that it requires careful balancing and fine-tuning. We should be proud of this model, while being very clear about exactly what it entails.

---

[4] Fareed Zakaria, *The Future of Freedom* (New York: W. W. Norton, 2003).

Can this special configuration be reproduced in countries that have not yet enjoyed democratic institutions? President Bush has suggested that this question smacks of cultural condescension. Every country, he argues, has a passion and a potential for liberty. This argument may well be true, but it does not mean that we can't ask questions about how to unleash it. President Bush and his advisers have found it easy to embrace democracy, but not the 'long, hard slog' it takes to get there. It requires constant engagement and a world, not of black and white, but of grey. It also involves questions about how institutions should be designed, and in what order. Such questioning is not just idle speculation by an academic in her ivory tower. It drives to the very heart of what we are trying to do when we 'build democracy' abroad. As we watch American, Polish, and Italian soldiers – not to mention Iraqi citizens – dying on a daily basis in the name of democracy, these questions become more important and more poignant.

My discussions with young Canadians suggest that while we hold the values of democracy, rule of law, and human rights very dearly, we are also deeply uncomfortable with the notion of imposing them on others. This is an aspiration associated with U.S. foreign policy, and one that has resulted in charges of hypocrisy and imperialism. Canadians, it has been said, take other countries as they find them, rather than seeking to transform them. Nor are we confident in our ability to rebuild other societies overnight. Perhaps this derives from our own very gradual experience of building Canada – a process that we see as ongoing. Part of the magic of being Canadian is the recognition that our country is still a work in progress. With this recognition comes a sense of humility, but also a sense of empowerment that an individual can make a difference to the shape of her society.

IV. Canada As A Model Citizen[5]

By way of conclusion, I'd like to propose a new way of think-ing about Canada's foreign policy. My vision is simple, but ambitious: that Canada will become a Model Citizen in the community of states in the 21st century. Both words capture important realities about our contemporary world. First, the notion of a model suggests a different approach to effecting change. A crucial aspect of Canadian foreign policy today is *simply being what we are*: a particular, and highly successful, model of liberal democracy. Our model values pluralism, as reflected in our federal structure, our official policy of bilingual-ism, and our immigration and refugee policy. It prizes mixed government, by balancing legislative decision-making with an activist court and a robust human rights culture. Our model makes risk a collective problem for society, by establishing a set of state-funded benefits that Canadians can draw upon in their time of need. It seeks a balance between providing greater security for citizens in a world of terrorism and other transnational threats, and respecting hard-won civil and politi-cal liberties. The Canadian model is also extremely civil, as seen in our crime levels, the vitality of our cities, and the suc-cess of our artists. Most of all, our model of democracy is inter-nationalist, in embracing free trade and multilateral co-opera-tion, but is also confident in our ability to sustain a unique national identity.

All these aspects of the Canadian model are exceedingly attractive. And what is attractive creates a magnetic effect. It induces others to emulate what we do, and to forge better and closer relationships with us. But this magnetism is a form of for-eign policy, and one that we overlook at our peril. While the effects of modelling are seen only gradually, they are nonethe-less real. Canada as a model democracy effects change in a way not unlike Western Europe did for Eastern Europe in the last years of the Cold War. The very success of Western Europe – and the increasing ability of those in the Eastern Bloc

---

[5] I first introduced this concept in my 2004 Hart House Lecture. See 'Where do I belong? Exploring citizenship in the 21st century', Toronto, 29 March 2004.

to see that success, thanks to the revolution in technology and communication – contributed to the fall of communism as a less attractive way of organizing society.

But Andrew Cohen is right: modelling from afar isn't enough for a country of our wealth and stature. So Canada must model in another sense. It must actively demonstrate how to establish the foundations of a strong society – much as a teacher or consultant might do. Rather than transplanting our model into other countries, our foreign policy can seek to help others help themselves. To contribute to regime building, rather than imposing regime change. In this task, Canada is ultimately a collaborator or partner, rather than an imperial occupier. In short, we are *a* model, and not *the* model.

This idea of partnership is captured by the second word: citizen. Citizenship, as I conceive of it, is a fundamentally social phenomenon. It is a status given to those who are full members of a community.[6] And with that status come rights and duties, which all citizens – in legal terms at least – enjoy equally. My vision for Canada's future entails modeling, for other countries around the world, what those rights and duties entail within the world community. But it also involves other attributes of citizenship, such as tolerating and working with others who are different from ourselves, and exercising self-restraint in terms of how we use the global commons.[7]

Understanding Canada as a Model Citizen steers us away from the problems associated with the lexicon of power used so frequently in international relations – and you will hear much about this on Sunday from Robert Kagan. Power is inextricably linked with the idea of control: getting others to do what they wouldn't otherwise do. But because the ability to control is often determined by the possession of certain resources, we end up defining power – and debating the status of certain countries as great, middle, or small powers – in terms of those resources (such as population, territory, or military force). Citizenship, by contrast, is an inherently egalitarian concept, better suited to

---

[6] T.H. Marshall, 'Citizenship and Social Class', in *Class, Citizenship and Social Development: Essays by T.H. Marshall* (London: University of Chicago Press, 1964), p. 92.

[7] These attributes are discussed by Will Kymlicka in *Multicultural Citizenship* (Oxford: Clarendon Press, 1995).

the common problems faced by countries in the 21st century. While some citizens are clearly more active than others, we do not think or act in terms of 'great citizens' or 'small citizens'. The language of citizenship also helps us to avoid choosing between 'hard' and 'soft' power. Citizenship can be exercised in a myriad of ways, depending on the problem or issue at hand; in extreme circumstances, it may require giving one's life for the cause of the community.

Let me make two caveats. First, my vision is aspirational. In describing Canada as a Model Citizen, I am not ignoring or downplaying the serious and growing cracks in our model. The most glaring example is the condition of Canada's 1.4 million First Nations, Inuit and Métis people, who lag well behind the national average in terms of life expectancy, health, and educational attainment. To date, Canada's profile on the world stage has been largely unaffected by this domestic 'black mark' – but this is likely to change in the coming decades, particularly as Aboriginal groups increase the effectiveness of their lobbying efforts within international organizations. Indeed, on my flight here yesterday, reading the British newspaper *The Guardian*, the only story about Canada, which came from Reuters, was one which pointed to growing concerns about the disappearance of close to 500 native women over the past fifteen years in Canada – and the inability of our law enforcement officials to get to the bottom of these cases. Once we begin to think of ourselves as a Model Citizen, the domestic and the international become closely entwined.

Second, in advocating the notion of Model Citizen, versus Middle Power, I am not leading us into a utopian sunset. I do not for a moment believe that the world of international relations is, or can be, devoid of power considerations. In fact, many commentators on the Iraq crisis seemed to forget that the United Nations Security Council itself, though an important institution of international society, is rooted in power politics. The vision of the Founding Fathers of the UN in 1945 was to bring together the world's greatest powers to manage threats to the international system – by making the prospect of their collective response a deterrent to those who sought to destabilize the post-war order. Power is an eradicable feature of international relations, and will continue to be one of the means that states, organizations, and individuals use to achieve their objectives. In this, Canada is no exception. But this does not mean that power should define everything about who we are, or what we can do, in the 21st century.

In order to realize the vision of the Model Citizen, Canada must think more strategically about its role internationally. And a strategy requires choice. Not being all things to all people. Not trying to steal a newspaper headline on every international issue. But choosing those areas where we want to make a contribution and where we are willing to apply our resources (human as well as financial) to make a difference. I don't have time to go into detail about what a Model Citizen agenda would look like, but for me three key tasks are to encourage countries to meet the UN's Millennium goals on development poverty reduction; to act as a watch-dog for human rights, particularly in the context of the 'war on terror'; and to reform the structures that govern us on a global level.[8]

In the end, however, the government's formal agenda is not enough. I want to encourage us to conceive of our country not just as Canada with a capital C – the corporate entity represented by the flag or government officials – but also as Canadians. Foreign policy is not something others do, 'out there'. Many of us, in our own way, are already contributing to it. In so doing, we must not be afraid to talk about values, and engage in a dialogue with others about the best way to realize them.

Thank you.

---

[8] This agenda is developed in further detail in *At Home in the World* (*op. cit.*)

·II·

CANADA IN A
NORTH AMERICAN PERSPECTIVE

David J. Bercuson

In his recent award-winning book *Fire and Ice: The United States, Canada and the Myth of Converging Values*,[1] Michael Adams tackles the difficult question: are Canadians and Americans becoming more alike, or less? As the title tells us, he found that the idea of "convergence" is a myth. If he were sitting on this panel instead of me, you would likely hear that Canadian values are growing more un-American by the year. He might even say that Canadians are now finding a new identity that makes them more liberal, more tolerant, perhaps more sophisticated in their understanding of world events, than are Americans. If he were to put it into a Jonathan Swift framework, he might say that we Canadians have become the Houyhnhnms of the world, while the Americans are the Brobdingnagians.

Adams' book is quite revealing both for what it says, and for what it doesn't say, about the confluence and/or convergence of Canadian and American values. His book measures values that are largely social and religious. He finds a growing divergence. Even the most liberal Americans – now to be found in New England according to his data – are more conservative than the most conservative Canadians – who live right here in Alberta.

I do not question either Adams' research or his conclusions. With my son living in the "heartland" of the United States – Miamisburg, Ohio – I can read a bumper sticker as well as the next person. Reading those bumper stickers tells me that religion plays a far more important role in the public life of the United States than it does here, even here in Alberta. That is one characteristic of Canadian life that makes me very happy to be a Canadian.

---

[1] Michael Adams, *Fire and Ice: The United States, Canada and the Myth of Converging Values* (Toronto: Penguin Group Canada, 2003).

But what Adams did not measure – and I suspect he did not because it would have been a waste of time, and made a very dull book besides – was the divergence, or convergence, of our political and constitutional values, our economic values, and our attitudes towards various forms of government activity such as education, social welfare, or environmental protection. I have not done any social science research on this, but I would wager that Americans and Canadians are largely in agreement on the need for an independent judiciary, an entrenched bill of rights, equality of citizens, the need to protect speech and expression, the market economy, a basic social safety network, and the desire that political leaders not betray the public trust and maintain certain standards of moral behaviour in doing the people's business.

Canadian attitudes toward gay marriage may be different from American attitudes – though I'm not so sure about that – but Americans seem far more protective of free speech than we are; witness our anti-hate legislation which has no parallel in the United States. What the historical record tells us clearly is that the United States was ahead of Canada in bringing government regulation to bear on some of the most immoral of business practises: in recognizing the right of workers to organize, in establishing a national non-contributory pension plan, in establishing social insurance, in instituting a written and entrenched bill of rights, just to give some examples. Canadians are now clamouring for their government to close the "democratic deficit" by bringing MPs into the process of judicial appointment, giving more power to Parliamentary committees, and setting fixed election dates. Those reforms all sound pretty "American" to me.

I would suggest that in the basics of democracy, human and individual rights, and the maintenance of a civil society, Americans and Canadians – and for that matter Europeans as well – have few significant differences between them. There are differences of form that are largely rooted in our different historical experiences. There are some differences in the way the forms are addressed. But since the end of the Second World War at least, both nations have moved towards greater openness, greater accessibility, greater opportunity, greater rights.

On the world stage, the fundamental aims of Canada and the United States are the same: to encourage greater freedom for people, ideas, and commerce and – to a lesser degree – to more equitably distribute the wealth of the First World so as to help create greater wealth elsewhere. Both nations have deviated from those aims from time to time, especially in the last of those objectives. But deviations have been the exception, not the rule. Looking back over the past hundred years or so we find both nations fighting in two world wars and Korea, both nations opposed to the Soviet Union in the Cold War, both nations as founders of NATO and defenders of a free Western Europe.

There is no doubt that the massive power imbalance of our two countries and the consequent tremendous imbalance in global responsibilities have sometimes led Canada and the United States to deviate in the means they employ to achieve their basic ends. What we Canadians need to ask ourselves however, is whether we truly believe that our international behaviour would deviate much from that of the United States if we were the nation of 260 million people with a globe-spanning presence and world-wide interests and they were us. I suspect it wouldn't.

Canada's global mission seems difficult for many Canadians to discern. It has been said that Canada's main strategic problem is that it has no strategic problems. In fact, Canada's main strategic problem is that Canadians refuse to recognize that their foreign policy must be based on the achievement of strategic aims that may be more subtle than those of the United States, but are no less self-interested. Those Canadian interests ought to be manifest. We must sell most of what we produce outside our borders to maintain our living standards. We know through the more than 100,000 Canadian combat deaths in the last century that global peace is indivisible. We are ever aware of the towering presence of the United States in our front yard and of our responsibility to protect our own independence by making sure that their back yard is adequately protected. Those three imperatives alone ought to translate into a formidable set of national interests that Canadian foreign policy ought to address. Foremost among those interests is the maintenance of the universal values of democracy and decency that we share with the Americans and other liberal democracies.

The problem is that Canadians have come to believe that the words "national interest" are somehow tainted and that Canada's primary role in the world today ought to be to teach everybody else how to be as "nice" as we are. We've done that before. As any beginner in the study of Canadian foreign policy knows, it was Canada's ambassador to the League of Nations in the early 1920s – Senator Raoul Dandurand – who uttered those now timeless words that Canadians lived "in a fireproof house far from flammable materials." Or as one observer put it in that same decade: "the toad beneath the harrow knows exactly where each tooth point goes; the crow that flies above the road teaches contentment to that toad." We were the international toad eighty years ago and we have become the international toad once again.

It is absolutely essential for a liberal democracy to base its international relations on its closest held values; it is insufficient to have its international relations consist of little else but an attempt to disseminate those values to a supposedly waiting world. It is also vital, to borrow a phrase, to recognize that "the high degree of subjectivity in the use of the term 'morality' often makes its application to problems of international policy nearly if not wholly meaningless."[2] That has certainly been the case where Canada is concerned

Let me give you some historical examples. At the end of the Second World War Canada found itself in possession of one of the world's largest militaries. There were literally thousands of planes, ships, and other items to be disposed of worth hundreds of millions of dollars. The government of the day decided

---

[2] Katherine S. Van Erde, "Morality and Politics". Queen's Quarterly, Vol. 65 (Summer 1958), p. 298.

that it would be immoral for those surplus weapons to fall into inappropriate hands. The weapons were, therefore, not to be sold to nations that were governed by dictators or which oppressed colonial peoples. It was all very moral, very Canadian.

When the Canadian government discovered, however, that the Americans and the British were selling surplus weapons to dictators such as Juan Peron of Argentina, Canada got into the game as well. After the formation of NATO in 1949, Ottawa transferred major stocks of weapons to France, Belgium and Holland, knowing full well that the weapons were to be used in the Congo, in Indonesia, in Algeria and in Indo-China to put down nationalist rebellions and to help those NATO countries maintain their rule over colonial peoples. How was this activity squared with Canada's moral position? It was reconciled by the simple expedient of adopting a policy that the end use of this equipment was beyond Canada's control and therefore not of Canada's concern. The moral issue was defined out of existence. Our actions and our words were not consistent. Nor were they consistent with our sale of nuclear technology to India. Or with our ongoing efforts to open or expand markets in nations with oppressive regimes, which we are still doing. Canadians do need jobs, after all. But then Canada isn't perfect, despite our occasional protestations to the contrary.

Canadians are not a people who are inherently morally superior to others. Canadians have built a nation that is decent, democratic and liberal, with a high standard of living, despite incredible obstacles of geography, climate and historical circumstance. We can and should celebrate that. We cannot claim with any evidence to be a nation that is morally superior to Britain or France or the United States or Australia or any of the other bona fide liberal democracies. Our nation is unique only because of those very factors of climate, geography, and history that have moulded us.

Canada ought not to claim, nor to seek, a phoney moral superiority in its foreign policy. But Canadians should seek out those roles that history and national temperament have best prepared us for. For example, we are a nation that has truly had no colonial past nor a history of "gun boat" diplomacy. We are

not a nation founded upon ethnic nationalism. We do not –
because we cannot – aspire to a single culture emerging out of
many cultures. Our foreign policy ought to project the things we
have truly learned, based upon our history, and not a veneer of
values that we don – when convenient – simply to appear different from our neighbours.

We are, I believe, better able than many nations to see the
ambiguities of international affairs because we are an ambigu-
ous people ourselves. Until recently we were not apt to spin out
political or constitutional principles to the nth degree before we
applied them to everyday life. The new post-Charter Canada is
more apt to do that, but the ultimate Canadian compromise –
between English and French speaking Canadians – could only
be undone at the basic peril of the nation. So we may indeed
be better suited to some international tasks than our neighbours to the south, but not because we hold superior values,
just a slightly different set of values.

Whatever the underlying truth about Canadian values, there
is one lesson that we must learn sooner or later. Good works
can only be done in an environment of safety. The standard of
living of the world's destitute, for example, cannot be raised
while they are being preyed upon by their rulers, by their neighbours, or by their enemies. There are many ways to bring safety to an international environment. Canada can take considerable credit, for example, in doing just that both by helping to
defeat the Axis 60 years ago, but also by being one of the very
first western industrialized countries to support the international boycott against South African apartheid in the early 1960s.

The topic of this Symposium is "Canadian Values in the
World Community: Building Trust, Balancing Global Power."
Real trust, in international affairs as in civic affairs or in our daily
lives, grows not from an absence of power, but from its responsible use. It is easy to trust the weak. If Canada is to seek the
world's trust in international affairs, it ought to be via the
responsible exercise of a combination of military, economic,
and moral power, and not from a lack of any power at all.

George Russell

It is impossible to separate Canada's place in the world from a single geographical fact: for all intents and purposes, it has only one neighbour. And that neighbour is the United States, the world's foremost military power, its foremost economic power, the keystone of the world economic order, and the world's foremost defender, however imperfectly – and at the moment those imperfections are uppermost in many minds – of democratic values. There is no Canadian external reality bigger than this. And in general, it is a characteristic of Canada that many other countries in the world would be very happy to trade for, even though Canadians themselves are often more ambivalent about it.

To be in Canada's place is to be at, or near, the centre of the modern global order, the centre from which much of the important change in the global order has emanated, for better or for worse, particularly in the past two decades. For the United States' partners on the continent, this location offers enormous advantages and many frustrations and constraints, which are mostly outweighed by the advantages. It is a particularly privileged and challenging place to be.

In these remarks I'd like to focus on one of those frustrations in particular, what I would call the political frustration, and suggest ways that I think we need to address that frustration in light of our new realities. And the central nature of that reality is the accelerating economic, social and cultural integration of the main North American partners, coupled with a lack of symmetrical political integration.

I should immediately stress that integration is not the same thing as convergence, as many Canadian nationalists fear. Indeed, it is one of the many ironies of Canada's situation that we have no difficulty in recognizing that loss of identity is not a problem in the case of Europe, where economic integration is accompanied by a project of political integration; yet in North America, where political institutions are not being superseded, uneasiness remains in some quarters.

Yet we all agree, or I hope we do, on the enormous success of the frameworks for economic integration that were set in place by the Canada-U.S. Free Trade Agreement and its successor, the North American Free Trade Agreement. The enormous increases in trade volumes, the equally important increases in capital flows, and the transformation of the corporate sectors in all three nations as a result have amounted to a fundamental reorientation of the smaller economies in this partnership, and a fundamental recalibration of the aspirations of their citizens. The U.S., too, has been affected, as it increasingly realizes.

Other elements of this reorientation now include the overwhelming issue of border security and freedom of movement in the wake of 9/11, which has changed our criminal laws, police procedures, privacy codes and a host of other arrangements, and focused us all dramatically on the need for further changes to regulate and improve the development of the North American continental space. Indeed, our narrow focus on trade sometimes obscures how densely interactive this continental space has become, even without a European-style project to drive it.

Let me give you a small example, based on a Canadian success story, the federally funded chairs in science, technology, medicine and other disciplines that are bringing lustre back to Canadian post-secondary education. These chairs are intended to make Canadian universities competitive in the competition for international scientific and academic talent, and they have succeeded brilliantly. But they have an interesting side-effect. They tend to support the further specialization of academic skills and institutional expertise on a continental or even global basis – a specialization that reinforces a continental division of labour even as it strengthens Canadian institutions. Our universities are getting better precisely as they become part of a more-than-Canadian scheme of things.

This is just one example. There are countless more. In the U.S., the debate about importation of Canadian pharmaceuticals online has grown from a minor facet of electioneering in some American states to a full-scale debate at the national level on the nature of U.S. drug development policy, and the challenges of the American health care system. Less visible is the effect this same debate is having on North American venture capital markets and the long-range impact on the vibrancy of Canada's present and future biotechnology industry.

What all of these changes point to is something that I think is under-discussed at the moment: the North American cultural, social and economic space is becoming increasingly INTER-ACTIVE. That is, after all, what integration is about. It is dynamic, it is ongoing, and it is really, at this pint, beyond anyone's ability to halt, not that that would be a good thing. But it also calls for many new ways of thinking and acting, especially on the part of Canada, the smaller partner in this enterprise.

Why? Because this is integration North American style. Most importantly, this means there is no parallel or guiding set of political or bureaucratic institutions that focus and modulate integration, or, just as importantly, keep it constantly in the public eye. There is no European Parliament, no European Commission, no Maastricht Agreement, no Euro, no regular structure of summitry or clearing house for the exercise of pooled sovereign will. Of course, there is nothing like the devastation of World War II either, which called all of these institutions, and the dream behind them, into existence. And pan-European institutions have their own problems, as we increasingly realize.

North American integration is very different. Beyond the broad instruments of trade agreements, which have long been surpassed, there is what I would call a dynamic and evolutionary system of micromanagement, of accords and legal instruments of cooperation, of interdepartmental deals and cross border understandings that have eased and aided the process of integration and given it shape and direction. Many of these understandings are discussed and formalized in practice, but many are left in the shadows. Many of them are less than formal – the fact that the City of Toronto now has a member of the New York City police department in its anti-terrorist unit, for example. Most of these bonds of integration only erupt into the public eye when there is a problem of some kind – when the U.S. Securities and Exchange Commission, for example, has problems with Nortel accounting, and a publicly traded North American company must react.

This extremely pragmatic way of doing things has tended to accelerate integration along the lines of least resistance – and it has done a fantastic job. North America has managed to avoid a huge amount of the stress that has afflicted Europe as it copes with continental integration, in areas ranging from institutional corruption to the democratic deficit that is now being debated around the European constitution to the monetary contortions being imposed by the adoption of the Euro. This uniquely flexible North American arrangement of integration works so well that most of the time we don't think about it at all – except when a catastrophe like 9/11 makes us see how important integration has become.

At the centre of all this, however, is an enormous asymmetry: not the relative size of the continental partners *per se*, but the separateness of their political systems. This is compounded by the fundamental principle that drives the American political system (and to a lesser extent, the Mexican and Canadian ones), the separation of powers. Differences in size, population, area and power come after this fact. By definition, the preponderant decision-making apparatus of North America is the government of the United States – and as we know, in important ways this is also the preponderant decision-making apparatus of the global order. And this separateness makes the solution of many of the day by day problems that integration throws up all the more difficult.

There is nothing new in this in the post World War II order, but it has been thrown into dramatic highlight since the demise of the Soviet Union, and the emergence of the U.S. as the sole global superpower. How long this singular situation will last is a matter of much speculation, but it is the current North American reality of this state of affairs that we must most energetically face. We can't reject it, ignore it, deplore it – well, we can deplore it, but let's be smart about it. Too often, these critical attitudes keep us from doing anything about it, in the proactive sense of thinking about how to manage it in the interest of our increasingly integrated lives. And too often, when this rejection of reality is posed in terms of real or imagined erosions of Canadian sovereignty, what we drive out of the discussion is the reality of our integrated existence.

This is something we cannot afford to do, since solving the political, economic and social problems that integration throws up becomes ever more important. And sometimes these problems aren't small. The integration of the Canadian and American forestry industries, for example, has thrown up the problem of softwood lumber duties when the Canada-U.S. exchange rate causes pain to politically important U.S. producers. The problem of mad cow disease exposed the vulnerability of a continental market for cattle in the absence of harmonized regulations and safeguards.

The point is that all of these joint issues, and there will be many more, are and will be exacerbated by the separateness of the U.S. and Canadian political systems, which can't be changed by outside pressure even as the rest of our societies move more closely together. So we must work as much as possible from the inside to deal with them – from the new inside, which is not any longer merely national in scope.

From the point of view of the smaller partners in North America, I would suggest, this points to the absolute necessity of developing what I call a "strategy of influence" to deal with the imbalance of political decision-making on the continent. It's based on the recognition that influence, to be effective in a North American context, must move away from the notion of competing sovereignties and zero-sum games and toward pooled decision-making where integration dictates. To do that, it must focus on bringing new perspectives within the decision-making apparatus of the U.S. government, which is already the world's most powerful machinery for integrating and reconciling the conflicts and conflicting values of America's tumult of interests. We must stress commonalities more than differences. In short, we must build shared interest into the American political system. And we must focus on this all the time.

This is a challenging thing to do, and an even more challenging thing for some Canadians to conceive. It's a challenge that calls for more closeness to American decision-making, not less, even when disagreements are profound. It calls for a broader and more long-term definition of our interests than short-term politics, or business economics, may always allow. It calls for a much deeper and more active engagement with the U.S. decision-making process than we previously thought feasible or politically defensible at home. It calls for recognizing the need to create new partnerships within the American political system to help guarantee that the collective interest is both noticed and satisfied. Above all, it calls for being proactive and vigorous in looking at where current and future problems are, and locating the points in American society and politics that are opening to a mutual interest and will embrace it – and there are lots of them. This is a big job, but it is also a strategic necessity, and an enormous opportunity.

What I am suggesting is that all decision makers – federal, provincial, corporate, whoever – need to build this necessity of influence into all of their cross-border decisions. And they must be proactive about it. They must build it into their earliest considerations of what they want to do, in the context of the future directions of further integration; more closeness, not less. It should, in fact, take on the elements of an unofficial national strategy. And parts of it are already in place.

Let me give you an example of what I mean. To an interesting extent, the lack of formal North American political structures has led to a new, "off the balance sheet" kind of political science between Canada and the U.S. It's focused on the provinces. As trade between various Canadian regions and the U.S. has grown faster than trade between those regions and other parts of Canada, provincial premiers have become increasingly active participants in regional U.S. governors' conferences. This is enhancing broader regional perspectives that cross the border, and bring Canadian voices into previously all-American discussions about lobbying for federal attention and funds, the disposition of services, developmental priorities and a myriad other matters. In effect, Canadians have become junior partners in a number of American regional development discussions. The voices do not have the same status, but increasingly, they are singing from the same songbook.

In another current case of blending interests, the government of Quebec and the government of New York State have created a $100 million transportation corridor and other elements of economic interweaving. This initiative is celebrating its first anniversary in a few weeks, and both Governor Pataki and Premier Charest will salute that fact in Montreal.[1] This joint venture is increasing their mutuality of interest and perspective, a closeness that will remain no matter the political stripe of any government that may succeed them. Quebec interests will get a better hearing in Albany, and the mayor of Plattsburgh, New York, is learning French. There is an important model here to follow.

Prime Minister Paul Martin, of course, has announced that better Canada-U.S. ties are a priority, and has created a Cabinet committee to foster better relations. Alberta is opening its own representative office in Washington, another useful

---

[1] This address was delivered on May 15th, 2004.

development. And Prime Minister Martin has also announced that Ottawa is creating a new position for diplomat Colin Robertson in Washington to foster greater parliamentary-congressional ties and also assist the provinces with their representation in Washington. It remains to be seen how successful this effort will be, but it is welcome.

This only scratches the surface of the integrative process that is underway, and the challenges it poses to Canada to create the strategy of influence that I propose here. The fact that EnCana, for example, is becoming the second-largest U.S. energy company of its kind is, in many ways, more important than any of the government developments, since it points to the centrality of energy strategy in the North American relationship over the next decade, and the further integration that is likely to provoke. Gaining seats at U.S. industry conference tables is vital, as is the harmonization of many regulatory regimes, which does not necessarily involve any loss of national objectives or goals.

Probably every person in this room is involved in similar integrating activity on another scale: through U.S. subsidiaries that have become active players in U.S. industrial associations, through participation in trans-national professional groups, lobbying associations and countless other organizations that seek to affect opinion and political decision marking. This is the very stuff of our continental dialogue.

What you may not yet have done is elevate this to the strategic level, of a persistent, systematic and, as much as possible, coherent effort to bolster the influence that flows from integration in the places where influence matters. And by persistent, I mean an effort measured in decades. Jean Monnet had bigger things in mind when he began to write position papers to promote the European Coal and Steel Community. But he also knew how long it would take to get to them.

Former Canadian Ambassador to Washington Alan Gottlieb has written passionately and intelligently about the importance of influence in Washington to Canada's global interests, and to

Canada's national interest. As Gottlieb observed, the most important aspect of that influence is the relationship between the President and the Prime Minister. It is the waste of an immense resource not to take advantage of this relationship to the fullest extent possible. It is also possible that too much closeness will backfire from time to time. But the risk must always be weighed against the opportunity

Nothing of what I am suggesting needs to work in any way against any notions of Canadian independence or Canadian sovereignty. Contrary to what many nationalists may feel, nothing in North American integration so far points in the direction of the kind of meta-state merger that Europe is attempting, in which the very real danger exists that a few major states may come to dominate the lesser ones. Neither Americans nor Canadians want that kind of blending. The dilemma is the opposite: integration is virtually unstoppable, but we will pay greater penalties for our political separateness than Americans ever will, unless we learn how to cope with that separateness better.

Where do Canadian values fit into all of this? In two ways. Canadian values are nothing if they are not expressed, and they will not be expressed in particularly practical ways if they do not take into account the realities of North American bonding. And secondly, because Canadian and American values are in most ways virtually indistinguishable, it is in the political expression of those values that we usually differ. That in many ways is what Canada has been from the beginning: the differing political expression of North American values.

Clifford Krauss

After living in Canada for two years, I feel like the question of whether the United States and Canada should draw closer together or not has probably been asked a thousand times before. Maybe ever since Benjamin Franklin tried to lure Quebec into the American Revolution, a diplomatic Hail Mary whose failure helped found what we know as Canada today. As a reporter for the New York Times I cannot really opine on such matters. And frankly, as an American who lives in Canada I don't have a strong opinion one way or another. If Canadians want Queen Elizabeth on their twenty dollar bill or allow the U.N. Security Council to decide when Canadian forces should be deployed in battle, that's fine with me.

So I am going to punt on the question of what we should do and rather comment on what I see is actually happening. The economic and geographical ties that bind us are growing inexorably and that will certainly continue whatever our differences on marijuana and Iraq. Canadians continue to express concerns about losing their sovereignty and their cultural independence to American domination but I think that debate has lost its zing since the days of the bitter NAFTA discussion that dominated much of the political debate a decade or so ago. That is so even though political relations between the two countries have been more tense in recent years than during the Mulroney years. And it is so because, despite predictions to the contrary, Canadian culture was not subsumed by American culture. If anything, Canadian literature is surpassing American literature at the moment. Denys Arcand, after failing with a number of Hollywood style English language films, has created a classic with his Barbarian Invasions that is recognized on both sides of the border. We Americans may be eating poutine at McDonald's before too long.

This is only natural.

Like it or not, I think most Canadians and Americans agree that we are obliged to find a way to upgrade our mutual electrical grid, our common cattle market and our security coordination because we are always going to be joined at the hip. It would be such even if there were greater cultural and political differences between us. It is the same between the United States and Mexico, where there are more suspicions that divide. Canada and the United States both need to find ways to boost exports to markets around the world, but in the end, despite all the friction over softwood lumber, I think we are destined to be each other's best customers for a long time to come. When NASA goes to Mars, there will be Canadian technology aboard the space ship. When the United States needs a helping Francophone hand in Haiti, Canada will be there.

Developments that draw us closer — particularly economically — will come, perhaps in an *ad-hoc* way, no matter what. Only an NDP victory might slow that, and that is not in the cards. A victory for Stephen Harper's Conservatives in the next election,[1] still highly unlikely, would stimulate the integration and trigger a whole new rethinking of security policy. After the election, should the Liberals prevail, Paul Martin will move ahead with coordination on anti-missile defense.

What I think would bring us together really fast, and trigger a revolution in perceptions throughout Canada would be a terrorist attack here, especially one that would reveal Canada's security apparatus to be impotent. Imagine American troops crossing the border, after a request from Ottawa. It's almost unthinkable, but I think it would catalyze a revolution in perceptions here.

It's easy sometimes to miss the big picture, especially recently: Canadians booing the American national anthem at

---

[1] This address was delivered on May 15th, 2004. The Canadian federal election referred to took place on June 28th 2004.

Montreal Canadiens hockey games; Liberal officials calling George W. Bush a moron and saying they hate the American bastards. We are not exactly totally comfortable neighbors, as I discover and rediscover almost daily.

Douglas Coupland, the great Canadian observer of global cultural trends, told me the following in his characteristically graphic way during an interview last year: "In the 70s, we were taught Canada would be absorbed by the United States and in the '80s it looked like it was happening. Then came the latter part of the '90s and it was like some high school class 16 mm. film where you see the chromosome duplicates, then realigns, and finally the cell splits. And that process only seems to be quickening."

Canada's decision not to join the American-led coalition in overthrowing the Saddam Hussein regime was a milestone, though far from the first time our countries have disagreed on foreign affairs. As far as I am concerned, Canada has every right to pursue its interests as it interprets them and history may prove the Canadian decision to have been right. I don't think many Americans paid that much attention to the divide, though obviously it damaged relations between the Chrétien and Bush governments. It also made anti-Americanism stronger in Toronto and some other parts of Canada. I will not bore you with the repeated incidents of rudeness that I have experienced over the last year or so due solely to the fact that I am an American.

But the divide has been deep. It had nothing to do with me, but I will tell you an anecdote that you may find difficult to believe. A few months ago a couple of young boys — maybe 12 or 13 — were carrying a placard outside my house in Rosedale. The sign read: Honk if you hate President Bush (this is a school assignment). The word 'hate' struck me. And I wondered if any students would carry the same sign replacing Bush with Saddam Hussein or Fidel Castro. Maybe in Alberta! But not in Toronto, where the anti-Americanism is prevalent and, for me at least, difficult to explain.

Of course there are some differences, even if Mr. Bush and Mr. Martin get along. Loosening of marijuana laws in Canada comes in contrast to the much more traditional approach of the Clinton and Bush Administrations. The government-financed injection site in Vancouver and experiments in distributing heroin to hardcore users in several cities is an approach tested in Western Europe, but one that the United States continues to reject.

The comparative ease with which three Canadian provinces have legalized same-sex marriage comes in stark contrast with the heated debate over the issue in the United States, though I would argue that Canada's actions have served as a catalyst for pro same-sex legal and social developments in Massachusetts, California and elsewhere.

But there is a paradox here, one that heightens the intellectual debate in Canada over whether Canadians and Americans are growing closer or more distant. Those who believe the two countries are growing closer and the differences are blurring note that Canadian public policy in recent years, at least in some provinces and partially on the federal level, has shifted toward cutting taxes, tentative privatizations, and balanced budgets. (On the last point, Canada is ironically more in tune with a more conservative Democratic policy on this, rather than with the deficit busting Republicans). The growth in Canadian venture capital activity is one example, and the Jean Coutu pharmacy chain's willingness to test the waters of the U.S. market is another example of how the Canadian private sector is becoming increasingly like the American private sector.

Not surprisingly, perhaps, Canada and the United States have by far the largest trading relationship of any two countries in the world — $645 billion Canadian last year. Canadian exports to the United States have expanded at an average yearly rate of 8.3 percent since 1989, more than a 300 percent increase. That's 80 percent of Canada's total exports, up from 71 percent in 1989. No matter disagreements over softwood lumber and opening cattle markets, which together represent a relatively small part of our trade and economic relationship. Meanwhile Canada is the number one export market for 39 of the 50 American states. Few Americans know this but Canada is the United States' number one supplier of energy, including 100 percent of our electricity imports and 94 percent of our natural gas imports. Canada produces more oil for the United States than does Saudi Arabia, and with all the global uncertainties how can that change?

If we are not getting closer psychically, we are certainly more joined together than ever economically. And who among us thinks that will ever change? Despite all the static, and even during the time when Prime Minister Chrétien sometimes seemed to be using relations with the U.S. as a political foil, Canada opened seven new consulates in the United States and upgraded two consulates. Deputy Prime Minister John Manley worked very closely with American officials in the wake of the 9/11 attacks to create the so-called Smart Border which quickly revolutionized management of the border and succeeded in keeping trade flowing soon after the terrorist attacks and during the Iraq war.

The recent report by auditor general Sheila Fraser pointed out a number of problems with Canada's airport security, intelligence sharing between agencies and keeping terrorism watch lists up to date. Nevertheless the relatively quick implementation of the FAST and NEXUS programs to ease the way for frequent travelers to give officials more time to look at less frequent travelers seems to have worked well. Sources on both sides of the border tell me intelligence sharing has deepened greatly over the last two years, and the Integrated Border Enforcement Teams, or IBETS, the joint border policing teams may be unprecedented in their reach for any two countries since the collapse of the Warsaw Pact. The new Canadian national security policy, which should improve coordination among different levels of government here, will help more.

Security relations remain a work in progress, one that I suspect will be driven as much by international events as bilateral relations. What form the American missile defense shield takes, and what role Canada will ultimately play in that are matters to be worked out in the next few years. But I think this is not such a big issue. We have learned the hard way that our security is more threatened by terrorist groups planting bombs or hijacking planes than rogue states with missiles.

One may assume that if Canada takes it for granted that the United States is responsible for protecting Canada from attacks across the American border, then the United States should be able to rely on Canada to protect it from attacks from the Canadian side. That seems logical to me.

But of course Canada does not give its military or other security forces the resources to do that. This will be a major test. Can Canada raise its military to the level it was twenty or thirty years ago, and still patch up health care? Again, an unthinkable attack on Canada by terrorists would force an answer. It is not unthinkable, especially with Canadian troops playing such a vital role in Afghanistan. And everything that the Islamic fundamentalist extremists hate about America, and Spain for that matter — democracy, the separation of Church and State, the liberation of women — they hate about Canada. Let's hope our countries don't have to draw closer by force of the violence from outsiders.

· III ·

Canada On the World Stage

Paul Heinbecker[1]

Thank you very much. Marsha and Joel have asked me to make a transition between the previous discussions and the broader international environment, to be discussed this afternoon. To do that, I will have to knit together some pretty disparate points. So I am going to ask for even more than the usual indulgence that a practitioner would ask for in a gathering of academics and experts.

I am going to set the Canada/U.S. relationship into a broader context, and make five points. One is <u>that values are integral to foreign policy</u> – above all to the foreign policies of democracies. In some important respects – and I do not want to comment specifically on the discussion which just took place, which was brilliant although complex – either Canadian and American values are diverging, or our behaviour is diverging. Either way, I think there is an issue there. The second point is <u>that there is a "perfect international storm" brewing</u> that could be very dangerous for Canadians, and <u>that U.S.A. foreign policy is integral to that storm;</u> and a corollary is <u>that we should stop blaming Canada for all of the problems in the Canadian-American relationship.</u> In fact, I heard a comment earlier that said, basically, in our bilateral relationship we should negotiate hard and tough, but as regards multilateral affairs our posture should be one of more civility and agreement. As a former director of Canada/U.S. relations – and we were dealing with the softwood lumber issue when I was a director in 1979 – I think I would like to say there is not a great deal of evidence that the harder you

[1] Paul Heinbecker is Director of the Centre for Global Relations, Governance and Policy at Wilfrid Laurier University and Distinguished Research Fellow at the Centre for International Governance Innovation. He recently retired after 38 years with Canada's Department of Foreign Affairs, most recently serving as Ambassador to the United Nations (2000- 2003). This paper does not necessarily reflect the views of the above institutions.

negotiate those bilateral issues, the more you resolve them. Nor do I think that there is evidence that circumspection on multilateral issues has delivered benefits in a bilateral relationship. I think those things are taken as separate in Washington. A couple of other points: <u>multilateral cooperation, not multilateral-ism, is still indispensable to the kind of world that most people would want to live in.</u> Further, <u>UN reform is necessary, but not sufficient.</u> There is a lot wrong with the UN; it would be a mistake to lay all of its problems at the door of the United States. Finally, – as Joel Bell has asked – I will provide some personal insights on Iraq and the International Criminal Court at the UN.

The debate over values and interests is sterile. Obviously, we make decisions because of who we are – because of our values. And we pursue issues abroad in part because it is in our interests to do so, and in part because they serve our values. Take, for example, international security; we want to protect the innocent, because we think, "there, but for the grace of God, go we". On the other hand, we know that if we have a stable world, Canadians can go about their own lives *more untroubled*, and in a more secure way. David Bercuson is absolutely right about the issue of soft power and hard power: It has been a bizarre debate in Canada, with practically nobody going back to figure out what the basic terms were supposed to mean. The distinction was invented by Joe Nye of Harvard, who was talking about the United States when he spoke of soft power. The idea was that you create a society that other people would emulate, and that would obviate the need to coerce them to do things, because they saw benefits in emulating your approach.

Obviously, that applies to Canada, albeit not as much to Canada as it does to the United States because Canada is not as big as the United States. But equally obviously, soft power is not enough. There is no substitute for assets, as Andrew Cohen was saying, for hard capability. I think where I would disagree with him is not on the question of whether we need to reinvest in our military capability; I do not think there is any question about that. I also think there is no question that we can afford it. Governing is about choices; it is about leading. If we want to have a military, if we want to carry a respectable share of the international burden, then we can do that. I remember taking a very senior Canadian official from the finance department, to the UN, to see (UN Deputy Secretary-General) Louise Fréchette. He said, "well of course you understand that we can't do very much on aid. We just can't afford it. And on defence we have problems also…" and so on. She just looked at him incredulously. She said, "I've been the Associate Deputy Minister of Finance of Canada. I've been the Deputy Minister of National Defence. I *know* you can afford it. The question is whether you want to pay for it or not. You may not want to pay for it, and you may not want to play a role in the world; but to say Canada cannot afford it is just not credible."

Where I would disagree with Andrew Cohen is that I think we have had a much better foreign policy record in the last twenty or thirty years – since the golden age – than he gives us credit for in his book. I can go back to the example of Prime Minister Mulroney's putting the issue of apartheid in South Africa, and sanctions, on the Commonwealth agenda, facing a lot of criticism from Margaret Thatcher, and pursuing it anyway. I raised with him later, at a certain point, whether it was now the time to end sanctions. And his answer was, "phone Nelson Mandela, and see what *he* says. And if he thinks the sanctions succeeded, then it's time. But if he thinks they haven't yet suc-ceeded it's not time." And I did. And he didn't. And we didn't. The same thing can be said for East Timor. The same thing could be said for the unification of Germany. The French and the British were very much against it and the Americans were wobbling on it. It was Mulroney, in part, saying to then President Bush that we really must be straight with the Germans. We have been telling them all of these years that they would be reunited; we cannot now renege. It is not the time to go back and fight the Second World War all over again. The Americans' position *did* subsequently solidify.

One could also, for example, cite the more obvious, current ones: the International Criminal Court, and land mines, and indeed Kosovo, where we played a significant role. Finally, we have a reputation for thinking innovatively and I think we deserve it. In response to the Kosovo crisis and the Rwanda issue and Srebrenica and Bosnia and the failures of the UN, we commissioned leading scholars and practitioners to reconcile national sovereignty, on the one hand, and the imperative of humanitarian intervention, on the other. The product of that is a report called *The Responsibility to Protect* which I commend to you. Anne-Marie Slaughter, who is the Dean of The Woodrow Wilson School of Public and International Affairs at Princeton, has called the book "the best foreign policy thinking in fifty years." That is not a small compliment. Also, she took that approach as a model, in a recent edition of *Foreign Affairs*, and emulated it – imitation is the most sincere form of flattery – with another idea: the duty to prevent. So I think the record is a considerable one. Likewise, I think the whole human security agenda has gained a lot of traction internationally – ironically at a time when the Canadian government was beginning to lose interest in it. Still, we do have to invest and put our money where our mouths are – especially when we are talking about intervention in places like Africa.

I also agree with Jennifer Welsh, because I think she made the case very convincingly: that indeed in some ways we can be – in some ways we already are – *a* (i.e. not *the*) model citizen in the community of states, that we are really an exemplar. I do not think that there is any question – from my own experience at the UN and others can comment on that – that we were listened to because of who we were (particularly in more recent years) at least as much as because of what we did. We have created (and this is the soft power part) an economically wealthy, culturally sophisticated, technologically advanced, socially compassionate society that has protected minorities and integrated immigrants as well as any on earth has. We are respected for that. When we talk, people listen. It is precisely what Prime Minister Martin said this week was "our major feat, an enormous feat, really…" in his most recent foreign policy speech, in arguing that Canada has exceptional qualities to bring to bear internationally.

So the conclusion is that neither power nor principle, neither soft power nor hard power, is enough. We need both. What we really need is *smart* power. That is both power and principle, intelligently applied. That is part of the agenda for the future.

Regarding the U.S. foreign policy, a few, not random, thoughts. Antipathy to the United Nations has not, until recently, been a basic operating principle of Washington. From Franklin Roosevelt to George Herbert Walker Bush, the United States has seen constructive participation in the UN as in its interests, and even as a kind of civic duty. It apparently no longer does so. There are many explanations for this shift. Most simply: the U.S. has changed, the UN has changed, and the world has changed. The U.S., whose domestic system of power is governed by a system of checks and balances, has progressively realized that, with the end of the cold war, it faces neither check nor balance internationally. I remember very well former Secretary of Defense Schlesinger, writing already in the 80s, about his concern that, in the absence of any check and balance, there was not going to be any foot on the brake, internationally, to American power. At the same time, the U.S. will and capacity for international leadership has continued unabated, and the disposition of others to let them do it has continued – in part because the others see no military threat that they think is worth spending that much money on. There is a notion that is current in some circles – including in Washington, including in Canada – that somehow it's a jungle out there, absent American power. That is *not* a view that is held in several regions of the world; in fact, there are many places where American power is considered to be the problem as much as it is considered to be the solution. I am thinking of Latin America and Central America, for example.

The U.S. national security strategy document – except for the "power" parts of it – could have been written in Ottawa. It starts with the idea of national values – the *propagation* of national values – that is one reason why I find it strange in Canada that some of our more pro-American fellow citizens want to get away from talking about values in foreign policy and be more mercantile. At the same time, they want to emulate the United States that puts 'values' at the opening of its national strategy document. In any case, because of this U.S. leadership role, there are a lot of people on both sides of the aisle in Congress, and in the U.S. more generally, who see the U.S. as bearing a disproportionate burden and meriting, as a consequence, exceptional dispensations from international law and practice.

The notion of America as exceptional is not a new one; it goes back to the Puritans. De Tocqueville commented on it in the nineteenth century; it was obviously present at the Paris Peace talks of 1919, as Margaret MacMillan has recorded. In fact, exceptionalism has been given a particular impetus in more recent years, starting with the Reagan presidency. Harold Koh, of Yale, has demonstrated that American exceptionalism has very positive, as well as negative, consequences. The U.S. has been an exceptional leader in the development of international human rights, and in the promotion of international law. But it is the more recent – and more self serving – expressions of exceptionalism that are the problem. They have eroded, among other things, the equality principle that most UN members consider integral to the democratic character of the UN Charter, much as the notion of equality of states is integral to the U.S. Constitution, even though in both cases, nobody is under any illusion that power is equally shared.

U.S. opposition to the International Criminal Court is a classic example of the U.S. seeking one law for the goose, and another for the gander. With the photographs-of-prisoners scandal in the Middle East, you might ask yourself whether that is a kind of dispensation you would really like to give.

It has not always been this way. In 1945 when the United States bestrode the world as colossally as it does now – even more so economically and militarily – President Truman told the assembled UN delegates in San Francisco that "we all have to recognize that no matter how great our strength, we *must* deny ourselves the license to always do as we please." People say 9/11 changed everything. I would argue that there was little in the post-9/11 reaction of the world that would justify – that would warrant – such a change in course, jeopardizing sixty years worth of development of international law, the development of most of which had been led by the United States. All of it was of significant interest to Canada. The consequent undermining of the UN was not, in some American minds at least, either incidental or unwelcome. Richard Perle, who was part of the President's Intelligence Advisory Board (and at one point chairman of it) wrote in *The Guardian* in March of last year, "Thank God for the death of the UN"[2]; there are two benefits to the war in Iraq: we got rid of Saddam Hussein and we got rid of the United Nations.

Right after 9/11, which is to say 9/12, the General Assembly passed a resolution of solidarity. The General Assembly does not make legal decisions, but at the first opportunity it had it issued a resolution expressing solidarity with the American people. The UN Security Council, which *does* have legally binding powers, within days proscribed cooperation with terrorists prohibiting the use of national financial systems by terrorists and giving refuge to them. They set up a process of monitoring the behaviour of countries ever since. Many governments, after 9/11, sent troops to Afghanistan to fight in combat. Canada sent ground forces into combat for the first time since the Korean War. Many countries, Canada included, sent a lot of money, also, to try to lift Afghanistan out of its failed state status, so that it would not revert to the chaos that served Al Qaeda's purposes. It was in our interest to do so for other reasons. Bringing stability to Afghanistan, which sits beside Pakistan, a government with nuclear weapons and the President of which has

---

[2] Richard Perle, "Thank God for the death of the UN". The Guardian Unlimited, (21 March 2003), www.guardian.co.uk.

been subject to two assassination attempts in the last months, is in the strategic interest of Canada. It is not a bizarre thing to have done, to invest in Afghanistan.

A further point. In declaring war on terrorism, the U.S. gave itself an unachievable objective. Terrorism is a tactic; you cannot win a war against a tactic. It is a heinous tactic, but it is a tactic nonetheless. Portraying terrorism in monolithic terms has probably made victory impossible. In attacking Iraq despite the absence of evidence of weapons of mass destruction and connections with Al Qaeda, and (unlike Kosovo) over the objections of, undoubtedly, a vast majority of the international community, the U.S. has isolated itself, claims of coalitions notwithstanding. It is not clear yet whether the war in Iraq, the war against terrorism, and all of those things which go with it, are morphing into a war between Islam and the West. But it certainly looks like a possibility. There are 1.2 (depending on how you count them) billion Muslims in the world. And if you "radicalized" one thousandth, one in a thousand, that creates, potentially, over a million militants. In these circumstances, in an age of asymmetric warfare, not even the revolution in military affairs and the high tech capability of the United States are going to bring much comfort. This is a war that should be avoided if it can possibly be avoided.

The cost to American interests of the war in Iraq has been catastrophic – and it goes well beyond Iraq. Already in December, Edward P. Djerejian, who was a U.S. Ambassador to Israel and a U.S. Ambassador to Syria, and a former senior official in the Reagan and (first) Bush administrations, carried out a survey of public diplomacy in the Arab countries. He found that "the bottom has indeed fallen out of support for the United States." According to a poll released this past March by the Pew Research Centre, "discontent worldwide with the United States and its foreign policy has continued and even intensified since last year." Even before the prisoner abuse scandal took place, vast majorities in predominantly Muslim countries held unfavourable views of the U.S. As regards Europe, transatlantic drift had become transatlantic rift.

One of the things that should cause us all pause is that there is no common international threat perception anymore. In the old days it was fairly easy to agree; now it is not. And there is virtually no consensus on how to respond to it. Subsequently, with its Iraq enterprise in jeopardy, and the November elections at risk, Washington has come to see a greater utility in the UN. What is not clear is that the UN is going to be able to live up to the expectations that a lot of people would put on it. Asking the UN to take over Iraq (and I say this as a former member of the august Department of Foreign Affairs) is like asking the Foreign Affairs Department to take over running Canada! The UN has about the same amount of resources and Iraq is about the same size of country as Canada. Only there has been a war in Iraq, in fact several wars. Also, there is an incipient civil war taking place. It is not at all clear that the UN would be able to handle this assignment. There is great trepidation at the United Nations about being invited in, and then carrying the can for the failure afterwards. By the way, that sounds a lot like Somalia. The business about Al Qaeda and Somalia is worth discussing. The American failure in Somalia took place when the United States – without reference to the UN command – went after General Aidid, one of the warlords.

On the question of Rwanda, I absolutely agree with David Bercuson, that no one's performance was glorious – other than Roméo Dallaire's himself. He did ask for help from the Canadian government, and the Department of Defence did take the issue forward, but there was opposition in Canada to getting involved until it was too late, actually, to do any good. We have to be circumspect in pointing the finger at others. But there is also absolutely no doubt that the Security Council's permanent members – not only the permanent members but especially the permanent members – failed on Rwanda. Warren Christopher authorized Madeleine Albright, when she was U.S. Ambassador at the UN, to talk about "acts of genocide", because if they had said there was simple genocide taking place, under the 1948 Genocide Treaty, there was an international legal obligation to stop it. With Somalia fresh in their minds they did not want to do that. They had forces immediately in the region, as did others. In 1999, when we had the presidency of the Security Council, we caused the first public discussion of Rwanda since 1994 to take place. The UN Secretary General and the UN Secretariat had admitted their share of the responsibility for it years earlier. None of the permanent members had, until the year 2000, when we caused that debate. They were content to let the Secretariat carry the responsibility, much as people are content to let the Secretariat carry it right now on the oil-for-food scandal. By the way, every single contract of the Oil For Food Program went through the six-six-one committee of the UN, with permanent members on those committees going over every contract with a fine-tooth comb. And people knew plenty about things being diverted – in fact it was the policy to let oil be diverted to Turkey, for example, because Turkey had lost $34 billion dollars, some say much more, in the Gulf War and needed to recoup some of that revenue.

I am not here just to criticize the UN. The UN is indispensable, starting with international law. The Charter is at the heart of international law. While there is no sheriff who can enforce international law and put bad countries in jail, the progressive adoption of laws voluntarily entered into through treaties has created a whole new system of laws and norms and customs and agreements, which make the world a much more civilized place than it would otherwise be. That goes also for security. I mentioned the UN's twelve counter-terrorism agreements. The same thing goes for human rights, women's rights, the environment, and so on. There are 76 environmental treaties. UNICEF has inoculated 575 million children against communicable diseases. The World Food Program last year fed 57 million people. The UN High Commission for Refugees sheltered 22 million people. The UN Mine Action Services destroyed 30.5 million land mines, saving countless lives and limbs.

Some people have said that this is international social work. One of the things that we have learned, however, is that well-governed states do not incubate terrorism, do not incubate disease flows, and so on. Well-governed countries in the third world are very much in our interest.

So what can be done about it? Actually there is a lot that can be done about it. The UN's biggest problem is that its strength is also its weakness. Its strength is its universal membership; that is what gives it its legitimacy. But also, a hundred and ninety-one countries mean it is a Sisyphean task to get anything done.

The UN has three basic challenges before it. The most fundamental issue is that the Charter was written in 1945. It was concluded in 1945; it was being written even earlier. In any case, it was written *in* another age *for* another age. Terrorism was not on the agenda. There were fifty-one members of the UN. The objectives were to manage relations among a very small number of countries to avoid another world war. Over time a contradiction emerged between the most sacred purpose of the Charter – "to save succeeding generations from the scourge of war" – and Article 2 of the Charter which prohibits interference in the internal affairs of member states. But intervention is necessary because increasingly, at least proportionally, those conflicts are happening inside states. So the most basic challenge for the UN is to come to grips with the idea of sovereignty and the idea of intervention for humanitarian purposes. Another is intervention for prevention purposes – forestalling the creation of a nexus of weapons of mass destruction and terrorism. When is that legitimate? Another question is the overthrow of legitimately elected democratic governments. Should that be a reason for intervention for the international community? The UN has to come to grips with these new challenges. It is not obvious that the UN is actually going to succeed. I think we can help in that process quite a bit. The most fundamental job we probably have to do is not 'brokering'

agreement between the United States and others, but explain-
ing things based on our particular insights we gain here as a
neighbour of the United States. To help the U.S. and the international community to reconcile their differences means that
we have to bring to bear insights into what motivates the United
States, why they feel uniquely threatened, why that is legitimate... but we also have to be prepared to speak truth to power,
and not shrink from dealing frankly as friends and as neighbours with the U.S. administration when we think they are
wrong.

I will conclude with a few remarks on the Iraq affair. It is evident from everything that you have read – from (former Bush
anti-terrorism advisor) Richard Clarke, from (former Bush
Treasury Secretary) Paul O'Neill, from (*Washington Post* journalist) Bob Woodward – that this enterprise was launched a
long time ago. It is also evident that the decision was made to
go ahead, all but formally, around the beginning of January
2003. At the time I was sitting in New York and I noticed that
U.S. discourse had changed. We were hearing a different discourse. The discourse changed from an impatience with the
time it took the inspectors to get going to a dissatisfaction that
they were there, to an impatience to get on with the war. There
was the famous case of the ambush of the Secretary of State in
the UN Security Council by the French about a week or two
later – the 22nd of January. But this followed discussions
between the French and the White House early in January in
which it became clear that whatever the French argued as a
reason for caution was being dismissed by the White House.
The French concluded, as did the Germans, that there was no
stopping the war. They were not going to allow the UN to
become an instrument of U.S. foreign policy and approve a war
they did not believe was necessary. We had the situation of the
Secretary of State being selected to be the U.S. spokesperson
in the Security Council – according to the Woodward book –
because he was an opponent of the war, or at least, not enthu-
siastic about the war. A good deal of effort went into his presentation; it took an hour and a half of explication.

There was talk of aluminum tubes of centrifuges; of magnets for centrifuges for producing uranium; of unmanned aircraft; of chemical weapons sites. There was, as Arnoldo (Listre) has reminded me, a vial held up with the assertion that that small quantity of botox could kill many people. One of the really great observations of the war came in an article by Maureen Dowd of the *New York Times*, in which she said that there was more botox on the upper east side of New York, than there was in Iraq. Botox is botulinum toxin. The UN weapons inspectors were portrayed as so many Inspector Clouseaus, wandering around a country the size of California, never going to find anything. There was a point in the Secretary of State's presentation in which he showed an overhead picture of a site with a decontamination truck. Then there was another picture which showed UN vehicles arriving and the truck was gone. The claim was made that "you see, the Iraqis are fooling the UN again". (Chief Weapons Inspector Hans) Blix, the following week, felt it necessary politely to point out that those pictures had been taken three weeks apart. There was also talk of a terrorist site. There were the infamous biological mobile weapons platforms. None of these things, at all, have been borne out by subsequent facts. Imagine! Nothing has been borne out. You can understand what that does to the standing of our neighbours in the rest of the world.

The case is instructive. The International Criminal Court discussion took place nine months earlier, in June 2002. The U.S. was seeking an exemption under article 16 of the Criminal Court Statute according to which provision the Security Council, acting under Chapter 7 (that deals with peace and security), can ask the Court to defer consideration of a case, if it feels, for example, that peace negotiations might be impacted negatively. As Chief Prosecutor of the *ad hoc* tribunals for the former Yugoslavia and Rwanda, Louise Arbour had indicted Milosevic in the middle of the Kosovo conflict. Some felt that that could have ended up costing a lot of lives if Milosevic had decided that he would continue the war, because he had been indicted and had nothing further to lose. In fact, the opposite effect happened; but one did not know that at the time. The U.S. asked the Security Council to act under Chapter 7 to give an exemption in perpetuity to people who had not signed the International Criminal Court Statute, and who were providing peace keepers. The difficulty is that the UN can only act under Chapter 7 when there is a threat to international peace and security. So what was the threat to international peace and security? Was the International Criminal Court a threat to international peace and security? Or was peacekeeping a threat to international peace and security? Despite the fact that they were turning the interpretation of the International Criminal Court statute on its head, despite the fact that the UN Charter was being misinterpreted blatantly, the U.S. still managed to get the Security Council to adopt – more or less – the exemption they sought, by a fifteen to zero vote. That was done by exerting *enormous* pressure on the Security Council members, including having Ambassadors recalled who were not cooperative. The point was that the U.S. came to believe that it could get any resolution passed if it exercised enough pressure on the Council.

Back to the Iraq case. The British (but not the Americans) felt they needed a Security Council resolution authorizing military action. I received a phone call from Prime Minister Chrétien, saying Mr. Blair had said that this second resolution on Iraq was going to pass. I told him that it was not going to pass. My judgement was that the support was not there. Ultimately, the support was not there, as you remember. Not even a majority of the members of the Council were prepared to vote for the U.S./U.K. second resolution. That led us to propose our compromise. We could see this train wreck coming. War and no war cannot be reconciled. So what to do about it? We tried to build more time into the issue and to give Saddam Hussein some specific tests to pass. If he passed them there would be no war. If he failed them, there would be war, with UN approbation. We were being encouraged to proceed by many, including virtually every country represented on the Security

Council. There were individuals on the Council who were encouraging us to try to produce this compromise. Even Americans – and I will obviously not name which ones – saw it as in their interest if this compromise could be reached. In the end, of course, Washington would not cooperate and the compromise was not possible.

Someone said earlier that Canada and the U.S. normally get along. Something about the positive relationships between diplomats and how constructive and friendly they are. And by and large they are. But I would like to give you an insight into how the Iraq chapter unfolded. The attempt was made three times to have the Mexican Ambassador removed, because of the Iraq issue. Eventually he was removed. The Costa Rican Ambassador was recalled. The Chilean Ambassador was recalled under U.S. pressure because of the position he was taking in the Security Council against authorizing the war in Iraq. Attempts were made to have the German Ambassador recalled, because he was opposing the second resolution. Complaints were made about me, in Ottawa, for proposing a compromise. I asked for the American complaint in writing, because I thought it would "make" the rest of my career. I had been warned by an American diplomat, that this complaint was coming, and that they, the U.S. mission, had had nothing to do with it. I think that is correct; I am sure they had nothing to do with it. But the U.S. mission, also, is not always listened to, in these circumstances, by Washington. In fact, very often, the U.S. mission seemed to be on 'receive' vis-à-vis Washington and not very often on 'send'.

There are times when Canadian and American foreign policies are not going to coincide. It is not a case of being able to get along bilaterally, or, put the other way around, of having our conflicts on bilateral issues and being united against the world. If we have values, and if we act on those values, there will be times when we are going to disagree. This was one such time. It is rare, in public life, that you are vindicated for making that kind of a decision on Iraq as quickly as we were.

When I was in Ottawa, not very long ago, Foreign Affairs Minister Graham made the point in a speech that, actually, relations with Washington are quite good; that people were exaggerating the problems. I sat there thinking to myself "I do not agree with this, actually. I do not think relations are that good. I am still angry at the way sixty years of international law have been set aside; at the way an institution we consider central to our interests – the UN – was abused." Then I read, "The Know It All Neighbour" in a recent *Maclean's Magazine*.[3] This is what the author wrote: "There is a problem in Canada-U.S. relations, and the evidence suggests that the attitude problems are almost entirely our own." And what did the author adduce as evidence of that? "Sixty-eight percent of Canadians say that the U.S.'s global reputation has worsened." That's our fault? Canadians have an attitude problem when they recognize what the international community has told pollsters like Pew Research over and over again? My point is that we should stop blaming ourselves for everything that goes wrong in Canada-U.S. relations. We did not launch an elective, destructive war that has de-stabilized a region and caused countless casualties. We opposed it and counselled against it. We should stop beating up on ourselves for being right. Thank you.

**A question and answer session
followed Ambassador Heinbecker's remarks.**

Question: I'd like to say that was a very refreshing conversation, and some of the conversation this morning grated on me a little bit because of the "victim" stance. And I think that we do that to ourselves in Canada and that we actually are very powerful if we took the power and provided leadership to the rest of the world – whether it's soft power or hard power (I don't even like those terms at all). And I'd like to ask the Ambassador, how we can challenge Canadians to *take* power and *be* leaders around the world and take their rightful place in providing leadership around the globe.

---

[3] Jonathon Gatehouse, "The Know It All Neighbour". Maclean's Magazine, Vol. 117 No. 18 (May 2004).

Ambassador Heinbecker: I don't think Canadians are necessarily the problem. I think sometimes the Canadian government is the problem, sometimes Canadian academics are the problem, sometimes Canadian officials are. And I say that for a couple of reasons. One is, when I imagine Canadian officials, they become physically deformed in the course of their career – you may have noticed that about me (audience laughter) – and that is that you get one big ear, which is trained on Washington, and one blind eye, aimed at U.S. foreign policy. And that's the way you comport yourself. You don't hear, very much, what people elsewhere are saying, and you don't care enough about what's happening. How many Canadians are there abroad now – a million? – young people working in NGOs and businesses all around the world, many of whom come back – I think those people are, in some sense an international generation. They will have been out there; they will understand where we fit in the world. They'll know that we can do some good and we can do some not good. And I think that they will take things in their own hands.

What the Canadian government can do, to be perfectly honest, I think is what Paul Martin is doing. I think he has said relations with Washington are job one. We must get that right. I personally am not so sure about the idea of a cabinet committee on U.S. affairs because I think that could get distorting, but that's now been balanced by a cabinet committee on multilateral affairs, and he, I think, chairs both. I think that's important. Some of the steps they've been taking are important. I think the return of civility to the relationship, no matter how much you disagree, is important. A lot of what Americans – many but not all Americans – didn't like about Canada and Iraq was the widely reported comments of some Canadian officials, elected and otherwise. So I think he's doing that right. I think on the UN he's doing the right thing. I think the G-20 – I don't know if you're familiar with his G-20 idea, but the G-20 idea is that even if you reform the UN it's still not going to be sufficient because it wasn't created for the circumstances it now faces – the international community needs innovation. We need to create some other kind of group, and to have a leaders' level group of the G-20 that would be more legitimate than a G-8, and would make it easier to crunch some issues like communicable disease defences or agricultural subsidies and trade. It would make it easier to come together on some kind of common understanding of how you're going to respond to humanitarian crises and that sort of thing. I think that those are very good ideas. I think the idea of exporting "peace, order and good government" – people are making fun of it a bit – but I think the idea is that we have *succeeded* in this country in building a democracy, and we have a highly effective administration – even though, occasionally, we have things like the sponsorship scandal, but we have a highly effective administration – and we can impart some of our expertise to others. And it goes beyond the people from the department of corrections going abroad helping people. As we now know, running prisons properly seems to be a very important thing to do. And sending judges abroad, and sending police abroad to train police, and administrators to train people in the hospital system. We can also use our expertise to help others build civil society. Maybe there's a role for the Council of Chief Executives, if they'd like to take an interest. If they could stop going to Washington every April they could do some of these other things too – dare I say it, if they'd stop going to Washington apologizing for Canadian policy, there are a lot of things that Canadians can do. Maybe the Canadian Labour Unions could do more. I think Mr. Martin has it pretty much right: these *are* new, important things that he's proposing, and I think that they'll help.

Dr. Karl Henriques: Mr. Ambassador, I wonder if you could find us some insight, and also some segue into the next panel, on the potential role and symmetry of interests between Canada, which is burdened with the idea that it should be supporting international institutions and international law, and the new and emerging role that I think perhaps the European Union and perhaps particular members of the European Union can play in helping Canada and in Canada perhaps helping either particular members or the European Union in general to promote any greater role in the presence of international law.

Ambassador Heinbecker: I'm always slightly sceptical about cooperating with the European Union. I was Ambassador in Germany for four years, and I had the impression that they were so transfixed by the European process of creating the Union that they had basically lost sight of a lot of other things that were going on in the world, and that they had particularly lost sight of us. They were so internally oriented that they didn't realize that we were changing – that the Atlantic was getting wider, the United States was changing, that Canada was changing; and just because they'd spent the last twenty years organizing themselves didn't mean that the rest of the world was staying the same. Also at the UN I find the European Union to be a mixed blessing. On the one hand it irons out – especially in relations with the Arabs and some of the developing countries – some of the more egregious resolutions that we face. But on the other hand, it's a little bit like dealing with Washington.

It is so difficult for them to come to an understanding of what they're going to do, that once they get that understanding, they don't want to talk to anybody else anymore. It's almost the Washington syndrome – that which happens between the agencies in Washington – that the discussion whizzes around inside the beltway, and then finally stops, and everybody says, "that's it!" If it's a UN question, they take it to New York and say you can't touch it, because agreement in Washington has been so hard to achieve. On the other hand, the EU are all countries of the rule of law, and I think that they are individually having a very significant impact.

I'm sceptical, by the way – and you haven't asked this question, but I'll answer it anyway – that there will ever be a common foreign and defence policy worthy of the name as long as there are two permanent European seats on the UN Security Council, because that will mean that the British and the French will always have their own interests in mind. And I also think – this is pretty controversial – that there won't be a real European Union until such time as the British decide whether they want to be in it or out of it. And for the time being, they have clearly opted to be "best friend", no matter what, of American foreign policy. It reminds me of an apparently true story – although I certainly heard it about tenth hand – of somebody from the UK foreign office who had spent a year in the State Department, and was asked what the difference was. And he said, "Well, when something bad happens in the world, the Americans ask, 'What should we *do* about it?' and the British ask, 'What should the Americans do about it?'... and the Canadians ask, 'what should we *say* about it?'"

Joel Bell: Paul, one additional characteristic of the United States is that – if you agree – it also has some fairly open debate. Although it periodically "circles the wagons", and voids them of that, at the moment it is, now, again, going through with clearly wide open debate. It is a risk, that the U.S. will lose its resolve, particularly in a highly political period. But the sore has been opened and created in Iraq, with significant risks on the terrorist front, significant problems on a religious divide – that was talked about a bit this morning as well. Do you have any thoughts, if a European relationship is not one where you're optimistic that we can work together to do something, on where we go as it were? What are the methods by which we can try to bring things back together? Because there is a need to do so.

Ambassador Heinbecker: One of the great tragedies of the Iraq war would be if the United States decided that (Somalia-like) it's going to withdraw from the international scene. Because fundamentally, what we have seen is that the need for intervention is close to endless. If you talk to Africans, in particular, they have a great fear that their sovereignty is going to be overrun. But while they have a fear of too *much* intervention, they have the reality of too *little* intervention. Darfur is a current example where people are dying and nobody wants to do anything. When the Security Council debated our report *The Responsibility to Protect*, Kofi Annan asked permanent members, "if Burundi becomes Rwanda, if people start to slaughter each other, what will your governments do?" And the consensus was that they would do nothing. That it would be Rwanda all over again. One of the great difficulties, of course, is that, if the United States doesn't act, very often no one else will act.

I said "speaking truth to power". It is really not easy. Particularly now when, although there is a debate, the wagons are really circled, there's an election[4] on the line, the place is deeply divided. I think, until after the election at least, there isn't a lot we can do about it. I would not discount the possibility at all, that you will see a withdrawal from Iraq – even in disarray. I don't think anything like that can happen before the election, but these days things happen so quickly. With the news cycle, (the 24 hours news cycle, I guess), everything is much foreshortened. I think, as a practical matter, one of the things we can do, if the world will buy it, is to form this G-20, where the benefit to the American President will be that *others* will understand some of the pressures that he's facing, and some of the constraints that he operates under, and *he* will understand better why some of the others are saying what they are saying – where they are coming from – and you might get a little bit more of an effective multilateral cooperation.

And I think the other thing is that it was very difficult, during the Iraq war, to talk to Americans who even opposed the war, and defend our not being with them. I think we made absolutely the right decision. The U.S. is a free country and they're entitled to make their own mistakes, and this is a major mistake. They made mistakes when they overthrew Mossadeq in Iran. They made a mistake in Chile. They made a mistake in Vietnam. They make mistakes. It's a great country and they

---

[4] This address was delivered on May 15th, 2004. On November 2nd, 2004, George W. Bush was re-elected in the U.S. Presidential election.

have great successes: overthrowing communism without firing a shot; getting rid of the Soviet Union; preserving stability between China and Japan and the Koreas. These are enormous successes. Nobody else could do it. But they do sometimes make mistakes. I think that we have to be prepared to speak frankly to people, but it's painful, and you get a lot of static for doing it.

What can Canada do about it? I think we can try to explain to other people why the Americans are behaving the way they are. And we can try to tell the Americans why the rest of the world is seeing them the way the world sees them. No one has granted us those roles. No one is going to ask us to do it. No one is going to care if we don't. If we do so, we may be able to have some impact. But we shouldn't expect, at least in the short term, any thanks for it.

· IV ·

CANADIAN VALUES:
AN INTERNATIONAL PERSPECTIVE

Arnoldo Listre

I would like to thank the Sheldon Chumir Foundation very much for organizing this event and for giving me the opportunity of addressing this distinguished audience. I would like to make my presentation in the context of the very interesting issues that were raised yesterday and continued this morning and over lunch. Yesterday, we had a very interesting discussion on values and interests – the contradiction that sometimes exists between these concepts which guide – or should guide – the conduct and the action of states in international relations. After the very good presentations of Professor Cohen and Dr. Welsh, I will not enter into a discussion on the same subject, but will try to address the question from a phenomenological point of view. I will talk about the phenomena which I experienced while posted to the United Nations. You can afterwards make your own conclusions as to whether the conduct, and actions taken, were based on 'values' or 'interests'.

During the last tenure of Argentina in the Security Council, in 1999/2000, Canada was also a member of this body. I can attest that when I was Permanent Representative of my country, both countries coincided in every question brought to the consideration of the Security Council. These coincidences occurred not only in the context of public debates, but also in private meetings and on the odd occasions where members expressed themselves more openly and in a freer way. We also expressed many similar positions in the General Assembly. Unfortunately, the General Assembly is a body that does not represent the international community as it should. But this is beside the point of this afternoon's talk.

As a matter of fact, I remember only one instance when Canada and Argentina voted differently, and it was a procedural issue. We also passed a very important experience together, which was the crisis of Iraq. Neither country was on the Security Council any longer but both participated in every open debate called for by the Security Council. Canada played a very prominent role and proposed a method to address the question – a method which unfortunately did not prevail, as explained this afternoon at the luncheon by my very good and admired friend, Ambassador Heinbecker. The position of Canada and Argentina was the same. It was also basically the same position expressed by the two Latin American members who were members of the Security Council at the time (Chile and Mexico) and by Brazil who, though not a member of the Security Council, also participated as asked in the open debates. So we can say that Canada sustained the same position as these four Latin American countries who are, needless to say, very representative of the region. We sustained the multilateral approach and the principle that the UN Security Council is the only body that can authorize the legitimate use of force. We sustained multilateralism vis-à-vis a unilateral approach to the issue. In doing so, we were affirming our support of the United Nations. This was a Canadian value, and also a Latin American value in international affairs. Time has proved that we were right. We think that there is no alternative to this organization, in spite of its shortcomings, its frustrations, and its failures.

During the luncheon, Ambassador Heinbecker reaffirmed this position, reaffirmed what the United Nations means, what the United Nations could do and how it should be reformed. We all agree that it is an indispensable institution. We think that the United Nations has to be reformed to cope with the new realities and the new challenges of the world. We agree that the Charter was written in a different context, and for different problems in the world. But for the time being and, until the Charter is modified, we have to abide by it. We think that the main bodies of the United Nations should be reformed. Basically, the Security Council and the General Assembly have to be reformed in order to be more effective and representative, less discursive, more agile and more concrete; and the Security Council should reflect a more democratic world and transparency in order to be effective. We also believe that ECOSOC (United Nations Economic and Social Council) should be reformed. It should be less inclined to the confrontations that have paralyzed and made this body rather innocuous. Argentina shares with Canada the idea that the Security Council should be enlarged in order to be more democratic and representative and believes that the new seats on the enlarged Security Council should be only non-permanent members, and not new permanent members with the right of veto. Canada and Argentina share the idea that the veto is an institution that has frustrated and is responsible for many of the failures of the United Nations.

Our commitment to multilateralism is also expressed in other areas. That is the case vis-à-vis our support of the International Criminal Court. Both countries were very much involved and active in the formation of this international body which will help prevent, and eventually will judge and punish, crimes against humanity, of war, and genocide. I hope that perhaps someday aggression will also be included among the issues that could be judged by the court. We are also opposed to exceptions given on a permanent basis to the eventual jurisdiction of the Criminal Court. We think that a permanent exception could definitely cripple the International Criminal Court. The court was established in 2003, with a Canadian President and an Argentine General Prosecutor. Another coincidence that comes out of our common approach to multilateralism is the support for the Kyoto protocol on environmental affairs. We share the same idea of how to face the great question of the protection of the environment. This is a very important issue on the agenda of the world. Human rights is another field in which Canada and Argentina coincide. After the end of the military

government in 1983, a state policy was adopted, continued by
every government of Argentina: the support and international
protection of Human rights. This is a matter in which Latin
American countries basically coincide, and which we have also
faced, in different international fora, trying to strengthen the
International Committee on Human Rights of the United
Nations. We also share another very important common interest with Canada – the interest in free trade. We have fought
against protectionism and subsidies (especially in farming) and
we share this preoccupation with Canada, through the action in
the Cairns Group.

We have to face a very important threat to the world that
has appeared lately in a global dimension: terrorism.
Unfortunately, this is not a new thing for Argentina; my country
was a victim of terrorism, and was aware of this terrible crime
before September 11th, 2001. In 1982 the Embassy of Israel in
Buenos Aires was blown up and two years later we suffered
another attack on the main Jewish institution of my country –
also in Buenos Aires – which left more than a hundred fatal victims and hundreds of people wounded. Both were terrorist
attacks. So you see that we have this tragic experience as a
reminder of the problem of terrorism. The big problem with
international terrorism is how to deal with it. In order to legit-
imize the fight on terrorism, we think we should do it through
international cooperation based on international law. And
although this may take longer than a shortcut, in the long term
it will prove more effective. We have expressed this on many
occasions, and share this position with many of our neighbour-
ing Latin American countries.

Canada has given sustained attention (and Prime Minister
Martin raised the question in the last forum in January of this
year) to the question of humanitarian intervention. This was a
new idea proposed to the United Nations during the tenure
ofForeign Affairs Minister Lloyd Axworthy and Argentina was
invited to participate in this group. On that occasion, some of
the participants, including myself, made some observations

related to the word 'intervention'. The word 'intervention' is not very well received, especially in Latin America. Apart from this linguistic observation I have to confess that in spite of the fact that I shared the preoccupation of Canada in this regard I am not very optimistic that we are going to advance very far in developing this idea in the near future, especially in the particular climate existing in the world today with the events that are taking place in Iraq. I think that the moment is not very propitious for this kind of institution. For the time being, I do not think that this idea can prosper.

Another question which is very important, and where we also share many of points of view, is non-proliferation, arms control, and disarmament. We share the position of Foreign Affairs Minister Graham that sustains the need to revitalize the Committee on Disarmament of the United Nations, which is practically forgotten. In an inactive situation, as is the case of the First Committee of the United Nations, it seems as if nobody pays much attention to the question of disarmament. We think that it is the only universal body which can deal with the question of disarmament, especially under the new circumstances that exist. For the first time in thirty-five years North Korea has rejected the Treaty and new actors have appeared on the scene who could pose a threat to non-proliferation. So the question of the need to revitalize this body is more vivid than ever.

We agree completely with Canada's position on peace-keeping and human security. As a matter of fact, Argentina and Canada participate together in different United Nations Peacekeeping Operations. As we can see there are very important values that guide the conduct of Canada in international affairs that are shared by Argentina and other Latin American countries. I think that in the international arena it will be mutually beneficial if we can sustain our support and eventually the coordination of our actions in order to make these values prevail. At the same time, Canada's position and support will be helpful for us in order to balance the power in the world. Today the only superpower which exists is the United States. And it is the only country that has a political interest in Latin America. It is the only country that expresses such interest in our countries. None of the European countries, no other international actor, expresses interest in our internal affairs. And I think it will continue. We must be realistic. But we encourage Canada also to be more involved in the region.

Foreign Affairs Minister Graham has said that Prime Minister Martin has commissioned him to present a new program next year: a reformulation of Canadian values and a reappraisal of Canada's interests and programs in international politics. Therefore, I believe that the Latin American perspective could be included in this study, bearing in mind that it is a region where Canadian values and even interests could find support.

In this regard many unexplored opportunities exist for Canada in my country. We need investment, we need economic progress; and Canada is a country that does not raise suspicions – or 'reservations' – which other countries can. Indeed, Canada is welcome in Latin America and is one of the largest investors in Argentina. There are many opportunities for us to receive investment from Canada. The sharing of common values in international politics, good relations and common actions in the international fora, all contribute to a good basis of understanding that promotes investment and good bilateral relations between our countries. Thank you very much.

Ahmad Kamal

It was the best of times, it was the worst of times, it was the age of wisdom, it was the age of foolishness, it was the epoch of belief, it was the epoch of incredulity, it was the season of Light, it was the season of Darkness, it was the spring of hope, it was the winter of despair, we had everything before us, we had nothing before us...[1]

Never in the history of the world has mankind had such powerful tools at its disposal, in communications, in medicine, in armaments, in access to knowledge, in everything. The speed of communications has made space and time curve around itself as we move closer and closer towards cheaper travel, instant emails, and awareness of distant events in real time. Advances in medicine have tapped the remotest corners of isolated rain-forests to unfold the mysteries of natural chemicals and brought them to our doorstep in our local pharmacies, while at the same time unravelling the innermost secrets of our being in an effort to clone us into our bionic alter-egos. The destructive capacity of armaments has reached proportions that give us a glimpse into Armageddon and Hell. And for the first time in history, access to information and knowledge has become a universal phenomenon, with no differentiation of race or color or sex or belief. With such tools at our disposal, this should be about as close to paradise as we can get.

Alas, at the same time, never in the history of the world has

---

[1] from *A Tale of Two Cities* by Charles Dickens

there been a greater gap between the potential of the available tools, and the actual delivery of results in an ever-shrinking world. The gap between the rich and the poor continues to grow, and has in fact increased at an alarming rate over the past decade. In a world where much is touted about perfect markets and economic opportunity, one half of the world has no access to safe drinking water, one third of the world has seen its per capita income actually decline in just the last decade, one fourth of the world lives at less than a dollar a day. Conflicts and tensions abound; the death toll of the local, regional and ethnic wars of the last fifty years is greater than the total loss of life in World War I and World War II combined. Surrounded by poverty and pestilence and endemic disease, shunned or ignored by the rich and the powerful, for many in the world today life is a living hell.

The question then is, why this paradox in a co-existence of contradictory realities. How does it happen that with all the tools and the knowledge in our hands, we fall so short of the desired results? What prevents us from unleashing the pent up potential in vast populations for the betterment of humankind as a whole?

There may be many reasons for the gap between capacity and delivery, but shortage of resources and facilities is not one of them. We have an enormous surplus of wealth in the world, and to the extent that wealth is a fair indicator of the availability of resources, there is obviously no problem in the latter. So, what prevents us then from moving towards a more equitable world?

The main problem appears to lie in arrogant self-centrism, cultural intolerance, and an artificial division of the world into "we" and "they". Only our own problems and security and incomes and quality of life are important; the rest of the world becomes largely secondary or invisible on our radar screens. In many cases, even our basic knowledge of others, and of their problems and cultures, is sadly deficient. Slogans and sound-bytes become the basis of our assumptions about others, and with our minds thus made up, we do not then want to be confused by facts.

That is where Canada jumps to mind, in its commitment to principles and values, in the constant support that it has given over the years to a shrinking world in which the pain in any one part of the body can only resonate in all other parts, and as a bridge between the haves and the have-nots. Nor is it just a question of the values that Canada espouses as its own; its broad global interests, its support of a multilateral system built around the United Nations, its participation in by far the largest number of peacekeeping missions, its on-time payments into the budget of the United Nations, its constant referral to civil society as an integral partner in the international decision-making process, its efforts to strengthen international Rule of Law, its serious attempts to increase the value of trade-related financial assistance, its demonstrated contributions to environmental sustainability, its credible international influence in the search for better human rights and democratic governance, and of course its leadership in the elimination of anti-personnel landmines and in the establishment of the International Court of Justice. These are well known principles that many others also advertise as their own. What distinguishes Canada, then, is the fact that it manages to actually implement these principles, where others merely leave them as words on paper.

We know of no other country where the enunciation of foreign policy is subjected to a detailed and direct 'dialogue' with the whole population in an extensive program of consultations – through the media, through the Internet, through town-hall meetings, in fact through all available sources – in an effort to identify the true requirements of consensus and public support.

We know of no other country that has made multi-culturalism its defining way of life, where asylum is given to all in need, where fundamental safety nets are extended so hospitably to immigrants. This is truly unparalleled in our world of today. It came as no surprise therefore when 17,000 stranded passengers were taken care of so generously and at such short notice when their flights were suddenly diverted into Newfoundland airports as a result of the tragic events occurring next door on 11 September 2001.

For many of us, this Canada is not just a beacon of values and hope, but also an enigma. It is legitimate to ask, as many do, how it happens that a country that is located just across the border from its giant neighbour has turned out to be so different? Why has this country not been completely homogenized by ideas and values and procedures from across the border, and by the converse token, how does it happen that this same Canada has not succeeded in imparting some of its own principles to the latter?

In this context also, one of the constant questions in our minds lies in the debate between wealth and welfare, between conspicuous over-consumption and clearly demonstrated social responsibility, between brash over-statement and discrete under-statement, between new world riches and old world charm. There is no more than an invisible line that separates countries, but sometimes that virtual line can mark cultures that are worlds apart.

That specificity of Canada is well illustrated in the extraordinary diplomats that this country has always managed to send to the United Nations, and in the many initiatives that this country has taken both inside and outside that forum. All of us have benefited from the determined efforts of one of its most prominent diplomats in bringing the world together in Rio to ponder on the future of our planet. All of us have admired the decision of Canada not to follow in the footsteps of others in the attempt to isolate an island paradise which produces the finest cigars in the world. All of us remember the dramatic breakthrough in the issue of "blood diamonds" that was identified by another prominent diplomat of Canada in the Security Council a few years ago, and which has then led to an entirely new process in which these stones are now being stripped of their murderous heritage. All of us remember the courageous decision taken, and publicly announced, by Canada when the misjudging of events was starting to lead us into unrelated geographical directions in our fight against the scourge of terrorism, with results that are there now for all to see. History will never forget those signal contributions of this country.

Sometimes it is easier to look at countries from the outside. Canadians would be surprised at the respect that they enjoy among these outsiders, respect and affection and admiration. It is no wonder then that so many from the developing countries, including large numbers from South Asia, prefer to emigrate to this country with its multi-cultural ethos, rather than elsewhere in their search for a decent life. They have found it easy to be assimilated here, in jobs, in society, in way of life, in their aspirations for the future.

Many of us come from the developing world, where values are said to be rooted in family and tradition, where riches are measured not by how much you have, but how much you can share, where tolerance and respect for fellow human beings is the highest virtue, where reason must weigh heavier than conviction. To our audience here it can be rightly said, you are one of us in these values, and better than us, because you have practiced what we have only preached.

That being said, there is much unfinished business that remains, and in which Canada will be expected to take the lead. Despite its glorious contributions in international relations in the past, Canada remains an unfulfilled promise today. For quite some time into the future, we will have to face the unfortunate consequences of the new political paradigms now occupying centre stage, many of which are rooted in missionary zeal rather than in rule of law or in those principles of civilized behaviour that have taken decades if not centuries to crystallize. These will not be easy to displace once they gain an acceptability and a permanence as a result of the constant repetition that is being powerfully showered on them.

Similarly, there is much to be done as we attempt to reverse the disturbing economic and social trends that divide our world today, many of which can only be answered with the renewal and improvement of global commitments regarding aid and trade flows. With donor fatigue setting in, who will produce the creative statesmanship without which the situation can only worsen? We will all continue to look to Canada as a lighthouse pointing the way to help resolve these weighty problems as we move timorously into the future, a future which will hopefully be better than the present or the past. Canada itself will also have to look at how it can do even better in this sad world of ours. It may not be enough just to espouse civilizational values; far more important will be the need to find ways and means for building up tolerance and respect for other cultures, and perhaps a bit of humility, so that we can get a global critical mass that moves the world forward rather than backward.

Equally important are the lessons that we in the developing countries have to learn ourselves from Canada, in the respect for human rights, in the search for good governance, in building up credible safety nets for the under-privileged, in avoiding extreme opinions and actions, in building bridges rather than digging canyons, in working together as we move deeper into an increasingly shrinking and globalized world.

There are no problems that cannot be solved with dialogue and tolerance and the courage to take them on, and no problems that *can* be solved *without* these three. It should be easy for us to sit on the same side of the table as we go along the path of this decisive moment in history. We look forward to that opportunity, and hope that intellectual fatigue and diffidence will not stand in the way.

Karl Henriques

How do Europeans view Canadian values in the international community? Since 1976, Europeans have increasingly seen Canada as not only having kindred values and approaches to international affairs, but also as being a potentially vital strategic partner in helping to realize the application of such values in international actions.

The thrust of this paper is to suggest that a most significant and refreshing – but also rarely reported and poorly understood opportunity is emerging to help Canada apply its common values and achieve a more peaceful and just balance of power relations in the international community. This opportunity is due to several major factors such as the convergence of Europe into a more values- and politically-coherent and economically powerful global actor in the form of the European Union (EU)and other minor factors that I will address shortly.

I. Europe's View of Canada as a Positive International Actor

Canadians are much beloved by most Europeans, who remain deeply grateful to Canadian and American citizens for their extraordinary sacrifice to help defeat fascist dictatorships in Europe during the Second World War. I experienced this first-hand when I cycled for 20 months through 17 European countries, from Ireland to the former Yugoslavia, and from the fjords of Norway to the islands of Greece. In all these places, I was warmly welcomed, specifically as a Canadian.

European gratitude to Americans and Canadians has nonetheless developed into a deeper admiration for Canada owing to the perception of both citizens and political leaders that Canada has demonstrated a far more consistent commitment to seek and progressively apply noncoercive means of conflict resolution, both domestically and internationally. In foreign policy terms, Europe appreciates Canada's commitment to reach for, and continue to attempt to use, various nonviolent policy instruments – trade agreements, diplomatic, educational, and cultural exchanges – in order to provide a basis for continued dialogue and greater understanding of what different countries value, are concerned about, and work towards. Europeans appreciate Canada's demonstrated commitment to reserve the use – as a truly last resort – of coercive instruments to attain preferred foreign policy objectives. They admire the fact that, not only are our goals reflective of high ethical standards, but also that we have developed the diplomatic ability to maintain them: Canadian politeness combined with the determination not to forsake those lofty goals which we so value. We are often referred to as a model for how and why European integration can continue and enlarge, as it has with the ten new Members States (MS) as of May 1, 2004.

Europeans also appreciate and admire Canada's difficult but essential balancing act of maintaining a respectful, yet professional, relationship with its major economic neighbour while, at the same time, ensuring that that relationship remains based on mutual respect. Europeans cite Canadians' capacity to live judiciously, a quality which flows from necessity, good fortune, and our own sense of right. The capacity to live judiciously flows from necessity because we live beside a superpower. Our good fortune stems from the fact that we have benefited from living beside such a liberal democratic superpower. Yet, we also have a different sense and basis for determining what is right due to our historical and cultural attachment to more continental European notions of the importance of solidarity, social responsibility, and the necessity to all that it possible to encourage the rule of international law.

Europeans' respect for us also flows from the fact that they have had to live in a similar balancing act, where they have needed to maintain respectful relations not only with the United States, but also with the former Soviet Union and contemporary Russia.

II. Europe and Canada:
Beyond Shared Concerns to Strategic Partners

Most Canadians can also identify with European values, and how those shared values sometimes differ in important ways from the dominant political culture of the United States. In his book *Of Paradise and Power: America and Europe in the New World Order*[1], Robert Kagan has characterized the rather profound and growing differences in values and approaches existing between Europeans and Americans.

Kagan suggests that Europeans (who live as if they are already in Paradise) are tending to approach problems with great nuance. They are more tolerant of diplomatic failures, and more patient for solutions even when they do not appear to be coming quickly. Europeans generally favour peaceful responses to problems, preferring deliberation, negotiation, diplomacy, and persuasion to coercion and force. They are quicker to appeal to – and stay within the rule of – international law, international conventions, and international opinion to adjudicate disputes. They employ commercial and economic ties to bind nations together, and often emphasize process over result, believing that ultimately process can become substance. According to Kagan, because of their unique historical experience of the past century culminating in the creation of the European Union, Europeans have developed a set of ideals and principles regarding not just the morality, but even the utility of power to coerce others to one's will.

Nonetheless, Europeans consider Canadians kindred spirits in terms of shared values, and view Canada as a potentially crucial, strategic partner in promoting such values in common international efforts. Although the European Union has a much larger population, and the largest global economy, many European Union top officials feel that it is both right and more effective to pursue goals on the international stage with other international actors. It appears clear that they would be especially pleased to work more closely and thoroughly with those countries that have a reputation as an "honest broker". In other

---

[1] Robert Kagan, *Of Paradise and Power: America and Europe in the New World Order* (New York: Alfred A. Knopf, 2003).

words, countries that attempt, however imperfectly at times, to conduct their international affairs through international institutions such as the United Nations, and internationally agreed upon rules and laws such as those found in the UN Charter and the World Trade Organization.

While policy framers in the Department of Foreign Affairs and International Trade have generally recognized the Canadian affinity with European values and approaches to international affairs, it is understandable that Canadians have not viewed Europe as an entirely effective partner in the promotion of a comprehensive and positive international agenda. The fairly recent and dramatic changes in the global community and in Europe may be fundamentally changing that situation.

First, since the end of the Cold War, even friends and allies of the United States are openly questioning the permissive consensus towards US leadership in world affairs. And this is particularly significant due to the increasing shift in the basis and character of power and influence since 1989 from an emphasis on one's military capacity to one's economic capacity, and from an emphasis on the use of coercive tools to that of diplomatic tools for the resolution of conflicts.

At the same time, there is an economic and constitutional strengthening of historical proportions occurring in Europe. The convergence of Europe into both a larger and more coherent global actor in the form of the European Union signals a potentially monumental shift in the global balance of power.

A constitution for the vast majority of Europe achieved its unanimous political agreement among the leaders of the newly enlarged European Union of 25 Member States on June 18, 2004. The Constitution[2] highlights the importance of promoting international principles and objectives and provides European leaders with a renewed and broadened institutional capacity

---

[2] The full title of "the Constitution" is the "Treaty establishing a Constitution for Europe"; therefore, in strict legal terms, the Constitution remains a treaty. While on October 29, 2004 the constitutional treaty passed the difficult hurdle of being unanimously adopted and signed by the political leaders of 25 MSs (they each had a right of veto), the entirety of the Constitution will enter into force only when all states have ratified it, either through referendum or parliamentary votes. However, as has been evidenced in referenda in France and The Netherlands, while there will be certain challenges to the ratification of the Constitution by some MSs, and some improvements

and mandate to implement the values and international vision often shared with Canada.

The strengthening of Europe through the enlarged and improved governance system of the European Union provides Canada with an opportunity to develop values-based partnerships with Europe that are perhaps deeper, if less exclusive, than those they have with the U.S. And one should recall that the EU itself is an opportunity structure and a set of actors of far greater significance than could previously be found when there were just one or two like-minded and influential countries with which we could make common cause. And since Canada and Europe share many of the same international values and concerns, such as the need for a greater reliance on the rule of international institutions and law, the time may be ripe for even closer EU-Canada partnerships.

Some officials in Canadian and European foreign affairs offices recognize the opportunity to promote an alternative international agenda as a consequence of the significant institutional strengthening and widening of the European Union and, in particular, through its capacity to act as a unified, coherent, and principled global actor. This emerging opportunity for Canadians to influence a renewed international agenda flows, to a significant extent, from some of the institutional and policy reforms envisaged for the newly enlarged Europe.

III. Institutional and Policy Reforms Envisaged for the Newly Enlarged Europe

Why is there currently an attempt in Europe to achieve a more coherent, values-based, and decisive political system through such mega-constitutional reform? And what are some of the principal innovations in that new constitutional system?

---

to it may be required, the major institutional and policy reforms that European leaders have agreed to in it will largely come into effect. For even if as many as one-fifth of the 25 MSs have not ratified it in a relatively timely fashion, the political leaders of the MSs are bound by treaty to work out a political solution for the adoption of the major institutional reforms that I mention below. By August 4, 2005 over half of the MSs had already ratified the constitutional treaty.

European Council. Presidency Conclusions and Draft Treaty establishing a Constitution for Europe (Luxembourg: Office for Official Publications of the European Communities: UNIPUB, 2004).

First and most significantly, the EU expanded eastward as of May 1, 2004 with ten new members, bringing its total membership to 25 Member States. Yet, even with fifteen MSs, the EU was already considered the world's most complex system of governance. Now that the EU has welcomed ten more members into its fold, one of its most significant challenges is to maintain a balance between the twin requirements of liberal democratic political systems: input representation for an increasingly diverse population of some 455 million people on the one hand, and maintenance of relatively efficient and effective policy outcomes, on the other. In order for the EU to meet this challenge, its institutions had to change to fulfill the difficult twin requirements of democracy and efficiency.

The Constitution that is winding its way through the ratification process has four parts, preceded by a Preamble. Part One defines the objectives, the powers, and the institutions of the Union. Part Two includes a Charter of Fundamental Rights while the third part deals with the domestic and international policies of the Union, and the fourth lays out the general orientations of the Union[3].

The Preamble of the Constitution solemnly states that the Union establishes, as its fundamental values, "respect for human dignity, liberty, democracy, equality, the rule of law and respect for human rights." The Union is to work for a Europe of sustainable development, notably founded on "a social economy within a highly competitive market" which will seek to "fight social exclusion and discrimination." In the further construction of the EU, the clauses in the Constitution judicially and politically guarantee a space for a "social Europe" by ensuring that policies that will affect Europeans reflect their valuing of a socially responsible economic and political system.

All 25 leaders of the EU Member States agreed that the Constitution would give the Union a clearer set of values and objectives for both its internal and foreign policy; formal legal personality and legal supremacy; an enforceable Charter of

---

[3] European Council, *Irish European Council: Presidency Conclusions and Draft Treaty establishing a Constitution for Europe* (Luxembourg: Office for Official Publications of the European Communities: UNIPUB, 2004).

Fundamental Rights to protect and promote, among other things, minority rights; an efficient political and administrative executive system; a President of the European Council; and a single and powerful European Foreign Minister.

Complementary to entrenching a more coherent set of values and decision-making institutions to help direct and strengthen the domestic affairs of the newly enlarged Union, the Constitution states that the principles and goals of the Union's international policy must be in line with the same principles that have governed the development of European integration. This includes the principles of subsidiarity and proportionality which ensure that proposed EU rules will respect national and subnational cultural diversity. Despite the need for maintaining an eye on the European interest in international policy development, political leaders are at the same time also explicitly directed to ensure that such interest-based decisions do not violate the broader principles stated in the Constitution. The document provides a readily accessible and relatively clear set of high standards to which European international relations and policy development must adhere.

In sum, we are looking at the EU possessing many of the characteristics of any liberal democratic political system. Irrespective of the outcome of the ratification process for the Constitution by parliamentary or referendum vote in some individual Members States, the EU will find itself with a constitutional system that will give it a vastly improved framework to function as a more coherent international actor. These include a clearer and more defined commitment to a set of values and principles; greater domestic legitimation of decision processes and policy priorities; the ability to identify international policy priorities and to formulate policies coherently; the availability of and the capacity to use international policy instruments; and the ability to effectively negotiate with other international actors[4]. With these improvements, there will be an increase in both the internal and external political strengths of Europe.

---

[4] Bretherton, Charlotte and John Vogler, *The European Union as a Global Actor* (New York: Routledge, 1999), pp. 37-8.

IV. Canadian Foreign Policy Considerations in Light of a Positive and Strengthening Europe

As a partial consequence of the view of Canada as a logical and key partner for international reform, Europe has engaged in trust-building exercises by signing some privileged partnership agreements with Canada between 1976 and March 2004. For example, the Framework Agreement of 1976 between the EU and Canada constitutes the European Community's oldest formal agreement with any industrialized country. In view of the dramatic changes on the international stage since that time (and even since the Joint Political Declaration on Canada-EU relations of 1996), the Ottawa Summit in December 2002 launched a comprehensive review of EU-Canada relations. A report set out the results of that review and recommended new actions to enhance the Canada-EU relationship, with a number of specific priorities for enhanced and cooperative leadership on an international agenda.

The report acknowledges the fact that Canada and the EU share some fundamental values that underpin their societies. In particular, the report highlights cultural ties as well as a common "respect for multilateralism, that are the foundations of our partnership"[5]. As the EU enlarges, and as the EU and Canada both face diverse and evolving global challenges,

> it is critically important to expand our multifaceted relationship and build upon these foundations. The increasing frequency with which we vote together in international organizations – well over 90% of the time during the most recent session of the UN General Assembly – is a clear indication of our mutual understanding of the importance of the United Nations and other international and regional organizations. This strong demonstration of our like-mindedness[6]

---

[5] European Commission, *Declaration on Canada-EU Relations* (Luxembourg: Office for Official Publications of the European Communities, March 18, .2004).
[6] *ibid.*

has encouraged Canada and the EU to deepen consultative mechanisms still further across the multilateral system.

In March 2004, Canada and the EU agreed to enhance and strengthen contacts at the political level in order to achieve the following objectives:

- advance international security and effective multilateralism
- further economic prosperity throughout the global community
- deepen cooperation on justice and home affairs
- address global and regional challenges
- foster closer links between the people of the EU and Canada

There are good economic and political reasons why Canada should continue to engage in constructive and deepening dialogue on a range of policy issues with the Europeans. And the policy areas outlined in the Canada-EU Agreements from 1976-2004 provide an excellent and well-considered basis for extending such dialogue, and common international policy actions.

This values-sharing and potentially actionable international partnership may very well excite the imagination and efforts of citizens and policy makers in Canada to participate in the improvement of the international system. Aside from the fact that the values striven for by the European Union come closest to Canadian international values, Europeis also is of practical interest for those pursuing international reform: the European Union is the only liberal democratic global actor comparable to the United States showing hesitant signs of acquiring the legal, political, economic and social capacity to viably push for the insertion of such shared (Canadian) values in emerging international treaties and affairs. As a consequence, the EU is well situated "to take a lead in the WTO, for instance, in promoting social rights globally in parallel with the reduction of trade barriers"[7].

---

[7] Denis MacShane, *Left Out of Europe?* (London: Fabian Society, 1996), p. 9.

The new global frames of reference and the strengthening of Europe are likely to offer some hopeful opportunities to those who wish to realize some of their goals for greater justice in national, regional, and international fora. Canadian policy makers should not doubt the size, extent, and importance of the changes that are occurring in Europe and the policy options that they can increasingly afford Canadians. There is certainly a realization, at least by top American officials, that Europe is becoming much more than simply an important economic presence. More Canadian policy makers may wish to take a more thorough accounting of the potentially beneficial implications of the changing geoeconomic and geopolitical conditions and Europe's place in it. From both a values and an interests perspective, we may wish to at least question the wisdom of continuing to pursue a foreign political and economic policy orientation that remains, perhaps, excessively geographically focused.

Due to the EU's increasing input and output legitimacy, far more Canadian policy framers, at both provincial and federal levels, may wish to recognize and be better prepared for the significant steps the EU is taking to make itself an even more able and willing global leader. Europeans, at both the elite and mass levels, would welcome such recognition by Canadians. And we should perhaps also feel most encouraged that European have shown their willingness to forge ties with countries such as Canada to improve international affairs.

· V ·

INTERNATIONAL INSTITUTIONS: CANADA'S ROLE

Michael Byers

It's wonderful to be speaking here in Calgary. I'm not only a Western Canadian, I'm actually an Albertan, my parents live in Lethbridge and I'm a proud graduate of the Lethbridge Collegiate Institute. But I've been away from Alberta for twenty years, although I've come back for occasional visits. It seems like home but seen through a cloudy glass and it's nice to be back in this intellectually clear atmosphere. I missed yesterday's proceedings because I was speaking at the annual conference of the Organization for the History of Canada. What relevance does history have for public policy and the politics of international law? Of course it has enormous relevance. Doing public policy without an awareness of historical context is like planting cut flowers – it doesn't take you very far. And I'm delighted to be speaking today at a conference on ethics and leadership because the argument I want to put to you in the next fifteen minutes is that here in Canada we're going in entirely the wrong direction in a time of massive, dramatic, cataclysmic international change, and thus abdicating our ethical and leadership responsibilities.

But I want to begin by dealing with the issue or the definition of international institutions, because this panel is entitled 'International Institutions: Canada's Role.' I'm sure that many of you, when you first think 'international institutions', think the United Nations, NATO, the WTO, formal bureaucratized institutions that sit in buildings, have secretaries general, and hold meetings. Those are international institutions. But of course international institutions go beyond that. The Land Mines Convention is an international institution – it doesn't have a building, it has a treaty. The Basel Convention on the Transboundary Movements of Hazardous Wastes and the Third Geneva Convention Relative to the Treatment of Prisoners of War are international institutions. So indeed is NAFTA which doesn't actually have a bureaucracy, but has a profound impact on this country and indeed on the world. And there are informal institutions as well. Diplomacy is an international institution, diplomats operate in institutionalized, traditionalized ways and form institutional units and fulfill institutionalized functions. So too is something called customary international law, the unwritten but extremely influential body of norms that govern state behaviour outside of the framework, or in parallel to the framework, of treaties. International institutions are *everywhere*. They are multilateral, they are bilateral, they are visible, they are invisible and they interconnect and define our world. It's a pretty complex world. Instead of "International Institutions: Canada's Role," the title of this panel could be "International Relations – Canada's Role."

And yet in this country we sometimes tend to miss the complexity, the fact that there is such an inter-related, complex, multilateral web of relationships, of institutions, of norms, of risks, of opportunities, because we obsess constantly, excessively, repeatedly about the United States. It's pretty easy to obsess about the United States. It's very close, it's very big, and economically it means almost everything to us. It's also growing more important every day. When I left Lethbridge twenty years ago the train tracks that run past my parents' house on the way to Coutts and the U.S. border carried two trains a day; now they carry a train every few hours. We have become ever more closely related to the United States. But, as I have said, obsession tends to distract our attention from other things, particularly at a time when the leadership in our powerful neighbour is missing the boat in terms of the real challenges of this world.

President George W. Bush and his advisors repeatedly assert that the defining all-important challenge in our world is international terrorism. Since 9/11, international terrorism has been the framework of analysis and policy-making. And I want to suggest that on an objective, non-obsessive view of international risks, international terrorism is actually a long way down the list. I hate to say this – but I will say this – in Calgary, the oil capital of Canada: the number one risk to the human species is climate change. Unquestionably climate change. The survival of our species is at risk through climate change. Environment Canada is predicting a five degree Celsius average increase in temperature in the western Arctic within the next hundred years. *Five degrees* – that is, potentially, an extinction level of change. Good-bye polar bears, good-bye beluga whales, good-bye fish, good-bye trees, good-bye forestry, good-bye fisheries. It's enormous beyond belief. And yet our leaders, our *ethical* leaders refuse to make this the number one issue. Because the most powerful country in the world pretends it's not a problem.

There's an abdication of leadership on the part of our leaders to grapple with this change – and it's not just Kyoto that's necessary. I bought a Toyota Prius last month – a hybrid car that gets over forty miles to the gallon. Why? Because if we don't start changing our cars, if I don't start changing my car, if you don't start changing your car, hybrid forms of transportation will not become economically viable. And yet I pay more for my Toyota Prius than I would pay for an SUV because the tax incentives are skewed in favour of SUVs and not hybrid cars. That's a failure of leadership on the part of those who devise our tax structures and those who lead our country and provinces. And the lack of leadership by Washington is a weak excuse. Why, when we have something facing us of the magnitude of climate change, couldn't countries like Canada, Germany, France, Japan and South Korea and others around the world say: "We're going to deal with this problem on our own now, as much as we can, and maybe one day when the United States, China and Russia are ready to catch up, well, we'll have led the way, we'll have made that happen".

Other huge problems that we're ignoring, that we've been distracted from because of our obsession with the United States, include international epidemics – SARS was a warning; the next mutation could be a thousand times worse. What are we doing about it? Almost nothing. And yet if we're unlucky and at some point in the next decade a hundred million or a billion people are wiped out by some new strain of influenza, that will eclipse international terrorism as a threat to humankind. Almost nothing. We haven't eradicated polio yet. Antibiotic resistant tuberculosis is making significant inroads. My father had West Nile virus last summer. What are we doing about it? Almost nothing.

We obsess about the responsibility to protect and the need to come up with new conceptions of state sovereignty and humanitarian action. Genocide is occurring *right now*, today, in Darfur in Western Sudan. Is anyone going there? No, because the United States doesn't want to be involved. That's a failure of leadership, not only on the part of George W. Bush but on the part of Jacques Chirac, Tony Blair, and Paul Martin.

Other problems include the trade in small arms. Most of the people who die from violence in today's world don't die from tanks, or missiles, or precision-guided bombs, they die from AK-47's and other small arms. Yet we still don't have an effective treaty limiting the transfer and trade of small arms between countries. We *still* don't have a treaty on that. Instead we see an increased arms trade, increased sales of small weapons to the developing world and a proliferation of technology; the development by the United States of a new generation of land mines and a new generation of small bunker busting nuclear weapons. And the response of the Canadian government to the challenge of disarmament is to indicate a desire to sign up to ballistic missile defence. It's the antithesis of disarmament. It's armament, the development of new technologies. It's bizarre; it's the failure of leadership.

And then, finally, let's talk about international development. I know that the gentleman in whose honour this conference is held travelled frequently to the developing world, and that's something that I hope that you've all done. The inequalities in this world are increasing rather than decreasing. The anger and the resentment increases as well, particularly as poor people become more aware, in our interconnected world, of the opportunities that are not available to them. The resentment is a contributing factor towards international terrorism and ethnic strife. But it's also more than that, it's not just an interest, it's an obligation for all of us. And yet, Canada's foreign aid budget is less than half of what it was in 1984 as a percentage of GDP. We're spending less, not more. We hear fine words in terms of NEPAD and the new initiative on AIDS/HIV, but if you actually look at the numbers, we're going down rather than up. These are the real challenges. Yes, international terrorism is a challenge, but we can deal with it. Indeed, with cooperation, we can deal with all of these challenges. The problem, though, is twofold. First, these are collective action problems and it's very easy for countries to say: "Well, we can't do anything because others will free ride." Second, there are issues that require leadership and when there is one country that is so dominantly powerful and about whom we all obsess, when it chooses not to lead, it's very easy to follow that lack of leadership.

And so my suggestion today in terms of Canada and international institutions is very simple: it's time for us to lead and not to look to Washington. And it's time for us to put our money where our mouth is and stand up as an independent country that is a friend and ally of the United States but also a friend and ally of people everywhere. And to move forward in ways that are unexpected and yet necessary. To perhaps put a goal forward, a firm goal forward, to reduce CO_2 emissions in Canada not to 1990 levels but to sixty percent below 1990 levels, and thus become the global leader in the reduction of CO_2 emissions. To indicate that Canada is going to be serious about international development and return our spending to 1984 levels, and then go beyond that because it's still a small amount of money, and thus show the world that we can be a leader there too.

And perhaps to do something really bold with regard to the issue of Iraq. Let's create a force of five or ten thousand Canadian soldiers who are designated as international peace-keepers with heavy lift aircraft to get them where they need to go and then offer them to the United Nations Secretary General on a standing basis for deployment at his discretion. To fulfill the vision that the representatives in San Francisco in 1945 had of a standing UN force and to do it, not because we've managed to get agreement with other countries, but just because it's the right thing to do. It's a lot cheaper than buying into missile defence. Missile defence is going to cost upwards of half a trillion dollars. If Canada is required to pay for even five percent of that, the cost would massively exceed that of five or ten thousand blue berets. Will the United States be unhappy if we do this sort of thing? Of course, since those who abdicate leadership hate to see others fulfilling a leadership role. But that's okay, we've stood up to them before and proven that we can be their best friend and ally and yet be an independent country at the same time. That's been very well documented, not just in the Vietnam War but also with respect to Iraq.

So I urge all of you, especially the young people in the room: when you think about international institutions and Canada's role, stop thinking about the United States and start thinking about Canada. There's a great opportunity here, not just a great challenge; and in my view that makes it all worthwhile. This is why I'm coming back to Canada, because I've grown tired of the lack of leadership in the United States, while here I feel a sense of opportunity and restrained hope that is ready to burst forward again much as it did in the 1950s and 60s. And so I hope that you'll work with me – as together we try to make something happen here that isn't happening elsewhere, that is, to exercise ethical leadership in our world. Thank you.

Roy Lee

I spent two very pleasant years at McGill University in the 1960s and have many fond memories of the Law School and of living in Montreal. Forty years later, when I close my eyes, I can still vividly hear and picture buses climbing up Peel Street in the deep winter snow. I had an opportunity to claim compensation on behalf of some thirty Chinese sailors who were shipwrecked in the St. Lawrence River. As a gesture of their gratitude, they gave me a ticket to England where I completed my Ph.D. study. From there, I was recruited to work with the United Nations in New York.

It seemed that my good fortune started with my first visit to Canada. Coming here to attend this Symposium in Calgary is not only an honour; it also gives me an opportunity to revisit Canada and to renew my friendships here. I would like to mention, particularly, Joel Bell, Chair of the Board of the Sheldon Chumir Foundation for Ethics in Leadership. Our friendship goes back to McGill. I had fun at McGill in debating with Joel the values of democracy and human rights. It is good to see him and to participate in this event. I would like to congratulate him and Marsha Hanen for carrying out so ably the admirable visions of Sheldon Chumir and for organizing this discussion of Canadian values in the world community.

I was fortunate to work for the United Nations in the field of public international law and multilateral diplomacy. During the past thirty-two years, I was involved in several important multilateral negotiations dealing with human rights, law of the sea, settlement of disputes and the International Criminal Court. Based on that experience, I would like to identify a number of areas where I think Canada can play a significant role in the work of the United Nations.

Canada is unique in many ways. It is a large country endowed with natural and human resources. It has a bilingual culture and a legal system embodying both common law and civil law. The people of Canada relate to all parts of the world.

Canada has been a strong supporter of the United Nations and has kept a very active role in the organization. It has many able and qualified diplomats and has undertaken numerous admirable initiatives in the political, humanitarian and environmental fields. There is a need in the world organization for a country like Canada to build a coalition of like-minded States to spearhead multilateral diplomacy and collective decision-making, which is the basis of our present world community.

A fundamental UN Charter principle is Member States' commitment to the process of making collective policy decisions and undertaking enforcement actions through the Security Council. I believe Canada can help strengthen this process of collective decision-making in the United Nations.

Under the UN Charter, on matters that affect international peace and security, Member States have in law transferred their traditional competence in that area to the Security Council. The Council deliberates and acts on behalf of the world community. All nations are bound legally to pursue this process of decision-making through the Security Council and to act in accordance with its decisions. This process of collective decision-making and action-taking works well when general agreement amongst members of the Council is possible. For example, such conditions existed when the Council was able to act or authorize Member States to act on its behalf to expel Iraqi invaders in Kuwait, to stabilize situations in the former Yugoslavia, and to create a criminal tribunal to punish those who had committed atrocity crimes in Rwanda. Recently, this multilateral process broke down in handling the Iraq situation. I believe that this multilateral process of diplomacy needs to be reaffirmed and Canada, in association with other like-minded states, can play a critical role in restoring its proper place.

States need to be reminded of what they have committed to the UN Charter. The United Nations is the world community because of its universal membership. As a treaty subscribed to by 192 States, the UN Charter has become the constitution of the world. Being the black-letter law, it must be observed by all states. True, there are many inadequacies and shortcomings in the Charter. But until the Charter provisions have been changed according to the appropriate procedure, the black-letter law must be complied with. No one nation, or small group of nations, should be permitted to act in a manner inconsistent with the Charter commitment.

Another area in which I think Canada can play a significant role is to help the Security Council to avoid inaction or deadlocks in its decision-making. Let me explain.

Under the existing system, the Security Council will not deal with a situation unless it is formally brought to it by a Member State. Neither the victims nor an NGO has direct access to the Council. Since most states are preoccupied largely with their own affairs, it is not unusual to find that no state is interested in bringing a matter to the Council, no matter how atrocious the situation may be or how many civilians have been killed. Rwanda was a case in point. The situation in Darfur was not brought before the Council until some half million people had died or been displaced.

There is therefore an urgent need to find ways to bring those deserving situations to the Council. I cannot offer a solution, but I can offer a suggestion.

Every year, states campaign vigorously for a seat on the Council without making a serious commitment to the performance of the Council's duty. Perhaps, states could issue their support conditionally on that kind of commitment of candidates. Canada could actively endorse such a policy.

NGOs active in the field should be encouraged to make coordinated and consolidated efforts to urge states and the Secretary-General to bring a deserving situation to the Council.

The present Secretary-General may do so only if the referral is supported by irrefutable and overwhelming evidence. His task is made easier when the request is supported by several reputable NGOs. The government of Canada supports and gives grants for many active NGOs' projects in this field and could motivate them to take steps in this direction.

Even when a situation is brought before it, the Council may not be able to act because of insufficient votes, veto, or threat of veto. Consequently, no action is taken by the Council and States may opt to act outside the Council. This was the case of Kosovo where NATO members decided to bomb the Serbs without an authorization of the Council for fear that the proposal might be vetoed. This was also the case in the Middle East when some of the initiatives were vetoed. Recent military action against Iraq led by the United States and the United Kingdom is another example when it became clear that there was insufficient support in the Council.

There is no easy way to deal with these difficulties. The Security Council is a highly political institution, and national interests often come first. But if there is a genuine collective political will to seek compromise and to avoid deadlocks, a way may be found to avoid a deadlock. Small and medium States acting together can play a critical role as a driving force to seek compromises. Canada can play a leading role in this group.

I now turn to the third area where I think Canada can lead, paving the way for a more humane world. This is the protection of civilians in armed conflicts.

Hardly a day goes by without news reports of serious violations of human rights in some parts of the world. More than 86 million civilians have died or been disabled in the past 50 years, mostly resulting from ethnic fighting and ideological and political conflicts.

In recent years, we have seen:

- Mutilations in Sierra Leone, genocide in Rwanda, ethnic cleansing in the Balkans, disappearances in Latin America or killings in Liberia.

- In sub-Saharan Africa, more than 22 countries have been involved in wars or serious insurrections since 1994 and 18 countries have each lost lives in numbers just below 800,000. Angola, Congo, Rwanda, Sudan have each suffered more than 800,000 deaths.

- The war in Sudan between the north and south has claimed 2 million deaths. In recent months, some 700,000 peasants have been displaced in the north-western region of Darfur as the result of violence committed by the government-supported militias who were given carte blanche to shoot, loot, burn alive and rape the farmers.

- The brutal fighting in Columbia between the government and guerrilla forces has resulted in 157,000 internal refugees. Last year, over 16,000 suspected members of the country's two leftist guerrilla groups either surrendered or were killed or captured. Few people knew what happened to those who were still alive and how they were treated.

- Burundi's civil war between the majority Hutus and the minority (but generally better educated) Tutsis in the past ten years has claimed 300,000 lives. 1.2 million, or eighteen percent of the population, were displaced.

- The war in Congo saw 3 million deaths between 1998 and 2003. Dozens of micro-wars smolder unchecked in the east of the country. The combatants are mostly irregular militias, and their victims are mostly unarmed civilians. In the northeast, militias are trying to exterminate whole tribes. Throughout eastern Congo rape, including male rape, is routine.

Historically, since the previous century, our law governs, primarily, armed conflicts between states and maintains a legal distinction between military and non-military targets and combatants and non-combatants. Non-military targets and civilians are not subject to attack and are to be protected.

Conflicts within a state lay outside the purview of international law. It was not until 1949 that we established minimum standards for fighting between government and rebel forces.

Our law cannot apply to fighting between factions and between other non-State entities.

It was assumed that the government in charge would be able and willing to protect civilians in times of armed conflict and would be able to carry out that protection.

The reality is that the law is often not complied with or enforced. In addition, the traditional assumptions, which formed the basis of our existing International Humanitarian Law (IHL), can no longer be sustained because of changed circumstances.

First, the government involved in armed conflict is often unable or unwilling to carry out the obligations to protect civilians. In some other cases, there exists no government. The situations in Somalia, Haiti, Afghanistan, Sudan, Sierra Leone, Angola, Congo, Kosovo and Liberia are some of the cases in point. In all these and other cases, the legal obligations under IHL could not be implemented by the government concerned and IHL became irrelevant. Civilian casualties were high.

Second, ninety-eight percent of our existing law addresses international armed conflict. Only two percent of the law is applicable to internal armed conflict. But most of the conflicts we now face are internal and involve various non-State entities. Fighting is also not limited to government against rebel forces, but often flares up between paramilitary forces, insurgents, factions or mercenaries. The militias, guerrillas and warlords are not legally bound by the law. They may not even know the law, let alone observe it. Our most serious difficulty is therefore to require the governments, rebels, militias, warlords and armed groups to comply with the law.

Third, our existing law prescribes a much higher standard for fighting between sovereign states, but a minimum standard for 'conflicts not of an international character'. This distinction was considered necessary during the colonial period in order to give the colonial powers the maximum leverage to deal with armed conflicts emerging from the colonies. Such a distinction is no longer justified. Civilians need protection regardless of the nature of the conflict.

Fourth, most of existing law is based on treaty. Treaties are applicable only to those states which choose to become parties. Non-parties are not bound, unless a treaty has become a custom. In the absence of authoritative determination, it is difficult to establish the existence of a custom. Under existing law, governments can easily refuse to apply a law denying the existence of an armed conflict or the nature of a conflict. This tactic was used in the West Bank by Israel, in Kuwait by Iraq, and in East Tîmor by Indonesia.

Fifth, the application of the law is self-judging. The International Committee of the Red Cross is the main entity responsible for monitoring compliance with the law. Each state decides the nature of the armed conflict, interprets and applies the law, and judges its own behaviour.

Our challenges are therefore how to bring non-state entities within the realm of international law and enforce the law in fighting between or amongst them.

We need to extract from the existing treaties and customs those basic humanitarian principles, and transform them into a set of practical rules for the observance of non-state entities. Some might consider this step technical or merely conceptual. Such a transformation is indispensable in order to firmly establish that the behaviours of non-state entities are now the concerns of the international community and are governed by international law.

The General Assembly and/or the Security Council of the United Nations should proclaim this set of rules in order to demonstrate the world's determination and commitment to the enforcement of the law. Any persons violating the rules should be prosecuted and published.

Such rules should be publicized and widely disseminated to all states and non-state entities currently involved in an armed conflict.

We also need to discontinue the flow of arms into the conflict area. We need to cut off the supply of bombs, mines, weapons and ammunition from outside of the area. Since divergent interests and concerns exist in any conflict, an effective arms embargo is extremely difficult to implement unless it is supported by political determination and true international cooperation.

From the legal standpoint, an arms embargo can be secured by a Security Council resolution under Chapter VII of the UN Charter if it is supported by all its members, particularly the permanent members.

It is also important to curtail the sources of financial support given to the factions, insurgents and paramilitary forces. This measure should be taken only when sufficient evidence points to serious violation of human rights committed on the part of such entities.

It is time to review all these issues in the context of civilian protection. Canada has advanced the proposition that it is a state's duty to protect its citizens. When they have failed in that duty, the world community is bound to assist. This is an important initiative. Canada should go further in proposing a redevelopment of the law.

Our existing International Humanitarian Law was last examined in 1977. During this interim period of thirty years, many basic assumptions have changed and the need to protect innocent civilians is even more urgent. The old law should be updated in light of current developments. Canada should lead in this field.

I now turn to the fourth area where I think Canada should and can lead. This relates to fighting genocide, war crimes, and crimes against humanity. Criminal prosecution at the international level is making great progress. The atrocities committed in the former Yugoslavia and Rwanda prompted the United Nations Security Council to establish two *ad hoc* international criminal tribunals to investigate and prosecute such egregious crimes. Criminal prosecution is also the chosen method in East Tîmor and Sierra Leone for handling recent atrocities. Some kind of criminal mechanism is also under consideration in Cambodia. The establishment of the permanent International Criminal Court further advances the efforts of fighting abuses of diplomatic immunity.

Canada's contribution to the establishment of the ICC is well acknowledged. I can personally testify that the success was largely attributable to Canada's leadership, substantive preparation, and negotiation skill, together with the active support of like-minded states and NGOs. The Court is now fully operational. Close to one hundred States are parties to the Court. The ICC Prosecutor has now been invited to investigate serious violations in Northern Uganda and Democratic Republic of Congo.

In my view, the ICC is likely to encourage national courts to investigate and prosecute the most egregious crimes committed by their nationals or within their territory; for if they don't, the International Criminal Court will step in and take the necessary action. The Court is likely to provide sanctions for enforcing our numerous interdictions and prohibitions that have largely not been observed or applied. The mere existence of such a Court sends a strong warning to the would-be perpetrators and might help to deter or restrain their behaviours.

Most significantly, the Court helps to advance human rights and humanitarian law by creating a true international criminal justice system, and by addressing in a comprehensive manner rights of the accused, victims and witnesses, as well as issues of reparation and rehabilitation. The crimes over which the Court may exercise its jurisdiction are defined in detailed and concrete terms. Victims are allowed to participate in the proceedings, and are entitled to physical protection and to receive reparation. Persons under investigation or indictment are entitled to more expansive human rights protection than traditionally accorded under universal human rights instruments. While the system ensures the independent right of investigation and prosecution, there are also built-in checks and balances to make sure that this independent right will not be misused or unused. A Pre-trial Chamber consisting of three judges is entrusted with the task of oversight.

The fight against impunity and for holding perpetrators accountable for their acts is not just a matter of justice. It is also bound up with the search for lasting peace in post-conflict situations. So far, great attention has been given to prosecution and punishment at the national and international level. Criminal prosecution serves the purpose of establishing criminal responsibility of the individuals answerable, not the entire ethnic, religious or political group, and avoids collective retribution which often produces further cycles of violence. Decisions from the tribunal can also provide a public, judicial confirmation of the facts, and give victims and society a sense that grievances have been addressed.

I have doubts that criminal proceedings alone are adequate to deal with situations involving large number of suspects. Take Rwanda for instance. Half a million people died because of ethnic fighting. The International Tribunal established to prosecute the notorious criminals indicted 81 persons, conducted nine trials in 2002. In 2003, it delivered six judgments and 29 suspects were in the dock. At the national level, thousands were arrested and are still waiting for trials in over-crowded jails. According to reports, more are dying in jails every day than the number who have been tried.

I believe that a broad spectrum of measures and mechanisms should also be used in combination to deal with situations involving massive numbers of victims and offenders. These include lustration, seizure of property and assets, factfinding, investigation of criminal acts, acknowledging and publicizing responsibility, and compensation for victims and their families. Civil society can help in providing technical assistance, monitoring and following up on developments. All these measures are not mutually exclusive, but can be pursued in combination as complementary components of a larger system of accountability.

Over the past decade, several countries (including El Salvador, Guatemala, Uganda and South Africa) have established commissions of inquiry or truth commissions to investigate massive repression and violations of human rights committed by the previous regime or during a civil war. These mechanisms are employed as part of a peace or reconciliation plan. Individuals were called upon to testify before the Commissions of the evil and pain that had been inflicted and suffered by victims and their relatives. The objective for such Commissions is to establish an official record of truth publicly acknowledged through an impartial and reputable body. The South African Truth and Reconciliation Commission also has the power to grant amnesty to those individuals whose confessions meet the criteria for amnesty. In addition to establishing truth, such Commissions can more promptly begin holding hearings and collecting testimony and documentation, which can then be turned over for use in prosecutions if and when such a course is to be pursued.

Lustration is another measure often used for handling situations involving a large number of cases. This method usually means the dismissal, suspension, transfer, demotion or compulsory early retirement of persons in military, paramilitary, and police forces, or in other public services (including the judiciary) connected with the abuses. Such sanctions were used notably in the Czech Republic, Lithuania, Germany, Bosnia and Herzegovina. Such sanctions can provide victims and their families a sense that certain sanctions have been applied and increase confidence and credibility in the new establishment. However, the process may be subject to manipulation and other limitations because it is less public and formal.

I firmly believe that these and other complementary measures should be employed to enhance criminal prosecution. Having led the international community to the creation of the International Criminal Court, Canada should also consider and promote these additional measures in order to encourage reconciliation and peace-building in war torn societies.

David Wright

A special thanks to the Sheldon Chumir Foundation for organizing this wonderful event and for focusing our minds for a weekend on the question of ethics in leadership. I think it's a crucial theme that you've identified here.

I'm the only non-lawyer on this panel and so I'm going to speak about legal issues. This reminds me of "Yes Minister" when Minister Jim Hacker thought he would take a new initiative that his permanent secretary, Sir Humphrey Appleby, considered unwise. When he asked Sir Humphrey's view, the response was "very courageous Minister" and the Minister took it literally and said "well that's great". But he eventually got the body language. In any case I will refer to some legal questions. But what I'm really going to concentrate on is a contemporary issue – dealing with conflict, dealing with the question of intervention. Let's look at how Iraq has changed all of that.

There was remarkable progress made in the nineties by the international community on how to deal with conflict. Look back at the humanitarian challenges, beginning with 1993 when the U.S. in Somalia had the terrible Black Hawk Down disaster. It threw the new Clinton Administration completely off its game. What happened next was the terrible tragedy in Rwanda. The international community failed totally in Rwanda as we all now know. But it took a while for the international community to recognize just how badly it had failed in Rwanda. Now with Roméo Dallaire speaking and writing so eloquently, and with Kofi Annan having addressed his own role, we really do have an important record of how the international community failed, how the UN system failed, and how everyone failed.

But then we started to make some progress. In Bosnia there was a fairly weak UN force on the ground, UNPROFOR. The massacre in Srebrenica in July 1995 was a terrible tragedy and it toughened the international community and finally led to military intervention by NATO that in turn led to the Dayton Peace Accord.

Kosovo was the next challenge and there the international community, NATO in this case, acted very firmly and very promptly. It stopped Milosevic's ethnic cleansing, got the Kosovars back into their homes, and started a process that led to Milosevic's trial in The Hague. That was a very good result. So we saw a kind of upward curve in the willingness of states to act in cases of humanitarian crisis.

Some people were a little bit uncomfortable with this because they said "Well, it's all very well what you did in Kosovo but you really didn't have a UN Security Council resolution to do that. And so by what legal means did you take that action?" And even people who were not at all sympathetic to Milosevic were troubled by this legal gap. And so Canada commissioned a study, the International Commission on Intervention and State Sovereignty (ICISS) which looked at the question of when nations should intervene. It was an extremely important undertaking and the Commission published a paper called *The Responsibility to Protect* which some of you have referred to this morning.

The trouble was that as the paper was being prepared for print, September 11th happened and, really, the whole world changed. Rather than going back to the drawing board, the Commission decided to publish their paper. They noted in the foreword that their report didn't address the kinds of issues raised by September 11th.

There were some extremely important messages in that report, I believe. One of them was the concept of "just cause" for international interventions. The report referred to "actual or imminent large-scale loss of life" or "large-scale ethnic cleansing". And it also said that there must be reasonable prospects for success of an intervention, that the consequences of action were not likely to be worse than the consequences of inaction. This implicitly recognized that only a limited group of countries – pretty rich countries with lots of resources and significant military means – were going to be able to have a reasonable prospect of success. So you had to have these countries on board.

In discussing the question of legitimacy of intervention or action of this kind, the report bowed to the authority of the UN Security Council, as is the norm. But it did go on to say something else that's quite important. It said "If the UN Security Council fails to discharge its responsibility to protect in conscience-shocking situations crying out for action, concerned states may not rule out other means to meet the gravity and the urgency of the situation". What that means is that if the UN Security Council doesn't get its act together, some people may act on their own. It phrased that point very carefully and also had another reference to consulting the General Assembly which I'm not sure was as productive. But they did recognize that the UN Security Council will not always be able to reach an accord to do things that, in the view of the Commission at least, may have to be done. I think this was a very important breakthrough. On the back cover of their report the final words are "There must be no more Rwandas.' That was their message, essentially. So this report gave us a kind of blueprint to deal with future challenges like Kosovo, like Rwanda, and so on. I think it was quite important. It is not international law yet, but it's been accepted by international public opinion to a very great degree. I think eventually the lawyers will come along on this one. But it may take time.

So, how do we link all that to what happened on September 11th? When September 11th happened it *did* change everything and there's been no challenge to the right of a state – the United States in this case – to respond to an attack. And indeed the world rallied and offered immediate political and military support to the United States after September 11th. In fact, a lot more help was offered to the United States than they were actually willing to take. Canada, for example was willing to put much more up front in the immediate battle in Afghanistan than the Americans initially wanted.

The problem of course was complicated by the fact that somehow in Washington the war on terror became totally enmeshed with Iraq. The books by Richard Clarke, *Against All Enemies,* and Bob Woodward, *Plan of Attack,* give us much of the story of what happened. They may not have it one hundred percent right but they do set out a pretty good inside view of how Iraq got linked up to terrorism.

And now we're in a real mess in Iraq. The United States is primarily, but I think we are all in a mess in Iraq because what's happening there is going to affect all of us. While there was very wide support for the U.S. war on terrorism, the Iraq war has divided the West very deeply. What was the U.S. rationale in Iraq? If you leave aside the whole 'weapons of mass destruction' issue, the elusive WMD, the United States acted because it saw Iraq as a threat so it took pre-emptive action to stave off that threat. This is the rationale that comes through time and time again.

It's very difficult to imagine that we're going to be able to develop universally acceptable rules for intervention to counter threats. The international community has struggled with this for decades – centuries really – and we don't have too much as a result. We have the UN Charter and we have precedent. But perhaps we should work on, in a contemporary context, some criteria for intervention to deal with threats that might be broadly acceptable for most democratic nations. At least we should have a blueprint, a study, for how to respond to threats that is comparable to the one we got at the end of 2001 to deal with humanitarian intervention. So we need another chapter to the report on *The Responsibility to Protect.*

Now let me give you a couple of ideas that have come from distinguished scholars in this field. Dick Gardner at Columbia University has argued in the *American Journal of International Law* for an *evolution* of international law, for an interpretation of the Charter along the following lines: he proposes that "armed force may now be used by a UN member, even without Security Council approval, to destroy terrorist groups operating on the territory of other members when those other members fail to discharge their international law obligations to suppress them". And secondly, "armed force may also be used to prevent a UN member from transferring weapons of mass destruction to terrorist groups".

Those on the face of them are pretty reasonable. Now obviously, the problem is agreement on the facts. These criteria may be widely acceptable in Western countries but the proof and the facts are the problem. And there would be a burden of proof on the country or countries willing to intervene.

One other contribution came from Lee Feinstein of the Council on Foreign Relations and Anne-Marie Slaughter of the Woodrow Wilson School at Princeton University writing about pre-emption in the January 2004 edition of *Foreign Affairs.* Their article was called "A Duty to Prevent" and it built on the ideas of the International Commission on Intervention and State Sovereignty (ICISS) and extended them to deal with the question of terrorism and WMD. They talk about the duty to prevent, flowing from their premise that the rules on the use of force devised in 1945 and embedded in the UN Charter are inadequate. They propose a duty to prevent dictators from acquiring or using WMD. They focus on leaders who have no internal checks on their power.

Now all that they've done in these two studies is open the debate. They've described the question. But I think the international community, and the legal community in particular, *has* to work on this issue and has to be creative on this issue. There will always be questions of definition and proof and fact, and future cases are very unlikely to be clear-cut. However, we need some criteria to guide debate on future questions of intervention to counter terrorism, WMD or both.

I wanted to focus on this one question because we have to deal with it and we have the power to do something about it. So I would call for a study comparable to that of the ICISS to deal with this question of threats and in particular the terrorism/WMD nexus. And I think that the Gardner and Slaughter/Feinstein pieces give us a good starting point.

But all of this will go for naught unless we have enough political will. And here is where I'm very concerned about the consequences of Iraq. I think it's going to sap the political will in the countries with any ability to take action. Legitimacy of action is necessary but it is not sufficient for anything to happen. And I believe the danger from what's happening to the United States in Iraq right now is that it's going to discourage capable governments, future American governments or other governments, from meeting future challenges, particularly humanitarian crises.

The U.S. presence in Iraq was never a humanitarian intervention. But there is no doubt that its consequences will reduce the political will to get involved in future humanitarian crises, partly because of political risk, partly because of the drain on resources that a venture like Iraq involves. The American public is going to be less supportive of all U.S. interventions in the aftermath of Iraq. The only exceptions will be those where the threat to the United States is clear and widely accepted. So Iraq will suck all the oxygen out of any debate in the near term on intervention in a humanitarian crisis – for example, Sudan – especially when national interests are not engaged directly and when the intervention will be for humanitarian purposes.

So all the progress that we made, and I believe there was progress, to strengthen the willingness and the ability of the international community to do something in humanitarian crises is jeopardized by the current situation. The political will to do something about the next Rwanda may well be another casualty of the current quagmire in Iraq.

Kathleen Mahoney

First of all, I'd like to thank the Sheldon Chumir Foundation for inviting me to participate in this very important Symposium. I have observed over the past years that the Sheldon Chumir Foundation conferences on Ethics in Leadership have become very important events in Calgary and in Canada. I plead with the Foundation: please never stop organizing these events. Calgary and Canada need these conferences with these themes. In my experience living here in Calgary, this sort of Symposium is rare. High level discussions which engage a broad spectrum of civil society on ethical issues, attracting the quality of speakers you have in attendance are an extremely valuable contribution to the ongoing debate that must occur in healthy civil societies.

My presentation today is going to be focused on human rights and their role in foreign policy. Canada's foreign policy has traditionally rested on three pillars: security, prosperity, and Canadian values. I will elaborate on the values pillar, and how it must shape Canada's role with respect to international institutions. I agree with Dr. Byers' definition of institutions; it covers just about *everything* internationally. But I'm going to talk in particular about the institutions of the United Nations and the regional human rights institutions in this hemisphere, and try to identify the context and values which should govern Canada's approach to these institutions. Questions that need to be asked are: How does Canada's human rights role converge with our role in international institutions? What is the relative importance of human rights in Canada's foreign policy, especially in relation to the three pillars of security, prosperity and Canadian values?

In my opinion, Canadian foreign policy, with respect to international and regional human rights institutions, has never been so important as it is today. The current trends and enormous tensions in international affairs in the last fifteen years have seriously undermined the values and policies developed since World War II, "to protect" (and I'm quoting from the Universal Declaration of Human Rights) "the inherent dignity, and the equal and inalienable rights of all members of the human family."[1] The fundamental changes and dramatic events which have taken place have shifted the ground under the assumptions that we've taken for granted for the last five decades. Consequently, this topic is highly relevant and in urgent need of debate.

Since World War II, Canada developed a clear set of core values which define us, and which until now have served us quite well. They include compassion for those in trouble and for those who have less. As well, Canadians value the reconciliation and accommodation of cultural differences. We traditionally disavow violent conflict, human rights abuses, and the negation of democratic values. We also believe in collaboration with civil society domestically and internationally, participation, accountability, and transparency. We are proudly multi-cultural and have a long history of welcoming immigrants and refugees to our country.

The value of our traditional inclusive global vision and policy perspective cannot be overestimated in the current global context of rampant ethnic, racial, and religious strife and divisions. But as we witness, on a daily basis, the extreme violations of human rights all over the world, simply having a particular set of values is, apparently, not enough. It is clear that the international institutions designed to protect and promote human rights are failing us… miserably! If we are to achieve the goals of the Universal Declaration of Human Rights, there must be a more effective way of implementing the values we espouse. Canada must redefine its role in international institutions with more, rather than less, of an insistence on open,

---

[1] *Preamble, Universal Declaration of Human Rights* (Adopted and proclaimed by General Assembly Resolution 217 A (III) of 10 December 1948).

global, and universal human rights, sensitivity to cultural differences, and respect for other civilizations and heritages. Canada's role in international institutions must be biased in favour of the notion that international human rights institutions should be effective and capable of producing concrete, measurable results which reflect our values.

To do this, there must first be a clear understanding of the recent mutations which have both unified and fractured the world. Second, Canada must have a strategy which will give effect to our essential values; and third, this must be followed by an action plan, which will place human rights at the core of the world community, and which will produce concrete results. I will deal with each of these in turn.

1. Recent Mutations
(a) The End of the Cold War and the Beginning of Globalization

Since the Universal Declaration became the international standard for human rights over fifty years ago, some fundamental changes have taken place in the grand political scheme of things. When the Soviet Union imploded and the cold war ended, a model of global governance with its own codes, alliances, and power relations disappeared. Existing international human rights institutions lost the context within which they had advanced the human rights agenda. The doctrine, policies, and jurisprudence of human rights which informed the operation of international institutions created in the aftermath of World War II remained; but the tensions which allowed them to advance were transformed. Ironically, it was the doctrine, policies, and jurisprudence of human rights that caused the disintegration of the Soviet Union in the first place. The millions of dissidents who defied their governments in Russia and in Poland and in Central Europe used the powerful tools of human rights to claim freedom, the rule of law, and democratic institutions for themselves with the unintended consequence that when the dust settled, those very rights were globally weakened.

With the disappearance of the equilibrium that rested on the duality of the cold war, geographical, economic, social and environmental points of reference shifted. The map of Europe was redrawn, new independent states emerged, the roots of South African apartheid were severed and major changes occurred to the environment because of new technologies and economic growth.

The global vacuum created by the demise of the Soviet Union was quickly filled by a new conception of the world – the conception of globalization. Globalization involved an unprecedented desire amongst many countries to organize the world into one vast marketplace and to level any obstacles getting in the way. Norms of private enterprise were presented as principles of general application that could be used to structure all the economies of the world and the world community. Corporate self-regulation was promoted over regulation through international human rights instruments and international institutions. At the same time, a conscious effort was undertaken to constrain multilateralism at the regional and international levels in order to promote the objectives of globalization. The purpose of this free market offensive was to clear the way for new international institutions, such as the World Trade Organization. In the result, the priority, doctrine and policies of human rights fell by the wayside and became more symbolic and declaratory than substantive and enforceable. International and regional institutions were marginalized, as were the social and political dimensions of the economy.

This revolution – and that's what it was – this revolution and reconstruction of the world, created conditions and pressures for convergences and movements towards a unitary system of development and growth. Still unfolding are the struggles for supremacy between forces of democracy and inward-looking nationalisms; a fragile global ecosystem and the new world economic order. Challenges to gender, race and class inequities perpetrated by institutions with inherent patriarchal, racist and classist tendencies are creating tensions causing fear and uncertainty for many people.

But diversity in the world is resisting. And this is what is so important – diversity in the world is as it always has been. The forces of globalization have not erased history. Cultures have not disappeared. Plurality still exists despite the efforts to create a single economic, commercial and financial global system. As well, the lofty aspirations of the globalization movement of shared growth and development have not been met – by hardly any measure. Protectionist policies of the developed nations have kept poorer countries poorer. Too often, investment and the quest for productivity and profit have been pursued with disastrous social and environmental consequences, and disregard for the most basic human rights.

Since 1990, the report card on globalization tells us that extreme poverty has increased in South Asia, sub-Saharan Africa, and throughout Latin America. During the same period, development assistance dropped drastically, and the net balance of resource transfers to developing countries is negative. Individual income is lower today than it was in 1990 in the majority of developing countries. While globalization cannot be solely blamed for creating vast poverty that exists in the world, it failed to redefine the relationship between the haves and the have-nots of the world to arrive at a more equitable distribution of wealth. While it is unrealistic to think that the mass poverty of the third world can be eradicated in the space of a little over a decade, it could have been realistically expected that globalization would have redefined the relationship between the developed world and the impoverished countries outside of the global economy, as they are described by the Organization for Economic Cooperation and Development. The profound disparities which divide the world persist without a glimmer of hope that they will be addressed in any meaningful way in the near or far future.

As things stand, none of the Millennium Development Goals proclaimed by the United Nations General Assembly in 2000, including halving extreme poverty and hunger, achieving universal primary education, achieving gender equality and empowering women, reducing child mortality, improving maternal health, combating HIV/AIDS, malaria and other diseases, ensuring environmental sustainability and developing a global partnership for development, will be attained. Another thing we will never know – and this is the sad part – is what would have happened if the forces of globalization had converged with democratic values and human rights. Some are of the view that we have missed our one big chance to achieve the kind of civilization that is codified in the Universal Declaration of Human Rights.

(b) The 9/11 Terrorist Attack on the United States and the "War of Terrorism"

Since the terrorist attack on the United States on September 11, 2001 by al Qaeda, security has become a major preoccupation without historical equivalent. The "war on terrorism" has metamorphosed into military operations – first in Afghanistan and then in Iraq – creating profound divisions in the international community and ushering in a new phase of global re-armament. The new doctrine and policy of preventive strikes initiated by the United States when it invaded Iraq seriously undermined fundamental principles of international law. The inability of the well-established democracies, including Canada, to constrain the United States, underscores the new power dynamics which compromise the role and credibility of the United Nations and the conditions upon which the multilateral system of peace and security are based.

Military budgets are on the rise in both Canada and the United States. Next year military expenditures will amount to more than four hundred billion dollars in the United States alone, an amount eight times greater than the whole world community spends on international development assistance. In many countries, the threat of terrorism has been used to repackage repression, stifle dissent and provoke racial, ethnic and religious discrimination.

The democratic deficit has worsened in many countries since 9/11 as the gap between formal adherence to international human rights and obligations and their implementation continues to grow. Civil conflicts have increased in number and have been more damaging than ever before. In the 1990s, 3.6 million people, mostly women and children, died in wars within states and the number of internally displaced persons increased by 50%. Torture of suspected terrorists by coalition troops and American prison guards and open questioning of the relevance of the Geneva Conventions to the "war on terrorism" by American defence authorities are further examples of the erosion of human rights at the altar of security.

It has become obvious that the international human rights system is incapable in its present form of enlightening or changing the direction of the response to terrorism. The essential arguments presented, the negotiations undertaken, the investments made and the ends sought to contain terrorism are based on a different view of the future human family than existed prior to 9/11.

Globalization and the war on terrorism together have compromised opportunities for progress in major international negotiations involving Canada. Negotiations concerning the need for fair trade, the Free Trade of the Americas Agreement, the broader social and cultural concerns of free trade in the Americas, and the possibility of a free trade agreement between Canada and Europe and consequent regional convergences are less likely to be successful in the current security-obsessed environment.

2. The Need for a Canadian Strategy

Globalization and the security measures taken to counter terrorism have set the challenge for a new strategy for Canadian foreign policy development. The mutations described above have created uncertainty and insecurity in the world, including in Canada. Like most countries post 9/11, Canada fell into line behind the United States, passing overly invasive and far reaching security legislation which undermined or completely obliterated many well developed and ingrained fundamental principles of human rights and civil liberties. Similarly, for many years Canada has participated in world trade and globalization initiatives without insisting on human rights or humanitarian standards as a pre-condition to entering free trade agreements or as an integral part of them. Canada's security and prosperity, our vital interests, and our ability to contribute to the world community in our own way have consequently been called into question.

To meet the challenge global problems present, a global offensive on the same scale as that which supported globalization must place the doctrine, policies and jurisprudence of human rights at the core of reconstituted societies and of the world community. Without this offensive, human rights could enter a phase of formidable and lasting marginalization. Concerted, purposeful decision-making and common action on the human rights front, as well as a greater sense of equality must energize our foreign policy. Concrete and verifiable human rights policies must be promoted. This strategy means civil and political rights as well as social, economic and cultural rights must be recognized and respected as complementary and essential to the common dignity of each human person and peace in the world. Globalization requires that Canada and like-minded international institutions re-commit to this concept, and ensure that it is better and more widely understood. In other words, the totality of human rights must be promoted to counteract the negative effects of globalization and security.

When analyzed in the present context, the sufficiency of the underpinnings of our foreign policy, particularly the three pillars of security, prosperity and Canadian values are found wanting. It is clear that the underlying pillars are not being given equal weight or significance and are being compartmentalized when dealing with global issues. Clearly, the security pillar outweighs the other two pillars which respond to the ethical needs and human rights imperatives of this time in our history. If we are to address this imbalance and live up to our national values, we must re-interpret the pillars to more closely reflect our needs. This in turn may require a re-evaluation of our relationship with the United States, and force us to pay serious attention to the undesirable effects of globalization.

In addition to re-thinking the relative importance of the pillars, Canada must recognize her duty to contribute to the common goals of humanity through an overriding commitment to international human rights and democratic development principles. If our democratic ideals combined with international and humanitarian law principles informed our interventions in the world community in a clearer and more forceful way, political and ethical needs would be better addressed and respect for human rights, democratic and sustainable development, equality of men and women and recognition of cultural diversity would be enhanced globally. What must be avoided is a single market world subdivided by borders of security and prosperity that protect those with the most means to impose them. This scenario will only lead to increased instability, insecurity, poverty and despair, which in turn will fuel terrorism.

To ensure that foreign policy is more than a theoretical or academic exercise, resources must be devoted to its implementation. Canada must contribute generously to human rights defenders and international institutions to ensure they have the capacity to mobilize and propose alternatives, with a view to influencing the public debate and decision-making both at the local and global levels.

3. The Need for an Action Plan

From the strategy outlined above, it is clear that Canada's obligations for an action plan are global, continental and in relation to developing countries. Detailed action plans focussed on human rights, democracy, education, the eradication of poverty and discrimination as well as protection of the environment must be developed with these obligations in mind.

(a) Global Governance

Canada's global obligations relate to the new ordering of the world, the promotion of multilateralism through the reform of common institutions, including the United Nations itself, and multilateral commercial and financial institutions and civil society.

For the past fifty-five years, Canada has enthusiastically contributed to the United Nations system and global governance. A universal and comprehensive perspective underpins the multilateral framework of the United Nations which is consistent with Canada's values. This is why Canada supports the work of United Nations institutions. This does not mean that Canada should not pursue bilateral and regional relationships, as we do, or belong to other multilateral groupings. It does imply, however, that our actions and commitments outside the United Nations must not weaken the United Nations. Given the magnitude of the problems that face our interdependent world, from issues of security and terrorism to the marginalization of the poor to the fragile environment, we surely must realize that no single country, no matter how powerful, can face the future alone. Canada must remain strong in its position that the world cannot solve its problems unless we work together.

Today, there is a crisis at the Security Council and at the United Nations, putting it in real jeopardy of being sidelined. At the same time that the UN as a whole is being undermined, its human rights institutions have fallen into severe disrepair, and can offer little to commend the UN system. The international UN institutions with the mandate to protect and promote universal goals and values have become ineffective and radically obsolete. For example, the UN Human Rights Commission is totally inadequate. It has antiquated procedures, inadequate guidelines, and insufficient powers. Furthermore, it has been taken over by a group of states with an *anti*-human rights agenda which has undermined any credibility and effectiveness that it might otherwise have. Other institutions which have crucially important mandates, such as the Committee on Social, Economic, and Cultural Rights are largely ineffective and toothless.

Regardless of the current difficulties however, the international institutions must be protected if multilateralism is to survive and the UN is to remain at the centre of international affairs. Canada must continue to be a strong proponent of the UN and commit intellectual and political support to its day-to-day operations. Canada must also counter attacks on multilateralism and collective decision-making and work toward the reformation or replacement of these ineffective UN bodies. As an example, Canada could take a lead role in animating a coalition to revitalize and renew the grossly inadequate Human Rights Commission, restore its credibility, integrity and authority and consolidate all the human rights institutions into one overarching body. Something like a 'World Organization for Human Rights' could emerge from such a reform effort, replacing all of the many and varied ineffective human rights bodies that exist at the international level. An international institution for human rights could better enforce the obligations, requirements, and spirit of the Universal Declaration, and of the various human rights covenants. If such a body also had the responsibility to accredit national human rights institutions based on exacting criteria, the power to investigate violations and report to the UN General Assembly, and adequate resources, it could go a long way towards effectively addressing the problems of this millennium.

In spite of the set-backs and dysfunction at the UN, some progress has been made. The development of humanitarian law and the creation of the International Criminal Court to end impunity for massive violations of human rights, crimes against humanity and war crimes give some cause for celebration. Canada played a major role in the development of the International Criminal Court and was recognized as a global leader in this regard.

The Court will advance human rights by creating a deterrent to those who would commit mass violations and crimes against humanity. Canada must continue to promote multilateral efforts to support the Court by urging countries to ratify the Rome Statute for the International Criminal Court as well as encourage the implementation of domestic legislation to give it full effect. In addition to providing support for the International Criminal Court, Canada should support the important work of the *ad hoc* criminal tribunals for the former Yugoslavia, Rwanda and Sierra Leone. The work of these institutions will create the foundational procedural and substantive jurisprudence of genocide, war crimes and crimes against humanity that will assist the ICC in its future deliberations.

As well as supporting international, multilateral organizations, Canada must continue to support international civil society and the international human rights movement. This approach has served us well in the past, helping to define binding rules and nurture responsible management structures and transparent reporting mechanisms. Through strengthening and encouraging civil society, Canada nurtures important democratic principles such as accountability and the creation of a culture of social responsibility.

(b) Global Prosperity

By 2020, the populations of Africa and Asia will have increased by 2 billion people. Unless shared and sustainable development is pursued, equity, stability and security will be denied to these future generations. Our obligation toward global prosperity requires us to seek ways to make trade more equitable while recognizing the social and political ends of economic growth and development. Unless such commitments are fulfilled, the Millennium Development Goals promised by world leaders will not be met.

Canada has committed itself to work within a rules-based economic framework for globalization. Our foreign policy must include insisting on reforms to global financial institutions such as the World Trade Organization to ensure equity and viability of those rules. In other words, these institutions must reflect the plurality, level of development and needs of its member countries in their working methods, decision-making processes, and dispute-settlement and appeal systems. They must also incorporate policies capable of respecting the economic, social and cultural rights of the citizens of those countries. This means respect for such basic rights as the right to food, the right to water, the right to health, and the right to education. International institutions must also regulate the role of multinational corporations so that their actions are compatible with respect for human rights.

(c) Global Security

At the outset, Canada should deal with terrorism in a way that reinforces the conditions for security consistent with our overall foreign policy and commitment to human rights. Canada should commit itself to understanding the underlying causes of terrorism and work toward their elimination. It should also promote the creation of a comprehensive Convention On Terrorism to clarify national policies on the definitions of 'terrorist' and the means of addressing terrorism to ensure that they are coherent with other policies. Canada should also reinforce the UN's preventative capacities and ensure it has adequate resources to confront threats to international peace and security through monitoring, inspections and reporting capabilities. In addition, Canada should continue to define its security as part of a wider collective of the UN and NATO and defend these institutions and the international rule of law.

Where extraordinary security measures need to be taken to protect Canadian citizens, they must be developed in the overall context of our commitment to human rights. Proportionality in the design of security measures is essential so that detrimental impacts on fundamental civil and political rights are minimized. To ensure oversight and transparency, all security measures must be supervised by civilian institutions and regular reports made to Parliament.

(d) Continental Obligations

Canada's most challenging and demanding foreign policy consideration is its relationship to the United States. Canada has positioned itself as an ally in the "war on terrorism" although it has refused to endorse the doctrine of preventative strikes that was deployed in Iraq. Other differences are Canada's position on the Kyoto Protocol and the International Criminal Court.

At the level of global governance, especially with respect to the central place of the United Nations and the multilateral treatment of the issues and challenges that confront the world community, Canada must forcefully affirm both the areas of convergence and divergence with the United States. It must identify, justify and illustrate them.

(e) Canada and the Americas

As the prospect of closer inter-American economic integration draws nearer, be it through the possible free trade area of the Americas or regionally based developments, the need for vibrant and powerful inter-American human rights integration has never been clearer. Anything else risks fostering greater inequality, marginalization, and human rights abuses.

Canada must vigorously promote the conceptual linkages between economic and human development issues in future rounds of the Free Trade of the Americas Agreement negotiations which in turn must be linked to the regional human rights institutions: the Inter-American Commission on Human Rights and the Inter-American Court of Human Rights. Both the Commission and the Court have made crucial contributions in the past toward improving human rights, but both are facing ongoing challenges to their authority and continue to be woefully under-resourced. Canada must support them by providing political backing and financial resources which they need to become bulwarks in the struggle for human rights in the Americas. Throughout most of Latin America, political dissidents are being jailed, people are being tortured, children are working in exploitative conditions, and internal conflicts are claiming innumerable lives. Canada must recognize and defend its values in the regional institutions which can prevent violations and promote greater adherence to human rights.

Despite joining the Organization of American States (OAS) over a decade ago, however, Canada continues to stand on the human rights sidelines in the Americas. The failure of Canada to ratify the American Convention on Human Rights, its two protocols, and three OAS treaties dealing with torture, disappearances, and violence against women, means that Canada has yet to make a full commitment to crafting strong effective mechanisms for human rights protection in this hemisphere. The Canadian government has not been transparent concerning the reasons it is hesitant about proposing ratification of the American Convention on Human Rights. A dialogue should begin on this issue. The ratification by Canada of the American Convention on Human Rights would allow a unique opportunity for the entire continent to benefit from the values that have guided Canadian human rights policies and foreign policy. Additionally, Canada's participation in the Inter-American human rights system could contribute significantly to strengthening governments in Latin America by providing stronger guarantees for endangered rights at home, when business and security agendas are constantly in competition with the human rights agenda.

(f) Canada and the Developing World

In the developing world, Canada must pursue a comprehensive strategy based on an equitable system of international investment and increased development assistance. It must be stressed that development assistance should not be solely interpreted to mean "aid". Development assistance must include reforms which make trade, commerce and investment more accessible and equitable. The least developed countries must have fair access to markets in their own regions as well as to markets in the North. This means eliminating tariffs and quotas on almost all imports from the forty-eight least developed countries, of which thirty-four are in Africa.

Equitable investment must be promoted to encourage growth, development and the social conditions required to ensure the full realization of human rights. At the present time,

Africa, with 13% of the world's population, attracts only 3% of the world's investment, most of which is in oil and mining. This is not equitable. Equitable investment also means quality investment that will truly benefit the developing countries. If the investments in the developing world are designed to create exploitative enclaves or are used for tax avoidance and high profit repatriation, they do not bring the human rights benefits required to meet the values pillar of Canadian foreign policy. For example, there should be no barriers for access to medicine when it comes to combatting epidemics such as AIDS and malaria, and intellectual property rights should not take precedence over food security.

4. Conclusion

Canada must base its foreign policy on the bedrock of human rights, democratic development, a renewed and effective multiculturalism, and an equitable sharing of growth and prosperity. Canada must help to develop the understanding that the political, social and economic aspects of the world community are interconnected and that democratic values and human rights are the most effective protection from terrorism. The UN system of global governance must be strengthened and reformed. A new world organization for human rights should be the basis of participatory involvement of all members of the global community who desire common security and prosperity. The World Trade Organization should be reformed to reverse the present emphasis of globalization and instead place equity at the core of its mission and functions so that it could reinforce and contribute to the renewal of global government. A framework for a new globalization ideal that takes into account the social dimensions of the economy and notably the protection of the physical integrity of people, including the right to food, health, and access to medicine, and labour rights must be our goal. With respect to domestic security, Canadian foreign policy must be aimed at restoring the balance between human rights and security.

Canada has the vocation, interest, and means to create or join coalitions that want to make the connection between the need for growth and development in the world with the values of freedom, equality and security. What is required is the ethical leadership to take us there, and make the choices that need to be made.

International Institutions: Discussion & Commentary

Dr. Michael Byers: Well, I agree with almost everything that my colleagues have said. The only thing I wish to address is some of the comments on the responsibility to protect, and the duty to prevent. In a remarkable speech given in March in his constituency in Northwest England, Prime Minister Tony Blair embraced the responsibility to protect agenda, explicitly with respect to the situation in Iraq as it had existed prior to the 2003 war. The danger – and it doesn't mean that responsibility to protect is a bad idea – the danger with such a concept is that it may be twisted and abused by powerful actors seeking to justify, either *post facto* or prospectively, interventions that are motivated by other ends. And we therefore need to be very careful when moving forward in ways that might alter the existing checks and balances on the use of force in international affairs. And, without going into this in any detail, I think that the first step in dealing with these kinds of challenges is scrutinizing the existing rules and institutions and asking whether they are indeed broken, or whether the problem is, instead, one of a lack of political will.

The Security Council in 1994 actually adopted a Chapter 7 Resolution authorizing humanitarian intervention in Rwanda. It was too late, and it was given to France, and France's motives were questionable. But the Security Council itself was prepared to grant a Resolution. The problem was that countries weren't prepared to intervene. Kosovo is difficult. There was a dispute over the factual circumstances: whether or not the level of the atrocities was such as to justify an intervention – prior to the intervention taking place – and indeed, most of the atrocities occurred after the bombing started. But also there was the very real fact that Russia felt challenged. Just two weeks before, three former Warsaw Pact states had been admitted to NATO. The Kosovo intervention occurred in what Russia saw as its front yard. And one of the purposes of the checks and balances that exist and the veto that is accorded to the five permanent members is to protect the essential interests of those five nuclear powers so as to prevent an escalation that could amount, at one point, to a nuclear war. I would like to suggest that the Russian veto in Kosovo might be a reflection of how the system is intended to work rather than an example of the system being broken.

And today the situation in Darfur, in western Sudan, is horrifying. I was at a conference a little over a week ago in Montreal where, in some comments in the context of an award ceremony for Philippe Kirsch, the President of the ICC (International Criminal Court), Federal Minister of Justice Irwin Cotler (who happened to be my teacher of Constitutional Law at McGill), made the most passionate plea imaginable for humanitarian intervention in Sudan – a senior Cabinet Minister in the Canadian government speaking to the world federalist movement, at this conference in Montreal. Well, if that's the case, why aren't we there? What is the problem? Is it the rules that are stopping us from intervening in Sudan? The federal Minister of Justice thinks we should intervene. Is he really concerned that we might somehow violate Chapter 7? We haven't put a draft resolution before the Security Council, so we don't know whether the rules are broken. There's a problem of political will somewhere. It's not with Irwin Cotler. It may be in Washington and it may be in the PMO. But again, be careful here; and the same goes with respect to the duty to prevent, the duty to deal with weapons of mass destruction and the threat of international terrorism.

There's something called the Proliferation Security Initiative, which is a wonderful initiative – it's being run out of the State Department – and which is seeking to deal with the problem of the trafficking of weapons of mass destruction and missile technology on the high seas without breaking international law and without changing international law. To the degree that any international legal development occurs, it is through the negotiation of bilateral treaties with countries such as Liberia and Panama to allow for consensual search and seizure of ships on the high seas. A huge amount can be done. The rules aren't necessarily broken; institutions could work. And so before we throw the baby out with the bathwater I would like to suggest that when we move forward on these issues the first thing that we do is look at people like Paul Martin and George W. Bush and Tony Blair and call them to account and ask why, today, a genocide is occurring in Africa and no soldiers wearing our uniforms are there.

Dr. Roy Lee: Thank you. I'd like to pick up on Michael's point regarding the issue we face, which is as he describes. The collective problem is that we need to identify the black letter law before we develop exceptions from it. I agree with Ambassador Wright that humanitarian intervention is a valid claim, and that we should study and establish the criteria for humanitarian intervention. But I think states must be reminded of what is, at the present time, the black letter law, so that further exceptions are not a departure from a prior exception. By starting with the black letter law you establish the parameters and possibilities for dealing with the issues.

As I pointed out, the present day problem is, really, who is going to determine how to apply the force of humanitarian interventions. Even with the criteria, you need a kind of mechanism to determine that. Currently it is self-judging; that is really the rule of the game. And I think that is wrong; we must go back to the black letter law which calls for collective decision making and collective actions. We should always refer to this. Of course some would object that the present collective system does not work. I suggest that we work on the ways and means of breaking deadlocks, and come up with constructive suggestions of how to break those deadlocks and find compromise – there must be a willingness to find compromise – and continue with the commitment to the multilateral decision-making process. I think in that way we would establish a more consistent, systematic approach.

I would also like to disagree, if I may, with Professor Mahoney's suggestion that we should abolish the Commission of Human Rights and form a new body. Having worked in the UN for thirty years, experience suggests that would not work, realistically. The attempt to abolish it would, in the end, be futile, and would not achieve the objective. And I think what we need to do is to effect the change within that body. This calls for a coalition of like-minded states within the body, not working to abolish the body, but a coalition of like-minded states working together to combat what she refers to as "the anti-human rights group". At the moment I do not see a strong coalition to fight the anti-human rights groups. And that really calls for skills and multilateral negotiation to do that. And to me that is the major issue and the issue that we must address.

Ambassador David Wright: Just three quick points. On Tony Blair and the abuse of the responsibility to protect: I haven't seen his statement but one thing one can say is that nobody used that concept in advance of the conflict in Iraq; it was not abused there. If it was used by Blair in March then clearly there's an element of desperation, I think. There is always a risk that something like that will be abused, but in this case it wasn't abused prior to the conflict in Iraq.

On Russia and Kosovo, one footnote, and an interesting one here: of course the Russians were upset. They did not have to veto because they never got a chance to veto. There was no resolution put to them, although they would have vetoed clearly, and it upset them deeply. And it took them awhile to get their relationship back on track with NATO and the western countries. But it did get back on track fairly quickly. But what caused the Russians to come around completely, and in the end abandon Milosevic politically, was the indictment by Louise Arbour at the critical moment in the war. This was really important. As the war carried on and was dragging on many people were advising Louise Arbour not to move to an indictment because it would have given Milosevic nowhere to go. But others were advising, and I would certainly, urging that the sooner we get that indictment the better. Because then he is truly isolated. And that was Justice Arbour's decision. And then came a situation where Russia could no longer, really in any way, implicitly support Milosevic. And it was the beginning of the end. So I think that her step was very courageous and very timely.

Third, on the question of Sudan: the reason that nobody's there has nothing to do with rules. The reason nobody's there is because

- CNN's not there.
- The risks are high.
- It's remote, and
- it's a resource question.

And – what I was talking about earlier – one of the reasons they're not there is because of Iraq. Because the mood is bad for this kind of thing now. But CNN is not out there broadcasting this one every night.

Dr. Jennifer Welsh: I just have a comment, and then a question, to come back to the theme of the Symposium about making decisions within an ethical framework. My comment is that, as a political scientist, I don't know what this thing "political will" is. It's always struck me as a bizarre term. And finally about three months ago an eminent professor in my field, Robert Keohane, who had the same frustration, said "it's a cost benefit calculation." Why don't we talk about that? Political will is really a phrase used to mask what is really going on in the minds of decision makers, which is about costs and benefits. I wondered if the panel would agree, and what kinds of calculations they think are actually going on.

But my question is about the consequences of intervention. One of the themes that I think Andrew Cohen and I were trying to get across on Friday was that, when we talk about ethical action, and leaders making ethical choices, it's not just about goals. It's about means and about consequences. And so my question, specifically for David Wright because I think he was hinting at this, is "what have the changes in the last fifteen years done to our calculation about consequences?" I'll give you an example. We used to think, in moral decision-making about intervention, that consequences were about how many of your soldiers are going to die verses civilians in a given action. But if we look at Kosovo, and we take short, medium, and long term consequences, we have a very interesting situation. "In the short term" we might ask, "did we actually encourage the movement of refugees and more ethnic cleansing through bombing?" "But in the medium term", the defenders of the action would say, "well no, refugees came back to their homes, so this was a good action ethically." "But in the longer term" we say, "now we've got some oppression of Serbs in Kosovo, so what have been the consequences of that?"

But even more long term, we now have a mission in Kosovo, rebuilding this country, that may go on ten, fifteen, twenty years. And so I think there are a variety of consequences that have been added on to our calculations about ethical action and intervention over the past fifteen years. And I would agree with David Wright that this is precisely what's going on in the minds of the Bush administration with respect to Iraq. When you say you're going to intervene now, the consequences you have to consider include how committed you are to being in a country for twenty years. And so I think this has opened up a whole new debate about ethical and moral action because the whole realm of consequences, that third pillar, has become so much more complex. I'd like to hear what the panel has to say about that.

Ambassador David Wright: Thank you very much Jennifer. I think that the definition of "political will" you referred to is completely right. We do refer to political will as a kind of concept out there; it's very convenient, but what does it really mean? I think it is a cost benefit calculation; I think your colleague is completely right. It's a calculation by political leaders of what is going to be acceptable to the public in the next election and it's a judgment call. It is also heavily influenced by the media; there's no question that political will sometimes gets generated by the CNN effect. But that is a useful definition at minimum, and I think it's actually a very good definition.

As to the consequences of intervention: indeed, I think everybody has to calculate these much better than they have in the past. And the ten-fifteen-twenty year perspective is actually the correct one. The trouble is that when these decisions are made, if you ask a politician "how long are our troops going to be there?", the reply might be "Oh well, we'll be there as long as is necessary." And if someone asks "well is that two years?", the answer is "Oh, well, we don't know." And that's only fair because the political leader has to think in terms of the political horizon that he or she has. But the experience is that the presence is long term, and it's not just a military presence. It's a civil presence, and it requires tremendous cooperation between the international organizations, the World Bank and the UN system, the NGOs, and the military to get these countries back into any sort of decent shape. And we (Canada) have been in Bosnia militarily since 1992! So that's twelve years, and it's still not over, although the force has changed a lot. When there was fighting going on it was way up here; now it's down to a very modest number, and I think the numbers will become even lower this summer. But presence is long term, and the civil society will be present in Bosnia much longer still. Kosovo is at a much earlier stage; it's going to take a long time. The military presence is higher. We haven't even started to address the question of Kosovo's ultimate status in relation to Serbia, in relation to whether it's independent or a part of something else. People have talked about it but nobody has faced it. And of course there are consequences for minorities such as the Serb minority in Kosovo.

I think that one has to make all of these calculations. We have to have much more capability in the international community to deal with these things. Military organizations often resist the idea of peacekeeping. I think, frankly, we had better embrace it, because we're going to have more and more of it. And it's going to be a more robust kind of peacekeeping than the old style of Cyprus-type peacekeeping where you stand on a green line for thirty years. It's going to involve much more nation building. It's much more dangerous. It's much more multi-dimensional. And so we are going to have to have the resources to do that kind of thing. It's a very costly business, nation building, but I think people are learning. I think we've been in this game, in Canada, for a long time; and we should continue to be in it and we should do even better. The United States has always been very reluctant to get into this. Remember Condy Rice's article, before Bush took over, saying "Oh we're not going to do nation building, my God! We're not going to send the 82nd Airborne to take kids to school." Well often that's exactly what you've got to do. And they've changed their minds; they've realized that that is true. But I think all of us have to get much better at this whole area of consequences, at the long term nation building tasks that we have. And when you get into something like Afghanistan, we are going to be in there for a long, long time militarily and politically and economically. The problems in Afghanistan are because people went in, did what they had to do, and left; and it gets worse and worse and worse. Well this time we can't do that.

Dr. Michael Byers: On cost benefit analysis, rational choice theory, and my dear friend and colleague Bob Keohane: like any theoretical approach, rational choice theory is a powerful tool, but only provides part of an explanation. When we're dealing with the issue of how a country like Canada should behave in the international domain, I think that issues of self perception and self confidence are going to alter the cost benefit analysis considerably. If our leaders regard this country as a weak country that is highly dependant on the superpower, whose population is politically disengaged and doesn't really care, where the dominant political forces are the Canadian Council of Chief Executives and not the Council of Canadians, that's going to affect their cost benefit analysis. Now I happen to take the view that Canada is the most dynamic, tolerant and, indeed, wealthiest country in the world in terms of its resources, its educated and tolerant population, and in terms of its social- and infrastructure. I've lived in the United States for five years. There's a lot of wealth; there's a lot of public poverty and decay. It's not as wealthy a country as Canada, despite what the normal economic measures might tell you. We are one of the wealthiest countries in the world. And that provides us with opportunity to engage in cost benefit analyses that are dramatically different from those that our leaders have engaged in, in recent years. So that's part of an answer. I think we're far better positioned to be leaders than we think, or than our leaders think. And our current stance of subservience towards the neo-conservative administration in the White House is the antithesis of what I think this country's potential is.

Professor Kathleen Mahoney: I'll just make a short comment. I always get a little bit nervous when I hear cost benefit analysis being proposed, particularly joining it with political will. It reminds me of the time I spent at the University of Chicago, as a very lonely person amidst the hub of law and economics in the U.S., which is the law faculty at the University of Chicago. And there I participated in debates on everything from a cost benefit analysis of having orphanages verses social welfare for single moms, to a cost benefit analysis of providing drugs for HIV/AIDS victims, to a cost benefit analysis of sex-selected abortions. I mean if you separate cost benefit analysis from the social context and human rights it can take you a very long way down a road to places where I don't think Canada would ever imagine or want itself to be. So my response would be, fair enough, if you want to talk in those terms, but the cost benefit analysis must be done through the lens of human rights, and it must be done in that social context, taking into account our values as a baseline below which we do not go. And then, fair enough, talk about that. And I don't think General Dallaire would disagree with me, that certain cost benefit analyses were done about Rwanda. And there are certain cost benefit analyses done about Africa, on a daily basis. Africa is a huge casualty of the end of the cold war, because the same tensions do not exist anymore in Africa. Nobody cares about Africa, because it doesn't provide the same kinds of opportunities for advantage that it once did in the cold war. And so they're just left to their horrible situations that they find themselves in with respect to all sorts of things – health, leadership, corruption, you name it… and genocide – and also, it seems to me, had that issue been looked at through the lens of human rights I think the value of the lives of the black people involved would not have been calculated, frankly, in the way that they were compared to the white lives of Europeans which were involved in the cost benefit analysis that was done there.

Dr. Jennifer Welsh: I wasn't suggesting we should do it narrowly, because I agree with you. What I was suggesting is that if a kind of calculation like that is what political will is – people balancing things – then let's be honest about all of the things that should be on the table, and recognize that we affect political will; that if, in fact, public pressure is part of what governments account for, then we should recognize that. I think that when we just blame it on political will, then we're not really engaging in the decisions that people are making. So I agree with you. Then we should have a discussion about costs in a very wide context.

Professor Kathleen Mahoney: I'm glad that you said that because – and again I'll go back to my opening comments about how good this event is – this is political expression going on here, from the people in the audience and the people up here. This is the kind of dialogue that can influence political will, and it's very, very important that these discussions don't take place in the arid halls of "the academy" or behind closed doors in Ottawa. This is the kind of public discussion that's extremely important so that leaders – and especially now when we're in an election period – that our leaders understand what the civil society believes in. Maybe I'm being naive.

Dr. Michael Byers: Just a final follow up point on that: sometimes, cost benefit analysis aside, it's important to do what's right. And I think there are historical examples where governments have chosen to do things that are actually quite costly because they're right. Our entire refugee system is difficult to explain in cost benefit terms; we take refugees who are facing persecution because it's the right thing to do. The same goes for the enormous political capital that was invested by Canada in the International Criminal Court and Landmines Convention. Lloyd Axworthy and his advisors didn't do that because there were benefits to be made, but because it was the right thing to do. And yes, there were some benefits; but if you actually talk to the people involved, they did it because it was the right thing to do. And I think that the primary benefit of doing the right thing is, first of all, that it's the right thing; but secondly, it fulfils the country's need to do the right thing. And again it comes back to this question of self confidence and self perception. Canada has a long history of doing the right thing and feeling good about doing the right thing; and we need to do more of that.

Question: I wonder sometimes about the one public institution, or international institution, that we tend to keep a little bit sub-surface, and that's the multinational corporation. Are they now the new international institution, but not really recognized?

Because often, are these states not really being driven by those kinds of people? Is that who's pushing the agenda instead of them acting in the public interest? So my question, really, to the panelists is, is there something that they see that can be done to either expose thei level of activity of multinational corporations in the decision-making process, or to moderate the power that they have in decision-making processes?

Dr. Michael Byers: Well capitalism is a wonderful thing when it's regulated and directed towards the public good. Within any western democratic system, we do not have unregulated capitalism; even the United States has a highly regulated capitalism. Part of what's gone wrong in places like Russia is that we've essentially unleashed unregulated capitalism. And part of what's going on internationally is that we haven't designed a proper and effective system for regulating capitalism, and so we have incorporations of convenience, and tax evasion, and flags of convenience, and all sorts of other things that clever lawyers do to reduce the impediments and restrictions on the making of money. So I think you've put your finger on a real challenge for the twenty first century, which is how do we harness the power of global capitalism to do good things; and how do we do that in a way that protects against the abuses without limiting the considerable good that can be brought to people everywhere, particularly poor people.

And so I think if I had to identify a couple of immediate challenges that Canada, in its leadership role, could take on, we need to do something to open up our markets to developing countries; and I don't think we need to wait for the United States and Europe. Textile products from the developing world should be coming into Canada tariff free. A small cost to Canada; a huge benefit, a huge signal in terms of leadership. I think we should be more serious about addressing the problem of agricultural subsidies, and show more of a leadership role in that regard. Instead we follow on from what the European Commission and the United States do. And there's still the

Tobin Tax: the question of unregulated capital flows. It's a wonderful idea, and Canada should be pushing it further. To give
you another small example: there should be an international
system for the taxation of jet fuel. There is no system for the
taxation of jet fuel; we pay taxes on gasoline for our cars, but if
you want to fly to the United States or Europe, that fuel is tax
free. It contributes something like twenty percent to carbon
dioxide emissions. We all like to fly free; I like to say that we
should be able to fly and pay fifteen or twenty percent more, so
that we don't fly as much, and so we protect the environment,
and so we regulate the unrestricted, chaotic growth in air travel that has occurred over the course of the last fifteen or twenty years.

    Lots of things that Canada could play a leadership role on,
going precisely to your question. They are institutions. They are
powerful. But they're not nation states. And they need nation
states in which to live, in which to sell, in which to grow.

Professor Kathleen Mahoney: All I might say to that is that I
think that all of the riots all over the place in the last several
years, whenever there's been a meeting of global leaders,
speak to this question. There's a certain very, very strong dissatisfaction with this huge power that corporations have now
acquired for themselves in terms of addressing basic values
that societies have; and they see themselves as being run
roughshod over in many instances by these seemingly uncon-
trollable entities. And, increasingly, we're hearing the terminol-
ogy change from free trade to fair trade, which I think is a very
positive step. Again, at the risk of sounding repetitive, I don't
think it's beyond consideration that human rights could be a
part of international trade agreements. We've considered the
environment in some – not too terrible effectively, but at least
it's been considered and is a part of international trade agreements and regional trade agreements. Why aren't human
rights? This brings up the point earlier of the inter-American
system: why don't we develop our regional human rights sys-

tems to counter the trade agreements so that there would be checks and balances in international institutions, so that some of these issues could be litigated, and decisions could be rendered on them. Right now it's just free, as you were saying; anything goes as long as you've got enough muscle to do it. And that's not good enough, I would say.

Question: At the risk of not only flogging the dead horse but riding it around the stables, I too have a question about political will. I just finished reading *A Problem from Hell*[1] by Samantha Power, where she talks about a history of American responses to genocide, and the tendency for governments to say "never again" when they're opening holocaust museums but, at the end of the day, that political will isn't there. And so, listening to what Ambassador Wright was saying, I agree that the problem is political will. Paul Heinbecker talked about this yesterday, that Warren Christopher wouldn't let Madelaine Albright call something "genocide" because of the legal responsibilities that it invokes as a result. I don't know the legal framework; I'm not a lawyer, obviously, so I'm sure that there are steps that could be taken to improve the legal framework. I think that the steps need to be taken, need to be done with respect to improving our willpower to act, to acting when it is right, when it's necessary. So the question, then, is how do we do that? We can set up these frameworks but, at the end of the day, what does it take for us to stand up and say "this is genocide; let's do something about it."

Ambassador David Wright: I must say, I too found the Samantha Power book enormously impressive, and very, very sad to read; but it's a powerful work and it's really a superb study of how countries, and particularly the United States, have responded to instances of genocide in the past. My thesis has been that, actually, we were making quite a bit of progress on the political will front, and I think we did through the nineties, and I think that Kosovo was a good example of that evolution;

---

[1] Samantha Power, *A Problem from Hell: America and the Age of Genocide* (New York: Basic Books, 2002).

but we've been knocked off course. What will affect the political will in the future? I think part of it is, it's clearly public opinion driven, and a lot of that is very, very short term. A lot of it is CNN implication, the CNN effect, and it also requires a bit of courage on the part of some leaders. I remember there was a lot of dithering on Bosnia in 1995. The UN had been there, and that was the low point; remember when the peacekeepers were being chained to transmission towers, and everyone was saying that we should perhaps arm the Bosnians but stand back. And all of a sudden, I recall, Chirac came to the Halifax G-7 Summit and said, "this is ridiculous; we're being humiliated here." He kind of embarrassed everyone into doing something serious, and that's what led to the NATO action that summer, at the time just after Srebrenica. (Interesting that a French President's comments led to NATO action in ways that, perhaps, have not always been consistent with French policy.)

So, leadership is key. Public opinion is key. Media attention is key. I think it's also important that we develop a body of experience and law and precedent; and we've actually been doing some of that and it's been helpful. But the political will, will never be there without that kind of public attention, and especially media attention; I think that's going to be crucial.

Dr. Michael Byers: Just a little bit of thinking outside the box. There's a significant possibility that governments simply can't do this because politicians are afraid to put their careers on the line. I'm wondering whether at some point in the future we might actually begin to think about a non-governmental intervention force, a sort of free force that is not accountable to any government but is funded by civil society. And that perhaps, ideally, has a council of eminent people widely represented from around the world – men and women from all continents and all parts of society, who decide when and where this force will be deployed, probably in violation of international law but with the moral force behind it that will shame governments into letting it act. I don't think we're there yet; I think it's a long way down the line. But when I look at Iraq and the important role of mercenaries and non-military forces; when I look at the important role of NGOs in the provision of humanitarian aid, I don't think we need to confine ourselves to this black box of "well, you know, we can't get Paul Martin and George W. Bush to act". At some point we're going to have to say, if they continue to show this absence of leadership, "well fine, we'll do it ourselves." Civil society, not states. As I said, I think we're still quite a ways from that; but don't get trapped into assuming that states and governments are the only way forward.

Question: I have a philosophical point that was prompted by Professor Mahoney's remarks, and I think it actually bears on this question of political will. Out of lamentable professional habit I'm going to phrase it as an obnoxious objection to what you said about Michael Ignatieff, but it's really just an invitation for elaboration. It seems to me that to lump Ignatieff, saying that human rights sometimes need to be weighed in the balance, together with Dershowitz, saying that torture could be OK, is seriously unhelpful. It seems to me Ignatieff is probably following one of his mentors, Sir Isaiah Berlin, and saying that, given the complexities of human life, dreadfully important things can come into conflict, and the conflict can be simply brute, and we just have to decide. Let me give you an example close to home. A majority of Francophone Quebecers – certainly a majority of the Francophone Quebec intelligentsia – think that the flourishing of their culture requires certain laws limiting access to education in language of choice, limiting the putting up of signs in language of choice. That clearly comes into conflict with the right of individual Quebec citizens to educate children in the language of their choice or put up signs in the language of their choice. What are we going to do? Either way, something terribly important is lost. It's not an "in principle" conflict. If the majority of Francophone Quebecers became ardent Trudeauvian federalists, as I wish they would, the problem would go away. But given that they're not, the problem is there and we've got to weigh one against the other.

Professor Kathleen Mahoney: Fair enough. I think in Canada we have quite a bit of experience in balancing; but I don't think it's the kind of balancing, with respect, that Professor Ignatieff is suggesting. In Section 1 of the Charter we do it all the time; it is a given that rights collide. Freedom of speech collides with all sorts of things; security of the person collides sometimes with equality. And our lawyers and judges, and our public I think, are quite content to have courts balance these rights out because they balance them in the context of a "free and democratic society". That's part of the balancing process. What I see lacking in this new approach to dealing human rights out of the picture in terms of the outcomes – in freedom and democracy – is the problem. I'm not arguing against balance; we have to balance all the time. But when we start down this slippery slope of dealing out the human rights card, and balancing the greater evils, then I think we're in huge trouble, because then you've gone below the foundation upon which human rights rest. And we've spent the last fifty five years trying to maintain that foundation, to maintain that floor; and then we work up from the floor. The more advanced societies that have more resources and so on can protect rights more and more above that floor; but now, I think the suggestion is, we go below. And I think that's what's very dangerous. And Dershowitz has gone to a greater extreme than Ignatieff; he's farther down the slope, in my view, but they're both on the slope.

Question: I still want to pursue this notion of political will. In addition to responsibility to protect there is an evolving notion of responsible citizenship. And I wonder if, looking at various issues around the world through different lenses – and I, for one, do support Professor Mahoney's idea of looking at situations from a human rights point of view – I'd like to suggest that this idea of responsible citizenship, the connection between the public civil society and the state, can be enhanced to a point where decisions that are being made by our political leaders and by the state become an integral part of the thinking of the public and the thinking of civil society. And maybe not so much that there is a legally binding resolution between civil society and the state, but there is some other mechanism in the governance of the land that actually takes into account the opinions, or the views, of people who are doing research in human rights or other social political issues and that such views are actually taken with the seriousness with which they should be in events like interventions and abuse of human rights abroad.

Dr. Michael Byers: Well we have a major disconnect in this country, at the moment, between the government and civil society. Anyone who's observed a meeting of one of the House of Commons Standing Committees consulting Canadians will have observed this. I once testified in front of the Standing Committee on Foreign Affairs and International Trade. There were twelve members of the committee and three bothered to show up and there were only another five people in the room. There's a serious disconnect in terms of the consultation process that's engaged in. I don't know if you've been consulted about missile defense yet? Probably not. There's been an abject lack of consultation on many of the big issues in politics today. We have an election coming up. Maybe that will help focus people's minds. We also have media in this country that I think are abysmally lazy in terms of challenging government. I lived for seven years in suburban London, England, and can tell you that I've seen an engaged and competitive media. We don't have one here. Civil society needs to demand the creation of an engaged and critical media, because that's an important facet in calling these kinds of actors to account. It's not that we don't have a good political system; our political system is far from perfect, and we need to work hard to make it better. And the final plank in that would be: we need proportional representation in this country; we need it very badly. This first past the post system and the creation of majority governments that only have forty percent of the elected voting public's support is a real problem in terms of political disengagement. We need to get those who hold minority views to have their votes count as well;

we need to get youth engaged in voting again. Something like only thirty percent of people under the age of thirty five vote in this country. So those are challenges for civil society: to call governments to account; to change the system; and to make it much better than it currently is.

Ambassador David Wright: I just wanted to add a word on citizenship and idealism and young people. I've dealt with a whole series of crises over the last ten years – I think most immediately of the Afghanistan situation. The numbers of young Canadians who are willing to engage themselves somehow in rebuilding, in helping – young doctors, young aid workers, people who wanted to help on construction crews, all sorts of people – come from the youth of this country who are actually very willing to take the risks and make the sacrifices, to play a part in nation building. We saw it in the Balkans throughout the nineties, and it is still there; we saw it throughout eastern Europe in terms of the political rebuilding of those countries. We had ministers, and central bank governors, and others, all drawn from the educated ranks of young Canadians who had gone, at complete disruption of their lives, to be part of history and to be part of change; so the will is there. It's terrific, actually, to see the enthusiasm and the energy and idealism that comes from young people in this country, in terms of getting engaged in some of the most challenging problems on the planet.

Professor Kathleen Mahoney: I'd just make a couple of comments, and I've been thinking about the Ambassador's comment about CNN and Sudan. It's very chilling, on one hand, to think that some production manager or whoever at CNN is basically going to make the decision as to whether or not there'll be humanitarian intervention in the Sudan, because of the publicity they can generate around it; I find that chilling. But on the other hand, it also...

Ambassador David Wright: But do you find it unrealistic?

Professor Kathleen Mahoney: Well, I was going to say, on the other hand, it does address the point that you were just making, that there is, I think, a reservoir out there in society of goodwill and of human rights. But it needs to be engaged. That's where the disconnect is. The engagement isn't being made. And I can speak to this from our Institute for Human Rights and Democratic Development. We've recently started a network in universities for human rights, and this thing has taken off like wildfire. With a very modest investment of money and resources we now have human rights clubs on just about every campus in the country and in the Northwest Territories. The students want to do stuff like this. They're very interested, but the mentors of the students aren't engaging them. There's another example I can give you at the University of Calgary. I was asked by the Students Union organization to come and speak at an event they were having, and it was on war crimes – about Henry Kissinger and about others – and to see whether or not some of the people that we admire in the West, indeed, perhaps have been guilty of war crimes in the past. Well, they put this event on and the students ran the whole thing; they invited several professors to come and speak, and the theatres were overflowing. They had three full theatres and screens and everything, and it was the biggest event on campus that term. And it wasn't initiated by professors or by a guest speaker or anything; it was the students themselves. And that plus our experience with this network of university students, and other projects that I have observed, leads me to believe that there is huge potential to mobilize public opinion towards a culture of respect, a culture of human rights. But we're not initiating it; we're not, somehow or other, getting the right things together that would spark this movement to take place. We also see it in these anti-globalization rallies; they are almost all young people there, from all sorts of different NGOs and different interest groups. So it's there. Maybe this is what the Sheldon Chumir Foundation for Ethics in Leadership, at bottom, is all about: why aren't our leaders exciting our young people and engaging them so that they can put some of these ideas on our national agenda?

Sheldon Chumir 2003-04 Public Policy Fellow Kristen Boon:
I wanted to start out, first of all, with a comment on the responsibility to protect because, while it's an extremely interesting
and influential document, there's a legal obligation which predates that by about fifty years which is Article 1 of the Genocide
Convention, which requires states, parties to the Genocide
Convention, to both prevent and punish genocide. Now, inter-
estingly enough, this has never been put into practice; but two
recent proposals by the Secretary General to set up a Special
Advisor on genocide, and also to create some sort of committee of states party to the Genocide Convention, may in fact be
very influential and may address this issue of political will that
we've been discussing, if they become effective political bodies.

   But, to my mind, the question now is not so much about just
war or just cause of intervention, because I think that with the
development of standards in international criminal law we all
have a fairly good sense of when there should be intervention
by the international community, what acts reach the threshold
set out in the Statute of the International Criminal Court, for
example, or other crimes that are in international treaties. The
interesting question, from an ethical point of view, is what sorts
of frameworks, what sorts of values and issues should inform
post-conflict intervention, especially when international powers
are getting involved and are governing in these countries? And
I think that Iraq is a very interesting example of this. The United
States has taken advantage of gaps in the Geneva Conventions
to pass very wide reaching reforms. They, for example, have
introduced a flat tax; so they've privatized the economy. The
Geneva Conventions are virtually silent as to economic reform,
and yet international powers are taking advantage of this and
are engaging in very substantial domestic reform. And I wonder
whether you have any comments on what the ethical framework should be in that situation. Should we be encouraging
some sort of a fiduciary relationship, for example, between governors and governees? Should we be introducing clearer rules
as to how power should be exercised in an occupation context,
whether that's a unilateral occupation, like the U.S., or whether
that's the United Nations operating in situations like Kosovo
and East Timor?

Dr. Michael Byers: Well the Genocide Convention is, unfortunately, limited by the UN Charter which, in Article 103, trumps any conflicting treaty. So, from a purely treaty law point of view, any duty to prevent genocide does not create an exception to the prohibition on the use of force. That doesn't mean that imaginative international lawyers can't find ways to ameliorate that situation. For instance one argument that I've put forward is that, in a Rwanda type situation, rather than seeking to change the rules to accommodate the exception, you should violate the rules in the exceptional circumstance, which does less damage to the rules than actually modifying them for all subsequent situations. One also needs to be really careful in saying that we all know the circumstances when humanitarian intervention would be justified. I disagree with the Ambassador in his assessment as to the most critical passage in the Responsibility to Protect Report. In my view the most critical passage says something along the lines of, "it would be impossible to achieve consensus in the international community as to the conditions for intervention in the absence of authorization from the Security Council or the General Assembly." There is a tendency that we in the developed west have to think that we know when it's legally acceptable or right to intervene. In his speech at Sedgefield in his constituency in March, Tony Blair, ironically, deals precisely with this problem in saying that we have a problem in that many countries are opposed to the responsibility to protect; and then he reaches – as his tool for avoiding this problem of consent – for the conception of community, which is bizarre. There's a harkening back, almost, to a kind of natural law, on the part of people like Tony Blair: that we the civilized countries know what is right and what is just. And one has to be very careful about that. We are here in a very strong tension between our desire to help the oppressed of the world, and the concern that the oppressed have about the powerful abusing their military capacity to intervene. And we need to listen to those concerns at the same time that we try to do the right thing to stop oppression and genocide, mass expulsion and systematic rape. It's tough. It's really tough.

Question: I'd like to pick up on the last point that was made. I believe there's a growing tension between the western industrialized countries and the developing world; the gap is growing massively. We heard, yesterday, Ambassador Listre express concerns of the Latin American countries about intervention. My question is: we've focused very much on intervention by western nations and intervention under the UN Security Council; is there a growing role for regional organizations and should we be looking more at a partnership between the UN and regional organizations to try and sponsor more intervention on a regional basis, as opposed to international through the Security Council?

Ambassador David Wright: I think the answer is "yes"; I think that's a very good point. Regional organizations sometimes have fairly limited capability; NATO, theoretically, is a regional organization, although it's becoming much broader than that, and has become – during the time that I was there became – much broader than a Euro-Atlantic institution. But there are kinds of conflicts, of a certain scale, that lend themselves very much to regional solutions; often, however, what's needed is perhaps a little help from the wealthier part of the world too. So the partnership idea is good. I like that approach; I think it's good because you get the expertise from the region, the sensitivity to cultural and historical factors that is greater from those in the region than from the international community at large, and the usual suspects of ten or fifteen countries who tend to provide most of the troops for these kinds of events. But I think that's a great idea.

Dr. Michael Byers: With a small note of caution concerning regional hegemony, and the potential for abuse: whether it's Nigeria in West Africa, or whether it's Russia in the Caucasus and the central Asian republics, or whether it's the United States in the Caribbean and Latin America, there's a long history of regional hegemons intervening for less than benevolent ends, and one needs to be careful about moving to a regionally based order when, potentially, the regional organizations involved may be rather subservient to the dominant actor in the field. Chapter 8 of the United Nations Charter is designed specifically to address this problem; regional organizations may intervene, but they need the authorization of the Security Council. They need that global rubber stamp.

Question: I have three questions; I don't know if they're related or not, so answer any or all.
- Do you consider yourselves idealists?
- Ethics in leadership and ethics in international relations: are they ideals or are they operational values? And third,
- how do you turn ideals into operational values in the international system?

Dr. Michael Byers: Academically, I'm regarded as about as realist as you can get while still being an international lawyer; I'm not known as an idealist within my own field, but I do firmly believe, from a broader perspective, from the politics and the economics that surround international law, that when political decisions have to be made, idealism has a very important role to play, and my answer to Jennifer's question went exactly to that: you can be a realist and do cost benefit analyses until the sun goes down; but your analysis is going to be initially considered by how you view yourself and how you view your place in the world. It's that aspect, it's your vision of your self, that is the idealist aspect in this rationalist hard nosed world. And I can tell you that I do and say a lot of things that get idealist colleagues annoyed because, for instance, I actually think that power can change rules of international law, and that the foundational principle of sovereign equality is largely a fiction when it comes to the international legal system. I believe that because as an academic that's my objective analysis; but that doesn't mean that I think that it should be that way.

Ambassador David Wright: I must say I've spent most of my career as a practitioner; and so I'm a realist. But now, having moved to a university, I've become more idealistic, or at least I've put under the umbrella of idealism all the things that one is forced to deal with in a tough world. But I would say that, facing some of the biggest challenges that I've been involved in, in terms of transformations in Europe since the fall of the Berlin wall, and dealing with the conflicts in the Balkans, and dealing with Afghanistan, and so on, in the end the greatest satisfaction is knowing that you're pursuing ideals and that you're doing so in the best possible way. And I must say, when it came to the crucial moments I was always – and I believe our country was always – driven by ideals. I think that's really important. My part in that has been more to apply it, and to try to make sure it works in a tough world.

Professor Kathleen Mahoney: My whole life I've been an academic; but I'm also a practicing lawyer from time to time, and an activist. I've been an activist a good portion of my life. So I think my answer to your question would be that I'm both. You can't be an effective lawyer if you're purely idealistic; you must be realistic. You have to make deals; you have to make hard decisions; you have to be strategic. And also activists have to do that too, if they want to be effective; they have to be very strategic. And sometimes you have to let something go that you might, ideally, like to have on your agenda; but if it's not going to work it can sink the whole thing. So I think you have to be both. But I certainly agree with the Ambassador that it is utterly essential to be idealistic; utterly essential. We wouldn't be the country we are today unless we were idealistic. Ideals are what human rights are all about. After World War II the world had sunk to such a low and dismal dark place it was only ideals that brought us up and forward, and it was idealists who drafted the Universal Declaration of Human Rights – and there's absolutely nothing wrong with that document. It's an incredibly fine document, which is full of ideals; and what I fear is that the balances that are being struck today are pushing the ideals off the table. My metaphor about Canadian foreign policy, when we talk about pillars, is a stool with three legs: when you cut one of those legs off half way what have you got? You've got a huge problem. And that's what's happening. The ideals part of our three pillars is being cut off at the knees, and we're out of balance as a result, it seems to me. I love your question; it's a very important question, and nobody should be embarrassed to answer that by saying "I'm idealistic. And I hope you are too."

Ambassador Paul Heinbecker: I hesitate to say anything after all of that because it was so interesting. I just thought it might be worth the audience's knowing a bit more about R2P (the Responsibility to Protect). For example, I introduced, or tried to introduce, into the UN General Assembly a discussion of R2P. The opposition to my doing so came mainly from the developing countries, and mainly from the Africans. We couldn't even get Rwanda to support a discussion of the Responsibility to Protect. Our Resolution invited interested countries to meet among themselves, at their own expense, to discuss the ideas given in the Report. That resolution was not passable in the UN General Assembly. So the problem isn't always, and isn't only, with the rich, and industrial, and proponent side. I would add, though, that in the High Level Panel that the Secretary General has established, the Responsibility to Protect seems to be a central feature, and there seems to be a movement among the Commissioners to propose that the UN Security Council somehow endorse these ideas. So that will be some kind of progress.

    On Kosovo: I wanted to say one thing, and that is because Michael Byers and I had a slight exchange that not everybody might have heard. It was a discussion about whether the stakes were high enough, whether we'd reached the level where we should be intervening. Well if you read the UN High Commission for Refugees (UNHCR) report dated the day before the bombings, there were 450,000 displaced people and refugees. That was the day before NATO acted. There's been a certain amount of mythology that has obscured things; some of it's been contributed to by, for example, U.S. Secretary of Defense (William) Cohen who talked of a hundred thousand casualties. Where he got that number no one has any idea; at least I don't. But the fact that there were 450,000 displaced persons and refugees before the bombing began, and that Milosevic had a track record of crimes against humanity, really were grounds, as far as I'm concerned, to act. And the point I'd like to make is that, if there had been a vote in the General Assembly, if we had tabled a peace resolution, I'm told by third world ambassadors, we would have got 150 to 160 votes, out of 190, in favour of action in Kosovo. But I can tell you from my own experience that, on Iraq, you would have got 150 to 160 *against* action in Iraq. So there is something to be said for all that.

Last point, on the International Criminal Court, which came up at various times earlier. This I say with some regret: the United States is actively working against the establishment of the International Criminal Court. It has removed defense assistance and other kinds of assistance from smaller countries to coerce them: if they want the money back they'll have to sign agreements under Article 98 exempting the United States from coverage of the court. And one anecdote, which is a public anecdote though you may not have heard it, which I have on impeccable authority: on the eve of the Iraq war, which is to say February or March of 2003, Under Secretary of State (for Arms Control and International Security John R.) Bolton of the United States had the brass to write to the Government of Jordan telling them that the imminent visit of the King of Jordan to Washington, that is, the visit of the head of government of a country on which the United States was depending in the coming war, would be cancelled unless Jordan signed an agreement with the United States exempting Americans from the reach of the criminal court. The Jordanians ignored that threat and the visit took place, and nobody heard much of anything of it subsequently until I just told you.

· VI ·

Canadian Business
in an
International Context

Madelaine Drohan

The last time I was in Calgary there was a freak snowstorm and I had to go out and buy boots and gloves after the temperature went from plus 17 one day to minus 10 the next. So this time I was determined not to get caught out and called a friend in Bragg Creek to ask what I should be wearing. His advice seemed a bit unorthodox at first – wear something red, he said – it's Flames fever out here. Now I realize a chiffon scarf is not really appropriate for hockey gear, but I hope you will see that my heart is in the right place.

That last trip was to attend the conference on whistleblowing put on by the Foundation. And just like this conference, it covered all the angles with a broad range of thoughtful speakers and participants. I went away with a deeper understanding of the issue and a greater appreciation of the work the Foundation is doing. I welcomed the chance to participate in this event. Most of my career as a journalist has been spent covering business and economic issues. During the eight years I was European correspondent for The Globe and Mail and the five years after that when I was researching my book,[1] I interviewed hundreds of Canadian companies operating in Europe, Russia and Africa. Marsha has asked me to address whether such companies promote our values abroad.

I have to admit I have been struck this weekend by the implicit assumption that Canada's image in the world is shaped solely by its politicians, diplomats and foreign aid policy. We are forgetting a rather important group of players.

---

[1] Madelaine Drohan, *Making a Killing: How and why corporations use armed force to do business* (Random House, Toronto, 2003; Lyon's Press, U.S.A. 2004).

Consider these figures. In 2002 Canada's official development aid totalled about $2.5 billion. That same year, Canadian companies invested $431 billion abroad, much of it buying or building new companies. What this means in practical terms is that companies rather than politicians or diplomats are the more familiar face of Canada out there in the world. Their activities help shape people's perceptions of Canada.

Globalization has made them our unofficial ambassadors, whether we like it or not. Which leads me to the three questions I want to address this afternoon:

- Are Canadian companies promoting our values abroad?
- Is it realistic to expect them to?
- And if it is realistic, is there any way the government can ensure that they do?

The companies I am most familiar with are the ones I dealt with in my book. But that's a rather unrepresentative group. I only include instances where people were killed either by the company directly or by someone else on their behalf. I think we can all agree that this is not the type of behaviour we expect of Canadian companies. It would also make for a very short speech as the answers are pretty cut and dried.

So I plan to base my remarks today on a more nuanced situation – that of Canadian mining companies in the Democratic Republic of Congo. I was there two weeks ago and interviewed a number of them. I'm going to get specific, but the issues raised by their presence there have a broader resonance in the business community.

To set the scene, I will tell you about what I saw in the Congo. Please bear with me on this because it is important to understand the environment in which companies are operating. I will then discuss how the Canadian companies fit into this picture. From there, I will talk about whether they are promoting our values abroad, and – if they are not, what the government can do about it.

A bit of context first for those of you who do not follow the Congo. It is a former Belgian colony. It is fabulously rich in resources. Copper, cobalt, gold, diamonds – the Congo has it all. But it remains one of the poorest countries in Africa because thirty years of [former President] Mobutu's corrupt dictatorship was followed by five years of war. An estimated three million people died in that war, either from the fighting itself or the famine and disease that came afterwards.

There is now a fragile peace, although pockets of violence remain. A transitional government is in place and elections are planned for next year. Using the word 'government' conjures up misleading images for Canadians. In the area I visited – the mineral rich province of Katanga in the extreme southeast – the government is in control, but it is not governing. I lost track of the number of people who told me while I was there that it was like living in the Wild West. And not the romantic version of Hollywood movies, but the rough, ugly version where the people with the guns are in charge and everything, including justice, is for sale.

Katanga was once the centre of a world-class copper industry run by a Belgian company called Union Minière. Almost all the jobs in the province depended either directly or indirectly on mining. It governed Katanga. The copper company built all the roads, railways, houses, hospitals, schools, water and electricity systems. Mobutu nationalized the company in 1967 and its successor then ruled Katanga.

But in the latter years of his reign, Mobutu destroyed the company, first by siphoning billions from its bank accounts and then by encouraging a general plunder in 1991. He also engineered, for political reasons, the exile of its most talented workers.

The result is that today the state-owned company is barely functioning. It owns all sorts of rich copper and cobalt mines, but lacks the resources to work them. Where once it produced something like 400,000 tonnes of copper a year, its production last year was estimated at 8,000 tonnes. It's a disaster. It's a disaster for the company and more particularly the people of Katanga. So what is keeping the people of the province alive now that the main employer is bankrupt?

The main economic activity in Katanga today is artisanal mining, or what they call there hand-picking. It is exactly what it says: thousands of men, women and children go out to the unused mines and use picks and shovels to mine by hand.

Copper isn't valuable enough to mine this way. The current world price is around $1.50 a pound. But cobalt, which is found in combination with copper, currently fetches $25 a pound. So that is what they are mining. They sell it to shadowy middlemen, who sell it to others who export it to world markets. Somewhere along the line, the cobalt passes from the black market into the hands of legitimate companies.

The only good thing to say about this situation is that it is keeping an entire province from starving. But there are lots of problems. There is the legal question. The cobalt is being taken from mines that belong to someone. The actual owner of the mine does not see a penny from the cobalt taken from his property.

There is the question of health and safety. These artisanal miners work with no equipment. They can't afford it. They work in t-shirts, some wearing flip-flops. And when they dig a hole into the earth, they have nothing to shore up the tunnels to prevent a cave-in. They get a pittance for the cobalt they dig up in dangerous circumstances.

While I was there, I visited the old uranium mine at Shinkolobwe. This is the mine that produced the uranium used in the bombs the U.S. dropped on Japan during the Second World War. Technically, it was closed and sealed with a concrete plug many years ago. But because the area happens to be rich in cobalt, as well as uranium, the hand pickers have flocked to the site.

The current Congolese government was embarrassed by international coverage of these activities earlier this year and declared the mine was officially closed. But it is not. An estimated 6,000 miners are working there daily. Some have brought their families to live with them in a makeshift village on the radioactive site.

I won't claim that I saw 6,000 people the day I arrived at Shinkolobwe. I saw probably several hundred. There are two reasons for this: One, we were told by one of the hand-pickers there had been a cave-in and that work had stopped in sympathy with the doomed miner, whose body had not yet been recovered. They had to dig him out by hand.

But the second reason was that we were prevented from going further than the edge of the mine by the men who were controlling the workers. And who were they? I counted two members of the president's special security forces, six members of the army, and several policemen in plain clothes. They ran us off the site.

The government could shut this down in an instant. But there are too many vested interests at stake. Too many military officers taking a cut. Too many politicians being paid off.

Just as an aside, before I leave the story of Shinkolobwe, I should note that people concerned about terrorists and dirty bombs should be worried about this situation. Katanga is a free for all right now. The uranium is there for the taking. And its a snap to bring whatever you want out of the Congo. The day I flew out of Lubumbashi, the x-ray machines were not working. They looked like they had not been working for a while. And for 300 francs, which is about a dollar, a customs officer would not even search your bags. You could carry anything you want through that airport and fly out of the country.

I told you this story of the hand-pickers because it gives you an idea of the current environment in this part of the Congo where Canadian companies have secured or are negotiating for mineral concessions. Just to be crystal clear, I saw or heard nothing to suggest that the Canadian companies are participating in this hand-picking industry. If anything, they appear to be victims. Three of them own properties that are overrun with hand-pickers and overseen by the military. So what are Canadian companies doing in a place that many would describe as a hellhole?

I discovered in doing the research for my book that it's a myth that all companies require peace and stability before they set up shop in a given country. They would prefer it, and certainly if there are alternatives they would go elsewhere. But resource companies have to go where the copper, cobalt, gold, diamonds, etc., are located. And for some of them, conflict represents an opportunity.

Why? It cuts down the competition for starters. Not every company wants to take such risks, no matter how attractive the resource. This is especially true of large companies. This leaves the field open to small- and medium-sized firms. This is why Ranger Oil, now called Canadian Natural Resources, went into wartorn Angola in the early 1990s. It is part of the reason that Talisman Energy went into Sudan which had been in the grip of civil war since the 1950s.

The eight companies who had negotiated deals for the Congo fit this profile – they are all small or medium sized firms with a high tolerance for risk. You will have heard of some of them – First Quantum, Tenke Corp., Kinross, Banro and American Mineral Fields – but not of others such as Melkior and International Panorama.

The second reason why conflicts such as the one in the Congo may not put off foreign firms is that a government under pressure – which governments fighting rebel movements or foreign armies invariably are – is more willing to do deals to bring in revenues. They are more likely to put a lower price on concessions than they are worth and offer tax holidays to secure a signature on a contract.

So the lack of competition brings down the price a foreign firm has to pay for a concession and the eagerness of the host government to sign deals could reduce that price even further.

I have travelled extensively in Africa and I have never been to a country where corruption permeated every activity as completely as in the Congo. It started at the airport in Lubumbashi. The customs lady asked whether I had been to the Congo before. I said no. She said that will be $10 please. I had to pay $200 and this was U.S. money to get a permit to operate as a journalist there. When I went to pick up the permit, the security guards were taking watches and pens off everyone who entered the building – and you did not get them back.

The UN experts had a lot more to say, but you get the general picture. The debate here is between the companies saying that within their narrow sphere of influence, they followed the guidelines, did not pay bribes and treated their employees well, and the experts saying that in the broader context the companies were not living up to the OECD guidelines because of the impact of their actions. If this argument sounds familiar to some of you, it is the same one that surrounded Talisman Energy's investment in Sudan.

When the experts released their report all hell broke loose. The companies were outraged and pressed the government to get their names off the list. The panel of experts wanted the home governments of these companies to investigate further. There were public hearings held in Belgium, the former colonial power. But none were held in Canada. The matter was dealt with privately between the companies and the government and when a third UN panel of experts report was released, seven of the eight Canadian cases were declared resolved.

The third UN report did not specify how this happened in each particular case. There were all sorts of ways a company could have its case resolved. Being innocent was one. But admitting you had done something wrong and resolving never to do it again was another. I would have thought that from the companies' point of view, this was not a desirable outcome. It was not a public exoneration. If they had done nothing wrong – which all of them said publicly – why not support a public hearing to clear their name? But they did not push for one, preferring to settle their cases privately. The result is that a shadow remains over all the foreign activities in the Congo.

While I am using the specific example of the Canadian mining companies operating in the Congo, this speaks to the broader public debate about what companies should be responsible for and how we should hold them accountable. I'm sure most of you are familiar with the famous quote by the economist Milton Friedman, who said the

> *one and only one social responsibility of*
> *business [is] to increase profits so long*
> *as it stays within the rules of the game,*
> *which is to say, engages in open and free*
> *competition without deception or fraud.*[2]

But he said that in 1970 and since then the "rules of the game" have changed significantly. From just being responsible for making profits, companies have gradually assumed the responsibility for the health and safety of their workers, no matter where in the world they operate, care of the environment, to make sure what they do is sustainable. And that definition is expanding again to include respect for human rights.

I'm not saying we are there yet. But you can see this recognition has dawned on companies because they have been producing voluntary corporate codes of conduct that enshrine human rights. What needs to happen now is that the intent of those codes be translated into laws that are mandatory and have real teeth and apply equally to all companies so that there are no free riders.

So going back to the questions I posed in the beginning. Are they promoting our values? Yes, if you interpret their responsibility narrowly. No, if you take a broader view. Should they? Of course my answer is yes. Given their clout – remember those figures I gave you at the beginning that show how foreign investment dwarfs foreign aid – the definition of corporate responsibility must be expanded. And I believe that is slowly

---

2 Milton Friedman, "The Social Responsibility of Business is to Increase its Profits". The New York Times Magazine, (September 13, 1970).

happening. As speaker after speaker has said here these are not Canadian values, they are universal values. I see no reason why companies should be exempt.

What can the government do about it? Now this is a long discussion, so I will make three short points. Our government should

- become more proactive about using the controls that exist, however imperfect they are. Such as the OECD guidelines. I would also put in this category the International Criminal Court, which while it cannot prosecute companies, can prosecute individuals within companies for their actions.
- withhold its support for companies that do not promote our values by their actions.
- push for an international law, not a voluntary code, to govern corporate activities and fill the current vacuum at the international level. This would also give companies a clear idea of what is expected of them.

And we as citizens who want to make sure that our values are promoted all over the world should push our government to do these things. I am not pretending for an instant that any of this is easy – either for the companies or the governments. And the debate can get a little blurry when you are having it back here in safe, secure Canada.

But when you go to a sad, ruined country like the Congo, what's at stake becomes a lot more clear. Because suddenly you care desperately that Canadian companies are helping, not hurting, when they fly our flag around the world.

Thank you.

· VII ·

RECOVERING AMERICAN LEGITIMACY

Robert Kagan

Thank you very much, and thank you Marsha for inviting me to this and for setting all of this up; I can see what a wonderful Foundation this is. I must say I now approach my talk this evening with a great deal of trepidation. I feel I must spend the first fifteen minutes ensuring that you understand what I am and what I am not. My biggest trepidation though, is that, after watching the clips from your previous Symposia, I feel under enormous pressure to be uplifting somehow and to send you out on a mission to change the world. And if I fail at being uplifting tonight, at least you've eaten so you won't be too mad at me.

In thinking ahead about American foreign policy, obviously a great deal is going to depend upon what happens in Iraq, and more broadly in the war on terrorism as we, in the United States, refer to it. But I don't really think anyone can say with any confidence what is going to happen in Iraq. For all the failings of the administration in the planning for the post war phase in Iraq, and in the execution of the post invasion phase in Iraq (we have certainly dug ourselves a hole), I actually have, more than some perhaps, faith in the Iraqi people themselves. There's a great deal of talk in Washington and around the world, especially in Europe, about the impossibility of building a democracy in Iraq. And some have even taken recent setbacks as *proof* that it's impossible to imagine an Iraq living in a constitutional system where people are allowed to choose their leaders. I must say I find that rather odd since, whatever else is true about Iraq, the Iraqi people have not been given that chance. It's not democracy that's failed in Iraq, not yet. Perhaps

America has been failing in Iraq in terms of meeting its responsibilities, but I don't think it is time yet to say that the Iraqi people have failed because, in fact, I don't see that they have failed
in any particular way.

But tonight I would like to take a step back from the immediate events which are grabbing our attention. In the United
States we have a political campaign going on – a time of great
controversy – everything that can go wrong does go wrong and
is made much of in a campaign. And we all know about the genuine difficulties that we're having in Iraq and elsewhere around
the world.

I would like to take a step back and look at the international situation more broadly and ask: where is the United States in
the international system? Where is Europe? – those are the two
topics I focused on over the past year – and also, especially in
light of what you have all been discussing this past weekend,
we need to ask: where is Canada?

Now I think that the differences between America and its
European allies have never been more stark. I first began writing about this back in 2001, even before September 11th, and
certainly before the Iraq war. And if anything, what's happened
since then has demonstrated that we are even *more* at odds
than I might have suspected when I first started writing about
this. Even as you look at the American presidential campaign I
think (as someone who has just come back from Europe – I
came back from Europe this past summer after living there for
three years) it is striking what is *not* being debated in the campaign. You have two candidates who supported the Iraq war.
John Kerry voted for it, George Bush obviously executed it. You
have two candidates who agree that the United States should
not withdraw from Iraq and that it has an important responsibility there. And you have two candidates vying for American public support on the grounds that they are both better at fighting
the war on terrorism than their competitor is. John Kerry promises to fight it better than Bush has fought it.

Now I don't mean to minimize the differences between Bush and Kerry, although I think they can be overstated. But I think it's worth noting differences between them and what I take to be the common view in Europe. In Europe they don't talk about a war on terrorism. In fact, most Europeans object strongly to the whole notion that there is a war on terrorism, that one can wage a *war* on terrorism. And whether Europeans or Americans are right – I won't for the moment suggest who's right – let's at least note the differences.

The differences have been striking on issues that go beyond Iraq *per se*. I look at the difference between the American reaction to September 11th and the European reaction to March 11th.[1] Certainly the American reaction has been one of great belligerence and bellicosity and support for military action. And the European reaction to March 11th has been entirely different. Europeans have talked about increasing their police capabilities. There's no talk of increasing defense budgets, there's no talk about using military force. In fact there is continued aversion to that. And again I won't say who's right and who's wrong, but there is the difference. It's a striking difference, and it hasn't changed on either side of the Atlantic since the Iraq war.

Now I won't go on at length about the causes of these gaps. I once made the error of referring to the United States and Europe as being like Mars and Venus and I've never stopped regretting having made that argument since it's constantly leading people to talking about whether somebody's from Saturn. Or is it really Mars? Or is it more like Mercury? Or something like that. I also say that, since I've been back on this side of the Atlantic, when I do speak with Canadians, Canadians are constantly asking me "so which are we, Mars or Venus?" And my answer is always "yes." But I will give an answer later on in the course of this discussion. In any case, the disagreements are there; the differences in the approach to the world are there.

---

[1] On March 11, 2004 over 200 persons lost their lives in terrorist bombings of three train stations in Madrid, Spain.

Europeans do, as a result of their own history and the organization that they have set up on the European continent, have much greater faith in the international order, in the established, international mechanisms of the United Nations, and international legal mechanisms as a means of conducting relations in the world. Americans are more suspicious of that. And I think there are both historical reasons and structural reasons for that. Now, although my views have changed on a number of issues, my view has not changed particularly on whether Iraq was the right war or not. But since the time I first started writing about the European and U.S. relationship I have come to be less sanguine about the differences that I, that we all, can see and that I identified in my book;[2] and I have become more worried about their consequences.

Now, I wasn't sanguine before. It wasn't as if I was happy to see the gap that opened up between the United States and Europe. I was a child of the Cold War and remembered an era of great U.S./European cooperation that was now over and that was a sad thing, but I did think it was something that we could all learn to adjust to. Europe is very much focused these days on the issue of Europe. And it seemed to me it was conceivable at least, although we had these disagreements about strategic issues such as the use of military force and even international order as it relates to questions of military force, that despite these questions we could sort of move along on our paths. I even imagined a kind of burden-sharing in the world where Europeans worry about Europe and the United States worries about most of the rest of the world. It turns out it is not so easy. Indeed, the fact is that, because the United States and Europe (and here I certainly would include all of us in the West) are so intimately connected by our common culture, our common values, and our common political philosophies, it is not so easy for us to have fundamental disagreements on issues as important as war and peace and strategic questions and international order and just go merrily along our own ways. And in fact, this is a source of great difficulty in the relationship and a great difficulty within the West which, if it goes untreated, I fear will

---

[2] Robert Kagan, *Of Paradise and Power: America and Europe in the New World Order* (New York: Knopf, 2003).

gnaw away at what we used to call the West. And this is occurring in a time when we face perhaps greater peril collectively than ever before.

Now in the United States, when I talk about a term like 'legitimacy' and 'international legitimacy', I can tell you that I often find a very unreceptive audience. But I think that the question of international legitimacy is one that the United States must face, and in fact one that we all must face, in the new international system. It is precisely international legitimacy that the United States is now lacking and not just because of prisoner abuse scandals and not just because of the war in Iraq, but because of a whole series of historical events and structural changes in the international order which I believe have led to the undermining of the legitimacy, such as it was, that the United States once enjoyed. That's what I'd like to talk mostly about this evening.

Before I do so let me say that I believe legitimacy does matter to Americans and that it is a myth, in fact, that Americans are an isolationist, indifferent, people who do not care what the rest of the world thinks of them and can go along without the approval of their closest democratic friends in the world. I believe that is not true about Americans. In our declaration of independence, our founding document, Americans talked about having a decent respect for the opinion of mankind. And I believe that Americans have in fact always been concerned about the opinions, if not of all mankind, then certainly of the liberal world of which the Americans are part. And I believe that, over time, if the United States moves forward and is constantly being declared illegitimate by its closest democratic friends, this will eat away at America's capacity to act. Indeed, Americans will not be able to do the things that I think may be necessary for the United States to do in the coming years and decades if, at every step of the way, their closest friends are declaring that they are behaving illegitimately and immorally. And so it's an issue that the United States must deal with. It's an issue that the Bush administration, in my view, has paid all too little attention to; and it must begin to do so in the near term.

Now what has happened to American legitimacy? As I think about it, I try to go back to the Cold War and think about the legitimacy that America enjoyed at that time. And by the way, I don't mean to suggest that America behaved legitimately at all times. But I would say that, in the eyes of the majority of Europeans, the European public (perhaps sometimes a silent majority, but nevertheless a majority) and, I would dare say, in this country and among America's Asian allies, that American leadership and American action in the world enjoyed a broad blanket of legitimacy among its allies. That legitimacy was not, incidentally, based on the fact that the United States was a model citizen in terms of its behaviour in the United Nations Security Council. The United States went to war frequently, threatened war, undermined other governments, and did a whole host of things without UN Security Council approval during the Cold War. Nor did the United States abide with any particular fidelity by the UN Charter and what might be regarded as the laws of nations.

I would say that the legitimacy the United States enjoyed during the Cold War rested on three fundamental pillars. The first of these pillars was a common sense of threat. The Soviet Union posed an obvious threat, certainly, for Europeans. They didn't need to look very far to see the hundreds of thousands of Soviet troops or Warsaw Pact troops parked in the middle of Europe. And not only was the strategic threat commonly agreed, but so was the fact that the United States was the only power capable of deterring that threat. This was not a subject of great disagreement among the allies during the Cold War. And that conferred the kind of legitimacy that comes from self-interest. I believe that Europeans, and Canadians, and Japanese, and others around the world, accorded the United States a great deal of legitimacy by virtue of the fact that those countries depended upon the U.S. for their security.

A second element, the second pillar of this legitimacy, rested on the ideological conflict of the era. It was a kind of

Manichaean struggle between democracy and democratic capitalism on the one side and a totalitarian system on the other. And, although again there were dissenters in the West, by and large the majority of people in the West agreed that there was that struggle and the United States, as the strongest democratic power, enjoyed a great deal of legitimacy merely by virtue of that fact. It wasn't only Americans who spoke of the United States as the leader of the free world, and that was a significant factor.

And then the third pillar (which I think is one that we were inclined not to understand at the time and which has only become more apparent in retrospect) is what you might call a structural legitimacy, by which I mean simply that the world was bipolar. There were two great superpowers which checked each other. And so American power, as great as it was during the Cold War, was checked. The United States hegemony could not be exercised at will. The United States could not do whatever it wanted to in the world; far from it. It had to worry about the Soviet response in all cases. And while Europeans did not, in my view, welcome the existence of Soviet power, they nevertheless, implicitly and sometimes explicitly, understood that this balance of power gave them a little bit of freedom of manoeuvre and operating room. And if you look at the policies of Willie Brandt or Charles de Gaulle or France's foreign policies in general you can see how the existence of the Soviet Union checked American hegemony, and created some room in the system. It also created some sense of justice in the system despite the fact that the Soviet Union was not considered a friendly power. Because among democratic peoples who organize their own governments and their own societies in such a way that power is checked, most people assume such checks should occur at the international level as well. How can there be justice at the international level if power is not checked? Checks and balances need to operate in the international system as well as within individual nations.

Now I think it's important to realize, especially at this moment when one wants to focus on the policies of Bush or the policies of Chirac or the issues of the moment that, long before *this* moment – dating back to 1989-1991 when the Soviet empire fell and the Cold War ended – it was at *that* moment that all three pillars of legitimacy, all three pillars on which American legitimacy rested disappeared before any president took any action of any kind. The common threat of the Soviet Union disappeared and was not replaced at any time since the end of the Cold War by any other threat that could unify the West in the same way. Europeans, certainly, have not regarded weapons of mass destruction and international terrorism in the same way that Americans have come to. And in any case, Europeans do not believe they rely on the United States or depend on the United States to protect them from those threats to the degree that they do see them. The fact is that Europeans who were once dependent on the United States for their security are no longer dependent and I believe that as a result, the legitimacy that America enjoyed purely by virtue of European self-interest has disappeared as well.

Nor is there an ideological threat to replace communism as a unifying force in the West. Recall that, rightly or wrongly, during the Cold War people used to worry in Europe and the United States that certain European governments might go communist. That was a big preoccupation, certainly, of the early Cold War. Well, radical Islamic fundamentalism is not a replacement for communism as the same kind of existential threat that can unite the West. No one in Europe worries, with the occasional sense one gets of the exception of the French, that Islamic fundamentalism is going to replace their rule, the rule of democratic governments in Europe. That threat does not exist in the same way to unify us against a common ideological threat.

Thirdly, and again, perhaps most importantly, the structural legitimacy of the Cold War has disappeared. The Soviet Union is gone and the United States, at least in the eyes of many around the world, now enjoys a freedom of action which, frankly, makes many people extremely uncomfortable. And I want to hasten to say that this discomfort predates Iraq, predates September 11th, and predates the Bush Administration. If you go back to the 1990s and read the statements of French foreign ministers and Russian foreign ministers and Chinese foreign ministers there was great concern expressed in the 1990s about the emergence of a unipolar world. There was a great deal of talk in those days about needing to create a multipolar world by virtue of the fact that a unipolar world could not be just. And I would say that suspicion of the emerging unipolar reality began even then and has been and is a problem that we all must somehow grapple with, because the truth is that the unipolar world is unprecedented, certainly in modern history, and we have no experience in dealing with it.

I would suggest that part of the problem that we're all having as we move forward in the international system today is that we are all grappling with the problems created by what I would call the unipolar predicament. I emphasize that it is a unipolar predicament, because I would suggest that even a president of the United States with the best intentions cannot so easily solve this problem. We now have a situation where, on the one hand, the old threats have disappeared and the sense of dependence on the part of America's allies has disappeared and at the same time America has emerged as this great power that can act when it chooses to act. So how would it not be the case that one-time allies now look with suspicion on this power that has been unleashed in the world?

I must say I try to explain as best I can to Americans how it might look, even to the best friends of the United States, if they feel that this great mammoth superpower is out of control. I would say that much of the crisis that we've been dealing with, even over Iraq, has not been so much about the difficulties in Iraq or the opposition to the war prior to the war, but over this larger issue of how we grapple with a United States that is unchecked. After all, Iraq is not unprecedented in American history even if it goes as badly as some fear it might, because we had Vietnam as well. All through the years of Vietnam even despite the fact that Europeans thought it was an immoral policy, it was a wrong policy, it was a foolish policy; and even despite the fact, if I may say so, that some of the atrocities committed by American troops in Vietnam make the recent scandal over Iraqi prisoner abuse look rather small by comparison – I mean we had incidents like My Lai in Vietnam, which were far worse; and even despite all that the United States still continued throughout that period to enjoy fundamental legitimacy in the eyes of its allies. And so I believe this problem is not just about Iraq and would not be solved were everything to go perfectly in Iraq, although I think that would help.

Now, in the interest of ending on an uplifting point, let me try to suggest some ways that we can all begin to grapple with this problem of legitimacy. I do want to emphasize that it is a problem not just for the United States but for everyone in what we used to call the West, because it is likely the case that America's lack of legitimacy will ultimately erode America's capacity to act. It is in fact the case that we are faced with some serious dangers out there, international terrorism being one, the proliferation of weapons of mass destruction being another, and there are many other global problems that we could talk about. There are, for example, traditional geopolitical issues which may arise in East Asia and elsewhere. I believe we are moving into a very dangerous phase, if we have not in fact already moved into a very dangerous phase, in human history. If the West is divided as we move forward into this dangerous period, we are all going to be the losers, and that's why I believe that it is a problem we all have to deal with.

Now I don't doubt for a second that the primary responsibility for dealing with the problem of American legitimacy is America's. One way to deal with our legitimacy problem is to get Iraq right. Certainly to fulfill America's responsibilities, now that we've gone into Iraq, is to ensure that we stay and do what is necessary to leave behind, where we can, a stable and better Iraq than the one that we found. I think that would help America's legitimacy in the same way that our current difficulties in Iraq are obviously harming America's legitimacy.

I also believe that the United States can win some legitimacy by being more consistent in pursuing the values and principles that it claims, and has legitimately represented throughout its history. I believe that when we compromise our values, when we compromise with dictatorships, when we fail to support democracy overseas, that too has an effect on our legitimacy and there is much that we can try to do to be more consistent in support of our principles of both liberal democracy and international peace insofar as we have the capacity to do so. But I think there is another problem that has to be addressed, which is the distribution of power in the international system. I believe it is going to be necessary, somehow, for the United States and its allies to come to some kind of new arrangement that fits the current international system which can give allies some confidence that they are not completely without control over the vast power that the United States wields.

I don't think we can move forward and expect to have allies on our side if they believe that they have absolutely no influence over how the United States wields its power. So my hope would be for a new kind of bargain in which the United States does genuinely cede influence to its closest democratic allies over how its power is used. But I must say that I don't see how that bargain can be fulfilled on either side of the Atlantic, and perhaps in dealing with Canada as well, unless we have a more common sense of the dangers and threats. That is where I worry, precisely because we don't have a common sense of threat, that there is no bargain to be had. It is difficult to see how we can come to some kind of common strategy if we don't agree on the nature and the severity of our common threats. So to Americans I say, in a way that makes Americans uncomfortable, "we need to be willing to cede some genuine influence to our closest allies." And to Europeans, and perhaps to Canadians what I say, in what will certainly make you uncomfortable, and has certainly made many Europeans uncomfortable when I said it to them, is that "you have to take a more, as I see it, American view of the nature of the threats."

If Europeans insist on playing down the nature of the threats and not seeing that it may be necessary, on occasion, to use military force to deal with these threats, then the United States cannot afford to cede influence because then the United States is hobbled by the fact of ceding influence and the West is hobbled in dealing with this threat. Now the European answer to that is "you want us to adopt your worldview and we can't adopt your worldview." And I understand that. But I also would say that America cannot adopt the European worldview and believe that we can do what we need to do to keep ourselves and the West safe. So that is the bargain that is, perhaps, tantalizingly out of reach. But I do think it's one that we should strive for.

The place where this bargain can take place, I believe, is the North Atlantic Alliance, NATO, where the United States has, historically, ceded influence to its closest democratic allies. NATO is the institution that has most successfully reconciled the American hegemony with allied autonomy and influence. Unfortunately these days NATO is in bad odour in Europe. I fear that Europeans, in building the magnificent structures of the European Union (something that I wholly support) are looking less and less to NATO as a place where they should do their negotiating with the United States.

Now let me end by talking a minute about Canada; and I must say I'm not saying this simply because I'm talking to a largely Canadian audience. I believe Canada actually has an important role to play in all of this because, in answer to the question: "Is Canada from Mars or from Venus?" my sense is that Canada lies somewhere in between. I may be wrong about that but I would note that between Mars and Venus, in the solar system, is Earth. So it could be that Canadians are the only people standing on Earth, which would be a good thing. But I think that Canada's role can be as an international broker, to be a communicator between the European worldview, much of which Canada, in my view, shares and the American worldview with which Canada also has, I think, more affinity than do many of the European countries.

I believe that we need some serious statesmanship to try to bridge the transatlantic divide in the interest of all of us. I would say that that statesmanship is at the moment lacking in Washington. But it doesn't have to be lacking in the future, and Canada can play a very critical role in that. Now I know that this Symposium has been about the nature and role of Canadian ethics and Canadian values in the world. I don't pretend to know – I missed most of the conference, so I don't know exactly – what those values and ethics are. But I do see a role for Canada, a kind of bridging role, playing the mediator between the United States and Europe. And so I would hope that, if there is an uplifting message in all of this, it's that Canada actually has a role to play in helping us deal with the fundamentally new situation of the international order. It is a problem, a series of problems, that we really do have to address if we are going to pull together and act in concert against a whole variety of threats that we're facing in the years to come.

So again, thank you very much for having me. It's a wonderful occasion, and it's been a great pleasure talking to you. Thank you.

A question and answer session followed Mr. Kagan's remarks.

Question: You've taken some pains to explain how the evaporation of the Cold War has basically brought about a realignment of global forces and created new realities. My question is this sir: do you believe that, as a result of this realignment, there is legitimacy to failing to recognize and abide by well-established international tenets of law? I have in mind tenets such as that it is not legitimate to invade another country unless there is a real and imminent threat, and such as that it is not right for a country to interfere in the domestic affairs of another country. In other words, as you see it, are those still valid principles or do you think that they have been supplanted by the new reality in terms of legitimacy?

Robert Kagan: That's an excellent question. I actually think that those principles have never been honoured and certainly were not honoured during the Cold War and certainly not by the United States. But also, I would argue, not by any *other* powers. They've always been the dream of the people who wrote the UN Charter. But the UN Charter has been honoured in the breach, not in the observance. I also think it's interesting that, in the war that Europeans fought in 1999 in Kosovo, all those strictures were violated. Kosovo, by any standard or traditional understanding of international law, was an entirely illegal war: no Security Council resolution. There was no threat as you described external threats. I mean, you could make an argument that there was a threat but there was no direct aggression. It was entirely a domestic matter in legal terms. I actually believe, contrary to what you're suggesting, that what we really need to do (if we want to have an effective international order where there is greater legal control over the actions of nations) is to *expand* our understanding of when intervention can take place and when it cannot take place. Now that kind of thinking has, in fact, evolved over the past decade or so, largely as a result of the events in the Balkans.

But I think we need to move beyond the simple UN Charter's "perfect sovereignty" that nations have been supposed to enjoy ever since Grotius laid out the principles of international law. These are not possible, I would argue, in the modern age. Now, partly I think it's ironic that, at a time when sovereignty is becoming something that most nations are trying to move past – the sort of strict observance of sovereignty – that we want to enshrine an international legal system which is built around national sovereignty. But more to the point, in terms of humanitarian intervention, I believe most people of the West have come to realize that we've got to be able to undertake interventions in the domestic affairs of other nations when they are carrying out brutal, genocidal, or various other kinds of horrendous actions within their countries. And even if you look at the statements of Kofi Annan, the UN Secretary General, he's also been talking about this. Secondly, in an era of weapons of mass destruction, I've found thinkers from the liberal end of the spectrum like Michael Walzer all the way to Henry Kissinger, who is the quintessential realist and believer in the Westphalian order that you've described, agreeing that in an era of weapons of mass destruction, the old principles about preventive war and intervention have got to be re-written to take account of the fact that a nation, or a group of people within a nation, can undertake a catastrophic attack against other countries with very little notice. And so, I would say the better hope for international order is, in fact, re-writing the rules to accord more with the reality. But they won't resemble that faithful adherence to the UN Charter that you've described.

Ambassador Heinbecker: I have a question in the same vein. I'm struck by the extent to which you equate legitimacy with power. There was a time, in 1945, when the United States was even more powerful than it is now. President Truman is quoted as saying at a conference in San Francisco "we all have to recognize, no matter how great our strength, that we must deny ourselves the license to do always as we please."[3] We always thought that you (the U.S.) believed in those legal principles that we were developing together under U.S. leadership. But when the Cold War was over, and the United States found itself unchallenged in power, we discovered that you didn't actually believe in those principles anymore.

And the second point I would like to make is that you said, effectively, that we have to come to some kind of understanding so that the United States can help defend the rest of us against danger. But as a matter of fact, a good part of the world thinks that what you are doing in foreign policy is *endangering* the rest of us. It's not that you're protecting us but that you're endangering us. You talk about Kosovo; in the Kosovo case if there had been a UN General Assembly vote you could have got a hundred and fifty countries in favor of intervention. In the Iraq case you could have gotten a hundred and fifty countries voting against the Iraq war. But the U.S. went ahead anyway. Throughout that whole period there was a steady stream of

---

[3] Harry S. Truman addressing the United Nations Conference on International Organization, June 26, 1945.

deprecation emanating from Washington against the UN, against UN weapons inspectors, against the restrictions that you encountered. So the difficulty that I see is that we would love to think that the United States believes in what it used to believe in, and that international order is not going to depend on U.S. exercise of power, but on U.S. restraint in the use of its power.

Robert Kagan: Obviously there has to be restraint in the use of U.S. power. But, I'm sorry, I have to differ with your perception of the Cold War. I'm amazed sometimes at the now retrospective rosy view we have of American behaviour during the Cold War. I don't think America behaved particularly badly. I think America behaved quite well, for the most part, in terms of actually fighting the Cold War. But, you know, Kosovo wasn't a bad case. If you are suggesting that bad cases make bad law then the whole Cold War was a bad case. It's impossible to look at American actions as idealistic following of international law, beginning with Harry Truman, beginning with Dean Acheson who, by the way, had contempt for the United Nations. I mean, just go back and read the things that Dean Acheson said about the United Nations; read his books, read his comments. He had contempt for the United Nations. He believed that the only security that the world would ever know would be the security that came from American economic and military power. That was a principle, a cardinal principle of the Truman administration. You go back and read NSC 68 – the strategic document of the Truman years – you're not going to find any references to international law there. You're going to find references to the desire for the United States to attain predominant power. And then, if I were to go through practically every year of the Cold War with overthrows of governments and interventions and what have you, where is the respect for international law in all of that? And so, I would say that there is too much mythology about the past which leads to too much anti-mythology about the present.

Now I quite agree that the administration's approach to many of these issues, in the kind of deprecating manner that you talk about, was unfortunate and wrong. And if I were in the administration I would be arguing that we need to take the UN very seriously indeed, and I think I would be calling for substantial reforms in the UN and substantial re-writing of some of the rules of intervention. But I think it is a very serious historical error to imagine that the United States changed completely and utterly as a result of the election in 2000. I just don't think that's true. Even as John Kerry talks about the international system that he wants to invigorate, he has to insert a line in every single one of his speeches that his hands will not be tied by allies, the United States will act when it needs to act.

Now I just want to suggest that if you don't like this United States then you haven't liked the United States for a long time – which is a perfectly reasonable response. I just think you need to see that, in my view, there has been much more continuity and that what's happened since the end of the Cold War is not that the United States changed utterly. By the way, Bill Clinton bombed Iraq for four days over the objections of members of the Security Council. Europeans *did* go to war. And I don't agree with you about the one hundred and fifty nations that would have supported it. In fact, many, many, nations around the world objected strenuously to the new doctrine that the Kosovo war seemed to indicate was being accepted, mostly by the Western States because there was significant objection in the south of the globe to the idea that Western powers could take it upon themselves to intervene if they were unhappy about the behaviour of other nations. I just don't agree that if you had taken an international vote you necessarily would have gotten full approval for Kosovo. But in any case, that's not the way the international system operates. I don't think you would suggest that no nation can act unless it has the seventy, or however many nations you need voting "yes" in the UN General Assembly before you can take action.

Ambassador Heinbecker: What you need is that the Security Council has an affirmative vote of nine members and no principal members opposing.

Robert Kagan: Which you didn't have in Kosovo…

Ambassador Heinbecker: Which you didn't have in Kosovo, but which you *would* have got – without question – if you had gone to the United Nations General Assembly, whereas you would *not* have gotten that for Iraq had you gone to the General Assembly.

Robert Kagan: I'm sure you're right but I don't think that this is a numbers game. Either we're abiding by the Security Council as the main decision-making body or we're playing 'how many votes can you get that are not the officially sanctioned UN authorization'. Which is fine. I would rather that the United States act with the general approval of most of the world. But I do think that what we need to recognize is that, since the end of the Cold War it is not so much that the United States has changed; rather, it is the international circumstances in which the United States is operating that have also changed, and we should not look back on history through such rosy glasses.

Ambassador Wright: I was intrigued by your contention that, if a country shares the perception of a threat with the United States, the United States would be willing to share in the solution, to share in kind of "steering the car down the road"; and I think that's an interesting statement. I guess our fear is that even if we share the threat, if we share the perception of the threat, even if we're willing to contribute to the cost of the gas, in the last analysis the United States will be unwilling to share the steering wheel. That's the real fear – that even if we share that basic goal, and even if we contribute our resources and take the political risks, there remains that reluctance of the

United States to share. So I'm intrigued that you've kind of opened the door there but I'm not sure it's really an accurate representation of the situation.

Robert Kagan: Well I would say that it is uncertain whether either side of my bargain can be fulfilled. I agree with you. It's not clear to me that the United States would fulfill its part of the bargain or that the other allies would fulfill theirs. And we have a perfect test case that's going on right before our eyes now and will play out over the next couple of years, which is Iran. Iran is a situation where the United States – for a variety of reasons, not all of them noble – has been willing to cede some significant influence to the three European powers: Britain, France, and Germany, in conducting negotiations with Iran. We allegedly all have the same common goal of keeping Iran from developing nuclear weapons. As we head down this path we're going to find out exactly the answer to your question. I think we're going to find out the answers to two questions. One is, are those European powers truly committed to getting rid of Iran's nuclear program, even if it ultimately has to lead to the use of military force? Or are they simply trying to negotiate, to avoid the use of military force? And the other question is, on the American side, if they are making progress, will the United States continue to let them make progress even if it has its own suspicions? I mean this is, it seems to me, a test case to find out whether we can make this thing work or not in the future. But it is very difficult, I agree. I think it's very difficult for Americans to genuinely cede influence. And I also think it's very hard to ask the rest of the world to see things through American eyes even though, as an American, to me it seems very obvious that that's what the world looks like.

Question: You spoke at length Robert, and I think very relevantly, about power over legitimacy. And you spoke of seeing things through the lens of Americans. And my question would really be: are you looking through the lens of the American public or the lens of Halliburton Corporation and Lockheed Martin? And so who is, really, the lens of Americans that you are talking about, that goal that we're looking at when we are looking at these global situations?

Robert Kagan: That sounds like a kind of rhetorical question. You really think that all of American policy is being made by Halliburton?

Question: No. My question is what role do these large multi-national corporations play – and it's certainly not transparent when they play – in the decision-making process, and what is being done to minimize the effects that these large multi-national corporations have in these very important decisions that states are making around the world on security issues?

Robert Kagan: Well, look, there's a serious question embedded in there but let me address the other question first by reminding you that when Dick Cheney was president of Halliburton he did not favour the overthrow of Saddam Hussein. I mean Halliburton's policy, if it had a policy – like all of the American oil industry's policy, if they had a policy – was to lift sanctions and normalize relations with Iraq. And the oil community in the United States was opposed to this war for a variety of reasons – not the least of which was that oilmen like stability – they don't like unpredictability. And there were oil people who were supposed to be friends of Cheney screaming about the prospect of going into this war. The interests of oil were the interests of getting to Iraqi oil and you could have done that much more cheaply than going to war.

Now when I say the lens of Americans I do mean by and large American public opinion. American public opinion is divided on Iraq now, although not nearly as divided as I would expect it to be after the whole string of bad news. It was not particularly divided in the run up to the war; there was substantial support for the war in the United States – between fifty-five and sixty-five percent consistently leading up to the war which, by the way, was much higher than the support that Bill Clinton had for going into Kosovo and higher than the support that the United States had for going into the first Persian Gulf War. And then beyond Iraq, I just think its unmistakable: you have to filter out the partisan anger. You had to filter it out when Republicans hated Clinton and everything was about beating Clinton. And you have to filter out some of that now. A lot of Democrats hate Bush and want to beat Bush. But when you look at polls on the war on terrorism, there is a pretty substantial body of American opinion in favour of the war. And by the way it may be wrong. I'm not suggesting the Americans are necessarily right and the rest of the world is wrong. But it is a very substantial body of public opinion in the United States. So unless you subscribe to the view that Americans have been mesmerized and put to sleep by the media or something you'll have to take seriously what the American public seems to want.

Question: It has been a great weekend Symposium and we've heard a number of amazing speakers. I was wondering what progress you feel is going to be made with young people assuming responsibility. There's going to be a great deal of change going on in the next decade or so, and I was wondering what you feel may happen in American-Canadian relations?

Robert Kagan: Well that's a good question. We were talking a good deal about this at my table. As I say, I do think Canada has a role to play and obviously it is not a role where Canada simply falls into line with the United States. I mean, that doesn't seem to me to be true to what Canadians think, in the first place, and I'm not even sure that's the kind of influence that Canada should exercise. It seems to me that Canada's influence should be what one might call in normal circumstances, "constructive advice". And I would say that, insofar as

Americans feel that Canadians are fundamentally on their side, they are, I believe, willing to listen to a Canada that says "perhaps you might want to think about doing that this way." I don't make any promises by the way; we have a particularly obtuse administration right now so it's a little bit tough. But I think, in general, that influence is possible. And perhaps we can have a relationship between the United States and Canada that is neither constantly obstreperous – sort of denigrating each other, and calling each other's leaders names on the one hand – or simply falling into line as a loyal ally on the other. I can see Canada occupying that kind of middle position *if it chooses to do so*. I mean it's sort of up to Canada in a way what role it plays in the American policy process. I can tell you honestly: America is not going to be *asking* Canada what it thinks about things. But, if Canada wants to assert itself, I think it can have some influence. Thank you.

· Appendix A ·

A Summary Overview of The Symposium Sessions

Paul Heinbecker[1]

1.   I think all present will agree that this has been an exceptionally good conference, for which the organizers, Joel Bell and Marsha Hanen, merit particular praise. It is rare to have such an intellectually stimulating time.

2.   I did not detect any consensus or particular agreed conclusions. There were, nonetheless, an unusually large number of stimulating insights, which I will describe in more or less chronological order.

- There seemed to be general agreement that we need, as a country, to reinvest in the instruments of our foreign policy, the three D's of diplomacy, development and defence.
- It was felt that values were not enough, that we needed to give ourselves the resources to act on those values.
- I detected hope mixed with apprehension about Ottawa's international policy review. I personally hope it will be more balanced than the economically-dominated last review, and put more emphasis on security and on values.
- Others felt that, on the contrary, Canadian foreign policy was too values-oriented, by which they appeared to mean too moralistic and pious.
- Still others felt that the values vs. interests debate was sterile, that the two work in tandem.
- There seemed to be considerable agreement on the importance of being "an (not the) international model citizen," on being an exemplar (e.g. West Europe as a model to East Europe, EU as a model to Turkey).

---

[1] Paul Heinbecker is Director of the Centre for Global Relations, Governance and Policy at Wilfrid Laurier University and Distinguished Research Fellow at the Centre for International Governance Innovation. He recently retired after 38 years with Canada's Department of Foreign Affairs, most recently serving as Ambassador to the United Nations (2000- 2003). This paper does not necessarily reflect the views of the above institutions.

- One speaker argued that
    - ..."middle power" was an inadequate paradigm, that "model citizen" was better,
    - ...we needed to be both self and other regarding,
    - ...ethical actions must consider not just objectives but also the means and the likely consequences of action.
- There was some disagreement on whether Canadian values were uniquely Canadian or, rather, universal ones.
- In a North American perspective, some thought that Canadian and American values were diverging and others thought that the divergences were overdrawn.
- One particular contradiction appeared in our attitudes. We thought that Hispanic influence in the U.S. South was important but, on the other hand, that predominately Asian migration to Canada would not affect the national character as much because newcomers to Canada largely adopt values of the communities they join.
- Some thought that the real Canada-U.S. boundary was the Mason-Dixon line and others felt, on the contrary, that the U.S. was becoming more homogenous as the North became more religious.
- Some thought that Canadians congratulated themselves a little too quickly, that in numerous values-areas the U.S. was ahead. For example, some participants claimed there was a democratic deficit in Parliament as compared to the U.S. Congress.
- Some argued that if Canadian and American roles were reversed, we would not differsignificantly, but rather would act similarly. Canadian moral superiority was a conceit.
- Others thought that Canadian moralism was less damaging than American exceptionalism.
- One panelist observed that Canada-U.S. integration was profound and continuing but that integration did not equal convergence.
- Some argued that bilateral political institutions were inadequate for the degree of economic integration that was happening.

- At the same time, although Brussels-like pan-North American institutions were not likely to develop because of the North American power disparities, a wealth of *informal* relationships were springing up to help manage relations, e.g. cross border, and state-provincial initiatives.
- All Canadian leaders needed to take the necessity of influence-building in the U.S. into greater account. The new office in Washington was seen as a first step.
- The view was expressed that some of the bilateral discussion seemed to ignore what was happening in the wider world, that a perfect diplomatic storm had been triggered by the collapse of the Soviet Union, 9/11, U.S. exceptionalism, Muslim extremism, the war on terror, Iraq, and the conflict between Islam and the West.
- According to this view, we were living through a dangerous moment, that if just one Muslim in 1000 were radicalized by events in the Middle East that could generate 1,200,000 terrorists, an outcome best avoided. This view also held that U.S. standing in the world had suffered a major setback
- As a consequence, Canadians should both help to make the U.S. border more secure and be circumspect about identifying with U.S. goals in the world.
- It was argued that multilateral cooperation, international law and norms, remained indispensable.
- Some observed that Canada was indeed seen as living by its values, but these values were also shared by others.
- The world had never been richer, or possessed of better tools, but paradoxically was ineffective in closing gapsbetween rich and poor.
- One panelist professed surprise/satisfaction that Canada had not been more homogenized by the powerful U.S.
- Canadians would be surprised at how well regarded they were, but also Canada represented a promise that was unfulfilled.
- It was argued that Canada had a role to play in modernizing U.S. policies in the Middle East in addressing the causes of terrorism.

- One panelist saw an opportunity to work with the EU, with whom Canada was demonstrably more like-minded than with the U.S.
- Another panelist saw Canadian foreign policy on the Middle East as normative, based not on realities, but on political correctness.
- One panelist cited major failures of leadership by the U.S. so that, were Ottawa to align itself with Washington, it would be going in the wrong direction.
- One panelist argued that we needed to obsess less with the U.S. and see what needed to be done in the world, in concert with others. For example, Canada should focus on climate change, where truly catastrophic consequences loom, on international epidemics that could kill millions, on protecting civilizations in conflict, on trade in small arms, on international development. All of these were more important than terrorism where, in any case, the policy framework is too narrow.
- Some thought we would waste too much time and effort repairing old institutions and creating new ones; reform is needed.
- Others urged thinking outside of the box of simple reform measures.
- One observer remarked that we had made progress in intervention after several failures had occurred, but that Iraq had sucked the oxygen out of interveners.
- The observation was made that values were being cut off at the knees in Canada for politics; also that values were not enough. Canada must build effectiveness into international institutions to give expression to the values.
- Human Rights should be at the heart of international concerns. There were dangerous new theories, e.g., the "lesser evils" as proposed by Ignatieff. We needed to take care to maintain the foundation of our values.
- One question was posed about political will: Was it not more than just cost/benefit analysis?

- One panelist argued that sometimes it was important just to do what's right rather than analyzing costs and benefits.
- There was a role for Canadian companies in promoting Canadian values – especially those companies that flew the Canadian flag for business/brand purposes and that got government assistance.
- When Canadian companies were accused in the Congo of violating the OECD corruption and other guidelines, no public hearing had been held in Canada. There had been very little up-take in Canada on the UN's Global Compact on corporate behaviour.
- On the future, some wondered whether the first half of the 21st century would see a repeat of the second half of the 20th century, when the Germans were too big to be controlled by Europe but not big enough to dominate. Likewise the U.S. was too big to be controlled by the world but not big enough to dominate.
- Would the "German problem" of the last 50 years be replaced with the "U.S. problem" in the next 50?

Some participants expressed enthusiasm for specific themes and sought opportunities for further consideration of:

- rules and norms post-conflict;
- clash of civilizations risk;
- the privatization of intervention;
- creation of a new Human Rights committee;
- Canada's leading role in reconciliation efforts;
- strengthening UN collective decision-making;
- the distinction between insurgents and terrorists;
- African issues;
- UN reform;
- the role of the media;
- Canada's independent imperatives.

· Appendix B ·

DISCUSSION TOPICS

Introduction

During the final session on Sunday May 16th, 2004 Symposium participants were invited to reflect on what they had heard over the course of the weekend, and discuss their views surrounding five aspects of Canadian values and foreign policy. Each participant selected one of the five discussion topics. Educators, community leaders and professionals were recruited to co-facilitate each discussion group together with a youth leader. The facilitators ensured that the round-table discussions were kept on topic, and that everyone had a chance to express his or her views. The facilitators also prepared a short summary of the discussion in their group which was then reported to the final plenary session.

Facilitators were provided with sample questions to ignite the discussion; however the purpose of these sessions was to allow participants to drive the conversation with their ideas and their views. The goal was to assess Canada's values in the specific topic areas, to craft a vision of how those values can contribute to Canada's future international role, and to determine what can be done now and what paths must be taken in future to realize that vision. Though there was variation among the groups, participants all indicated that the means by which Canada participates in the international community is equally important to the goals we achieve, that while we work internationally we must continue to work at home to improve the implementation of our values in our own country, and that a values-based foreign policy is something that Canada should strive to achieve.

The following is by no means an exhaustive account of what took place during the discussion sessions, but is intended to give the reader an indication of some of the issues and themes that were considered by our participants. The Foundation is deeply indebted to all facilitators and participants for their contributions.

Business & Corporations

Participants were asked to address the question of what role Canadian businesses should undertake in upholding Canadian values, how business and communities can work together, where the responsibility of government lies in regulating business, and how socially responsible corporations can be encouraged and celebrated.

The starting premise for the discussion was that every time a Canadian company seeks to do business abroad, sets up an overseas operations, procures raw or finished goods or services, there is a potential opportunity for conveying Canadian values and having an influence on conditions in the globe.

Canadian values that businesses and corporations can uphold abroad include fair business practice, transparency, accountability, a community focus, and stakeholder engagement. The group envisioned a future for Canada where our businesses were the champions of engaging consultation processes, where they worked to ensure their presence minimized harm and maximized quality of living in their host communities, and where high standards of fair business practices were met. The vision extended to a Canadian government that pursued policies to make corporate social responsibility profitable, and provided sufficient education about international business to allow individuals to make socially conscious personal choices.

The group suggested that within Canada, better education and access to information was necessary. The general public, typically, lacks the information it needs about companies – international and in many cases domestic operations as well – to make fully informed choices. More transparency about how business and governments negotiate and work, in both the host and home country, is needed, as is better education in universities, workplaces and civil society about the circumstances and challenges faced in international business operations.

To achieve this vision, the group felt Canadians need to:

- bring Corporate Social Responsibility into the classroom, not only to business students at the post-secondary level but also into the elementary and secondary schools;

- work towards eliminating the vilification of corporations, and instead examine how they work, what they do right and what they can improve;

- endeavour, as employees and consumers, to make ethically and socially responsible individual choices about the companies

    to which we give our business, or

    for which we work, or

    from which we purchase services;

- support the development of independent and unbiased organization and information sources that analyze the behaviour of businesses and provide objective and sound information to the public;

- encourage Canadian businesses to develop closer partnerships with NGOs, which are usually already working in local communities and government departments (e.g. CIDA) which have extensive country-specific resources. Such groups could facilitate local engagement and dialogue about the differing roles a particular business could play before it actually moves into a country;

- engage with businesses in a way that acknowledges and builds on the economic argument with a view to showing them that being socially responsible actors and being profitable are not and should not be mutually exclusive;

- reinforce the positive standards within which many companies are working, and celebrate even those companies (e.g. Nike and Talisman) who have made mistakes but who have acknowledged them, and who are working to rectify and learn from them;

- work with foreign governments on a capacity-building form of engagement to assist them in setting up strict standards for the operation of domestic and foreign businesses in their countries;

- value business' efforts to assist local communities, such as the support of their local employees, as in the example of support for African employees with AIDS.

Justice & Peacekeeping

This group was asked to comment on the role of Canada's military, the quality and quantity of our participation in UN peacekeeping missions, the institutions and areas where Canada can promote human rights, and what improvements Canada might make in order to become a better example of a just society.

Focusing internally, the group acknowledged that Canada does have many social injustices to address, the largest being the poverty and poor quality of life of our First Nations populations. We also have to sharpen our tools for international participation, specifically by refocusing and rebuilding our military and our other international agencies.

The Canadian values of maintaining a just and peaceful society, of upholding human rights above all else and of caring both for ourselves and others are values that we must continue to bring to the international community. The group envisioned Canada as a "polar bear with two big arms reaching out to hug the world". Canada would be seen as a country continually working to improve justice and peace in our own society, while extending our help to the world. This vision of Canada sees us with a peacekeeping force that is strong and reliable, working not necessarily everywhere but where we are needed most and where we can be the most useful. Canadian organizations other than our military will also be recognized as being competent international actors, working throughout the world in humanitarian operations, education and community building.

To achieve this vision, the group felt Canadians need to:

- work simultaneously to improve peace and justice domestically and internationally;
- identify where we want to work in the world geographically, and what issues we want to focus on – Canada can no longer be everything to everyone;
- work in better and more competent ways in the internation-

al community – we need to concentrate our resources, focus on areas where we have sound expertise and work to maximize our international contributions while minimizing our strain at home;

- sharpen and focus our military power, and use the resources allocated to our military to create a force that can achieve our international goals;
- contribute to justice and peacekeeping through our armed forces, but also build our other international arms – humanitarian work, non-profit organizations and education;
- establish values-based criteria by which we can judge our participation in UN peacekeeping missions, and focus on quality peacekeeping participation;
- reconsider our role and our abilities not only in peacekeeping, but also in peacemaking, peace building and enforcing peace;
- continue to act in cooperation with others in multilateral international activities.

Aid, Trade, Non-profits, & Individuals

Asked to comment on Canada's aid and trade policies, and the role of non-profits and individuals in the international community, the group began by turning the microscope inward. They suggested that Canada needs to look at what is going on inside our country, and improve our internal society while working concurrently on external societal challenges. What the group felt we have to offer the world is the experience of looking at problems through a variety of lenses, and this is a unique contribution Canada can bring to the world.

Canada's 'best practices', or values, include participatory decision-making, working towards sustainability, and increasing international connectivity. The group envisioned a Canada that does what is right because it is the right thing to do. The vision sees Canada as a trusted partner in all areas, with substantial aid packages that work toward reducing poverty and focus on achieving long-term effects in local communities. We should foster strong trade relationships that benefit both Canada and her trade partners, without exploitation; and we should encourage dedicated individuals and NGOs who work throughout the world to build communities, enrich education and encourage diversity.

To achieve this vision, the group felt Canada needs to:
- work towards providing shelter, clothing, food, health care and education to meet basic human needs in the world, thus reducing both poverty and addressing many of the root causes of conflict;
- ask ourselves where we have the expertise to be working in the international arena, and focus our aid efforts in these areas;
- work simultaneously to improve conditions in our country, while helping places in the world with equally serious problems to develop their own solutions;
- recognize trade policy as situational, and continue to eval-

uate each situation based on who might be hurt and who can be helped;

- implement a clear trade policy focusing on our moral obligations to act so that there is no exploitation of us or of others;
- insist on accountability with all our international partners, including governments, NGOs and international institutions;
- create trusting relationships through communication and consultation at the local level;
- address openly the morally vexing question of cheap labour;
- aim for a larger and longer-term impact for our aid dollars;
- recognize that we are deluded about how much we can afford to contribute, and responsibly increase our available aid dollars.

Education, Arts, Culture & Media

Participants were asked to look at the role of Canada's media in expressing Canadian values, our role in education around the world, and how we can promote cultural exchanges. The group felt that internally, Canada needs to expand our cultural vision of Canada beyond a bilingual society, and emphasize internally our multiculturalism and our pride in it. We need to examine our values and clearly define them, then express those values through our art, culture, media and education.

The group acknowledged that how Canada sees itself and how we are really acting internationally has changed, but felt that we should remain dedicated to several of the values we see ourselves as holding: the primacy of the truth, the values of consistency, accountability and integrity, the importance of education and a commitment to multiculturalism.

The group envisioned Canada as a country that looks beyond self-interest in its international actions, and works towards something larger: a focus on human values inside our country and abroad. Canada can lead the world in new ideas; we should promote discussion, dialogue and diversity. We can work to build educational systems that incorporate the concepts of democracy, integrity and diversity. We can be bold about the inclusion of ideas, inspire discussion, face differences in politics and religion. Finally, the group envisioned a Canadian media that was respected internationally for objective reporting and a vigorous commitment to the truth. Through our example we can inspire ethical leadership, open dialogue and a commitment to human values.

To achieve this vision, Canada should:
- recognize itself as a country of balance, one which appreciates the distinction between doing what is right and doing what needs to be done, and works to find the common ground between the two;
- celebrate our historical cultural struggle between unity,

and diversity of opinion, and recognize it is our experience with that struggle that we can bring to the world;
- encourage diversity of ideas in the world, while finding common ground among its players;
- reject the "CNN Factor" and challenge mainstream media, seeking out a variety of opinions to educate ourselves about the true nature of international events;
- invest in education, art and culture;
- assist in the development of educational systems abroad that promote diversity, dialogue and idea-sharing.

Governance, Politics, Institutions & Reform

Participants were asked to comment on Canada's role in building good governance, both on an international scale and within other states. What is our role in developing democracy, how should Canada engage in international institutions, and how can our country work with other states to achieve balance between sovereignty and international co-operation? The group felt that Canada is at a point where we need to question how aggressive we should be in promoting our values, and question which of our values are uniquely Canadian and which are truly universal or human values. We should focus on promoting the latter.

Canada is dedicated to five core values that it should continue to bring into the international community: good governance, non-violence, consensus building, institution building and respect for multiculturalism. While we have little military or even moral authority to promote these values, Canada's authority abroad derives from our dedication to continuously questioning and struggling to improve these areas within our own country, and it is crucial we continue this process with our internal governance and institutions as we work internationally.

This group envisioned a Canada that was known internationally for its expertise in building sustainable institutions, for its government's partnerships with NGOs and local communities, and for its commitment to peaceful resolutions to problems. The group saw a Canada that demonstrated good governance and good citizenship not only through its politics and its institutions, but also through its civil society, developing strong local partnerships that enable us to focus on education and training, technical development and technology transfer, and capacity building within communities. Canada can be at the forefront of international assistance, institutional development and government reform. Finally, Canada should be known to be committed to high quality participation. While it is nice to see Canadians holding high and prestigious positions, it should not a priority for us – if we hold these position, we want to be there because we have earned it through our hard work and commitment "on the ground".

To achieve this vision, Canadians should:

- search for less invasive means by which we can promote our values;
- maintain and build strong partnerships between our government and NGOs;
- work pre-emptively through environmental scans and develop early warning systems in areas that may need our help;
- set an international example by ethically and responsibly dealing with issues that arise inside our country;
- focus our aid on local institutional and government capacity building.

Conclusion

The indication from the discussion groups is that a values-driven Canadian foreign policy could indeed work to promote balance in the international community and build trust among its many actors. Canada is not in a military or even economic position to balance other powers; however we are in a position to bring balanced dialogue to the table. We can lead through the example of our approach to international involvement, balancing realism with vision, internal and international efforts to improve peace, justice and good government, and a diversity of ideas within a unity of cooperation. We can build trust by acting fairly, consulting with individuals in local communities, building partnerships with accountable organizations, and striving to set an example through our own actions.

Contributors

Joel Bell is Chair of the Sheldon Chumir Foundation for Ethics in Leadership and of the Council for Canadian-American Relations based in New York. Born in Montreal, he was educated in economics and law at McGill University, before pursuing doctoral studies at Harvard. He was involved in the creation of Petro-Canada, serving as Executive Vice President until his departure to establish the Canada Development Investment Corporation (CDIC) as founding President and CEO. He was also Chairman of Power DirecTV, and subsequently founded and served as President and CEO of the Maxlink Group of Companies. Mr. Bell has served extensively as a consultant for the federal government, including among others: Senior Economic Advisor to Prime Minister Pierre Elliott Trudeau; Special Advisor to the Department of Energy, Mines and Resources; Special Counsel to the CRTC; Chairman of the Working Group on Foreign Investment; Special Advisor to the Minister of Consumer and Corporate Affairs; and Consultant to the Economic Council of Canada. He has also extended his work as consultant to the Government of Indonesia, the Province of Newfoundland and Labrador, the City of Montreal, and a variety of corporate and public sector bodies. He is the author of several articles and reports.

David J. Bercuson is Director of the Centre for Military and Strategic Studies at the University of Calgary, and Vice President of the Canadian Defence and Foreign Affairs Institute, also based in Calgary. He has published on a wide range of topics specializing in modern Canadian politics, Canadian defence and foreign policy, and Canadian military history. He has written, coauthored, or edited over 30 popular and academic books and does regular commentary for television and radio. He has written for the Globe and Mail, the Toronto Star, the Calgary Herald, the National Post and other newspapers.

In 1988, Professor Bercuson was elected to the Royal Society of Canada and in 2003 was appointed an Officer of the Order of Canada. He is also the 2002 winner of the J. B. Tyrrell Historical Medal from the Royal Society of Canada. From 1989 to 1996 he was Dean of the Faculty of Graduate Studies at the University of Calgary.

In 1997 Dr. Bercuson was appointed Special Advisor to the Minister of National Defence on the Future of the Canadian Forces, and was a member of the Minister's Monitoring Committee from 1997 to 2003. He received the 2004 Vimy Award sponsored by the Conference of Defence Association Institute (CDAI) which recognizes Canadians who have made a significant and outstanding contribution to the defence and security of our nation and the preservation of our democratic values.

David Bercuson's newest book, co-authored with Holger Herwig, is *A Christmas in Washington: Churchill, Roosevelt and the Making of the Grand Alliance*. It will be published in New York, London and Toronto in the fall of 2005.

Michael Byers has been Canada Research Chair in Global Politics and International Law at the University of British Columbia since 2004.

Prior to this, he was Professor of Law and Director of the Center for Canadian Studies at Duke University. Professor Byers is the author of *Custom, Power and the Power of Rules* (Cambridge University Press, 1999), editor of *The Role of Law in International Politics* (Oxford University Press, 2000), translator of Wilhelm Grewe, *The Epochs of International Law* (Walter de Gruyter, 2000), and co-editor of *United States Hegemony and the Foundations of International Law* (Cambridge University Press, 2003). Most recently, he is the author of *War Law* (Atlantic Books / Douglas & McIntyre, 2005). He is a regular contributor to the *London Review of Books* and *The Globe and Mail.*

Andrew Cohen is a native of Montreal, Quebec, and was educated at The Choate School, McGill University, Carleton University and the University of Cambridge. In a career of twenty-seven years, he has worked in Europe, the United States and Canada for *United Press International*, *The Financial Post*, *Time*, and the *The Globe and Mail*, where he was an award-winning columnist, editorialist and foreign correspondent in Washington, D.C. He writes a weekly column for the *Ottawa Citizen*, which appears in the Canwest Newspapers. Since 2001, he has been a professor of journalism and international affairs at Carleton University. He has written and edited three best-selling books. The most recent is *While Canada Slept: How We Lost Our Place in the World*, which was a finalist for the Governor-General's Award for Non-Fiction and a *Globe and Mail* Notable Book in 2003.

Madelaine Drohan is an award-winning author and journalist who has covered business and politics in Canada, Europe and Africa during a twenty-five-year career. Her work appears in *The Economist, Walrus Magazine, The Globe and Mail, and The Toronto Star*, among other publications. She has worked for *The Globe and Mail*, as a foreign correspondent and columnist, *The Financial Post, Maclean's* and *The Canadian Press*. Her book, *Making a Killing: How and why corporations use armed force to do business*, was published in 2003 by Random House of Canada and in 2004 by The Lyons Press in the United States. It won the Ottawa Book Award and was short-listed for the National Business Book of the Year Award in 2004. She is a member of the board of the North-South Institute, an independent research institute focused on international development, and of the Media & Democracy Group, which promotes good governance through a stronger media in emerging democracies. Whenever possible, she conducts journalism workshops for media in Africa and Southeast Asia, with a special focus on business and investigative journalism. She was awarded a Reuters Fellowship at Oxford University in 1998, and the Hyman Solomon Award for Excellence in Public Policy Journalism in 2001. She is a 2004-2005 Media Fellow at the Sheldon Chumir Foundation for Ethics in Leadership and the 2004-2005 Journalist in Residence at Carleton University.

Marsha Hanen is President of the Sheldon Chumir Foundation for Ethics in Leadership, having previously served for ten years as President and Vice-Chancellor of the University of Winnipeg. Prior to that she was Professor of Philosophy and Dean of the Faculty of General Studies at the University of Calgary. She has published widely in philosophy of law, philosophy of science and feminist theory and has spoken frequently to community groups on policy for post-secondary education, women and equality, curriculum change, interdisciplinary education and issues in ethics and law. She holds AB and MA degrees in Philosophy from Brown University and a Ph.D from

Brandeis University. A recipient of the Order of Canada and an Honorary Doctorate of Laws from York University, Dr. Hanen has served on Boards in the fields of education, women's equality, health, the arts, banking, community development and international affairs.

Paul Heinbecker is the inaugural director of the Centre for Global Relations, Governance and Policy at Wilfrid Laurier University and Distinguished Research Fellow at the independent research Centre for International Governance Innovation (CIGI) in Waterloo. These appointments follow a distinguished career with the Canadian Department of Foreign Affairs.

Mr. Heinbecker joined the Department of External Affairs in 1965, with postings abroad in Ankara and Stockholm, and in Paris with the Permanent Delegation of Canada to the Organization for Economic Co-operation and Development. In Ottawa, Mr. Heinbecker served, *inter alia*, as Director of the United States General Relations Division and as Chairman of the Policy Development Secretariat in External Affairs. From 1985 to 1989, he was Minister in Washington.

From 1989 to 1992, Mr. Heinbecker served as Prime Minister Mulroney's Chief Foreign Policy Advisor and speech writer and as Assistant Secretary to the Cabinet for Foreign and Defence Policy. In 1992, he was named Ambassador to Germany, where he promoted German investment in Canada. In 1996, he was appointed Assistant Deputy Minister, Global and Security Policy, and Political Director in the Department of Foreign Affairs and International Trade. Mr. Heinbecker led the interdepartmental task force on Kosovo and helped to negotiate the end of that war. He was also head of the delegation for the negotiation of the Climate Change Convention in Kyoto.

In the summer of 2000, Mr. Heinbecker was appointed Ambassador and Permanent Representative of Canada to the United Nations, where he was a leading advocate for the creation of the International Criminal Court and a proponent of compromise on Iraq.

Mr. Heinbecker received his Bachelor of Arts Degree (Honours) from Waterloo Lutheran University in 1965, and an Honorary Doctorate of Law from the same institution in 1993. He was Alumnus of the Year at WLU in 2003.

He is married to Ayşe Köymen; they have two daughters, Yasemin and Céline.

Karl Henriques was born in Winnipeg, Manitoba, and raised in Kingston, Jamaica. At universities in British Columbia, Nova Scotia, Ontario, Québec and Mannheim in Germany he studied both the external sources of the political turmoil that the island of Jamaica suffered during the 1970s and 1980s and, especially, the emergence of the European Union as a global actor. He is currently an Assistant Professor of Comparative Politics (European) and Political Theory in the Department of Political Science at the University of Regina.

Professor Henriques is an Executive Board Member of the European Community Studies Association-Canada (ECSA-C), and a founder of the newly established *EUCAnet*. (*EUCAnet* is a Canada-wide network of select experts providing analytic media commentary on emergent European affairs.) Professor Henriques presents and writes regularly on political, economic, cultural, and foreign policy developments in the European Union. His research with members of the Group of Policy Advisers (GOPA) to the President of the European Commission, and with European and Member State treaty and constitutional negotiators, will form the basis of a book he is writing that Claus Offe has already referred to as a "powerful synthetic effort". This work assesses Europe's potential as a model for strengthening political, economic, cultural, and foreign policy dimensions.

Robert Kagan is Senior Associate at the Carnegie Endowment for International Peace. His most recent book, *Of Paradise and Power* (Knopf, 2003), was on the *New York Times* bestseller list for ten weeks and the *Washington Post* bestseller list for 14 weeks. It was also a bestseller in the United Kingdom, France, Germany, Spain, Italy, the Netherlands, and Canada. It has been translated into over 20 languages including French, German, Italian, Spanish, Greek, Dutch, Danish, Polish, Czech, Portuguese, Hebrew, Korean, Finnish, and Japanese.

Kagan writes a monthly column on world affairs for the *Washington Post*, and is a Contributing Editor at both the *Weekly Standard* and the *New Republic*. He served in the State Department from 1984-1988 as a member of the Policy Planning Staff, as principal speechwriter for Secretary of State George P. Shultz, and as Deputy for Policy in the Bureau of Inter-American Affairs. He is a graduate of Yale University and Harvard University's Kennedy School of Government.

He is the author of *A Twilight Struggle: American Power and Nicaragua, 1977-1990* (Free Press, 1996), and is co-editor with William Kristol of *Present Dangers: Crisis and Opportunity in American Foreign Policy* (Encounter Books, June 2000.) He is currently at work on a history of American foreign policy, which will be published by Knopf. He was born in Athens, Greece, in 1958. He is married to Victoria Nuland, a career foreign service officer, and has two children: Elena, 8, and David, 6.

Ahmad Kamal served as a professional diplomat in the Ministry of Foreign Affairs of Pakistan for forty years until his retirement in 1999.

During this period he held diplomatic postings in India, Belgium, France, the Soviet Union, Saudi Arabia, the Republic of Korea, and with the United Nations both in Geneva and in New York. During his decade-long assignment as Ambassador and Permanent Representative of Pakistan to the United

Nations, Ambassador Kamal held many of the highest elective posts: Vice President of the General Assembly; President of the Economic and Social Council; Chairman of the Consultations on the Role of NGOs at the United Nations; Chairman of the Working Group on Informatics; Chairman of the Board of Trustees of the United Nations Institute of Training and Research; and a Member of the United Nations Advisory Committee on Administrative and Budgetary Questions. He was the chief negotiator of Pakistan in the Uruguay Round negotiations which led to the establishment of the World Trade Organization.

Ambassador Kamal continues to be a Senior Fellow of the United Nations Institute of Training and Research, and is also the President of The Ambassador's Club at the United Nations. He is the author of important publications, on disarmament, management, multilateralism, global economic issues, and on technical aspects of informatics and information technology, and is an Honorary Visiting Professor at several universities in the United States.

He has received numerous honours in Pakistan and in the other countries of his posting.

Clifford Krauss has been the Canada Bureau Chief of the *New York Times* since January 2002. In his previous 12 years at the *Times*, he was the Buenos Aires Bureau Chief and covered a wide variety of beats including the New York City Police Department, Congress and the State Department. He worked in Mexico in the late 1970s for *United Press International* and covered Central America for the *Wall Street Journal* between 1984 and 1987. He was the Edward R. Murrow Fellow at the Council on Foreign Relations in 1988-89. He has published articles in many publications including *Foreign Affairs, GQ* and *The Wilson Quarterly*. He is the author of *Inside Central America: Its People, Politics and History*.

Roy S. Lee has been with the United Nations since 1967, working in the fields of human rights, law of the sea, international humanitarian law, peacekeeping and settlement of disputes. As Director of the Division for the codification and development of international law, he was Secretary of the law-making bodies including the International Law Commission and the Sixth (Legal) Committee of the General Assembly. He was Executive Secretary of the United Nations Diplomatic Conference of Plenipotentiaries on the Establishment of an International Criminal Court and currently Senior Special Fellow of the United Nations Institute for Training and Research. Dr. Lee teaches at Columbia University Law School and has published five books in the field of space law, law of the sea, and the International Court of Justice, and some thirty articles on various subjects of international law.

Arnoldo Listre, a long-term diplomat in the Foreign Service of Argentina, began his career in the Cabinet of the Argentine Minister of Foreign Affairs in 1964. From 1966 to 1974, he served in Argentina's Embassy in Paraguay. From 1975 he served as part of Argentina's Permanent Mission to the Organization of American States in Washington, D.C. and then from 1979 as Ambassador Extraordinary and Plenipotentiary in Argentina's Embassy in Costa Rica.

In 1981 he became Chief of Cabinet in the Ministry of Foreign Affairs, and then Director of International Organizations. In 1982 he was Permanent Representative *Pro Tempore* to the United Nations in New York, and subsequently Director of Foreign Policy in the Ministry of Foreign Affairs in Argentina. Beginning in 1985 he served as Ambassador to Nigeria and in 1987 became Ambassador to Hungary.

Ambassador Listre was Chairman of the Argentine Delegation to the Rio de la Plata Administrative Commission in 1989. He served as Consul General in New York for three years, and from 1994 was Ambassador to the Russian Federation.

He was Argentina's Permanent Representative to the United Nations in New York for four years commencing in 2000. He is currently a Member of the Cabinet of the Minister of Foreign Affairs in Buenos Aires.

Kathleen Mahoney is a law professor at the University of Calgary, and has dedicated much of her research to internationally critical issues in human rights. She has been a professor at the university for 25 years during which she has held many international fellowships and lectureships throughout Australia and the United States.

Having published extensively in constitutional law and women's rights, Professor Mahoney has participated as counsel and advocate on projects such as the genocide action against Serbia and Montenegro in the International Court of Justice for Bosnia and Herzegovina. She has also organized and participated in collaborative human rights projects in Geneva, Australia, New Zealand, South Africa, Spain, Israel, China and the United Nations.

Kathleen Mahoney is currently Research Director for a major research project examining the substance and process of the Canadian government's Dispute Resolution Initiative to settle the abuse claims of Aboriginal residential school survivors.

Among the many awards she has received, Professor Mahoney was elected to the Royal Society of Canada in 1997 for her academic achievements. In 1998 she was selected as a Fulbright Scholar to pursue her research work at Harvard University and in the same year was also appointed by the Federal Cabinet to Chair the Board of Directors of the International Centre for Human Rights and Democratic Development. In 2000, the Canadian Bar Association presented her with the Bertha Wilson Touchstone Award in recognition of her outstanding accomplishments in the promotion of equality in Canada. In 2001, she was awarded the Governor General's medal.

George Russell is Executive Editor of Fox News, the largest cable news network in the United States. He was born in Calgary Alberta, and earned his B.A. (History) at the University of Calgary. He began his career as a journalist with the Toronto Globe & Mail, and in 1974 as staff writer for TIME's Canadian edition, based in Montreal. In 1978 he became Associate Editor in the World section for TIME in the U.S., based in New York, and in 1979 Buenos Aires Bureau Chief responsible for coverage of all of South America, for the Time-Life News Service, based in Argentina.

Mr. Russell has been Senior Editor for all of TIME's international editions, as well as for the U.S. edition of TIME, dealing with areas such as education, religion, and social policy. From 1997-2001 he was Editor, TIME Canada and TIME Latin America, and International Editor (The Americas) for the U.S. edition of TIME, responsible for the content and editorial budgets of the Canadian and Latin American editions. From 2001-2003 he was President and Editor, TIME Canada, responsible for both the corporate and editorial operations of the weekly newsmagazine in Canada.

Mr. Russell's professional awards include the 1988 Hancock Award for Business Journalism, co-winner, for helping to edit TIME's coverage of the 1987 stock market crash. From 1988-1995 he was a member of the program advisory board on Latin American Affairs, Center for Inter-American Relations (Americas Society), New York City. In 2003 Mr. Russell became special assistant (*pro bono*) to New York City Commissioner for Cultural Affairs Kate D. Levin, and in 2004-2005 he chaired the jury for the Lionel Gelber Prize for the best book in English on foreign policy.

Jennifer Mary Welsh was born in Regina, Saskatchewan. She holds a B.A. in Political Science from the University of Saskatchewan and a Masters and Doctorate in International Relations from the University of Oxford where she studied as a Rhodes Scholar. She is a former Jean Monnet Fellow of the European University Institute in Florence, and was a Cadieux Research Fellow in the Policy Planning Staff of the Canadian Department of Foreign Affairs and International Trade. Dr. Welsh has taught international relations at the University of Toronto, McGill University, and the Central European University. She is currently University Lecturer in International Relations at the University of Oxford, and a Fellow of Somerville College. In 2005, she was the Distinguished Visiting Fellow at Massey College, University of Toronto.

In addition to her academic career, Professor Welsh spent five years in the private sector – first as a consultant with the international firm, McKinsey and Co., and subsequently as a partner in d~Code, a research and strategy firm focused on the 'Nexus Generation.' She is a member of the Banff Forum, the Pacific Council on Foreign Relations, and the International Institute of Strategic Studies, and is on the Editorial Board of the Round Table.

Dr. Welsh is the author and editor of five books and a series of articles on international relations. Her current research covers Human Rights and Humanitarian Intervention, and the prospects for North American integration. Her most recent work is *At Home in the World: Canada's Global Vision for the 21st Century* (HarperCollins Canada, 2004).

David Wright is Kenneth and Patricia Taylor Distinguished Visiting Professor in Foreign Affairs at Victoria College, University of Toronto. He was Canadian Ambassador to NATO from 1997-2003. Previously he was Canadian Ambassador to Spain (1994-97) and Assistant Deputy Minister for Europe in the Department of Foreign Affairs. Ambassador Wright has held various positions in economic and policy planning bureaus of the Department of Foreign Affairs and International Trade, and is widely published on foreign affairs and economic issues. He is a graduate of McGill and Columbia Universities.

Sheldon Chumir Foundation for Ethics in Leadership

THIRD SYMPOSIUM AND GALA DINNER

Canadian Values in the World Community: Building Trust, Balancing Global Power

Programme - May 14th to 16th, 2004

Friday May 14th

Keynote Address and Reception

CANADIAN VALUES, CANADA'S ROLE: MYTHS AND REALITIES

Joel Bell - Chair
Chair of the Board of the Sheldon Chumir Foundation for Ethics in Leadership

Andrew Cohen
distinguished journalist, Associate Professor of Journalism and International Affairs, Carleton University, and author of *While Canada Slept: How We Lost Our Place in the World*

Jennifer Welsh
political scientist and expert in ethics in international relations at Oxford University; author of a forthcoming book on Canada in a post 9-11 world

Saturday May 15th
Panel

CANADA IN A NORTH AMERICAN PERSPECTIVE

David Taras - Moderator
Professor in the Faculty of Communication & Culture at the University of Calgary

David Bercuson
Professor of History and Director of the Centre for Military and Strategic Studies, University of Calgary

George Russell
Journalist with Fox News in New York, formerly Senior Editor Time Magazine

Clifford Krauss
New York Times Canada Bureau Chief

Luncheon Address

CANADA ON THE WORLD STAGE

Marsha Hanen - Chair
President of the Sheldon Chumir Foundation for Ethics in Leadership

Paul Heinbecker
former Canadian Ambassador to the UN, Director of the Laurier Centre for Global Relations, Governance and Policy at Wilfrid Laurier University

Afternoon Panel

CANADIAN VALUES: AN INTERNATIONAL PERSPECTIVE

(Saturday Afternoon Panel continued)

Michael Keren - Moderator
Professor and Canada Research Chair in Communication, Culture, & Civil Society, University of Calgary

Arnoldo Listre
member of the Cabinet of the Minister of Foreign Affairs, Argentina and former Ambassador to the UN from Argentina

Ahmad Kamal
former Ambassador to the UN from Pakistan and founder of the *Ambassador's Club*

Karl Henriques
University of Regina Assistant Professor of Comparative Politics and Political Theory

Sunday May 16th
Panel

INTERNATIONAL INSTITUTIONS: CANADA'S ROLE

Aritha van Herk - Moderator
Member of the Board of the Sheldon Chumir Foundation for Ethics in Leadership

Michael Byers
Professor of International Law and Director of the Canadian Studies Program, Duke University

Roy S. Lee
former secretary of the Commission to create the International Criminal Court, Professor, Columbia University Law School

David Wright
Kenneth and Patricia Taylor Distinguished Visiting Professor in Foreign Affairs, Victoria College, University of Toronto and former Canadian Ambassador to NATO

Kathleen Mahoney
Professor of Law, University of Calgary, and Chair of the Board, International Centre for Human Rights and Democratic Development

(Sunday continued)

Luncheon Address

CANADIAN BUSINESS IN AN INTERNATIONAL CONTEXT

Dr. Ronald Bond - Chair
Provost and Vice President (Academic), University of Calgary

Madelaine Drohan
well-known journalist and author of *Making a Killing: How and Why Corporations Use Armed Force*

Afternoon Discussion Sessions
Brief Reports, General Discussion and Summary Remarks

Colin Jackson - Chair
President and CEO of the EPCOR CENTRE for the Performing Arts

Paul Heinbecker
former Canadian Ambassador to the UN, Director of the Laurier Centre for Global Relations, Governance and Policy at Wilfrid Laurier University

GALA DINNER

6:15 pm Reception

Closing Address

Hon. Ron Ghitter Q.C. - Chair
former Alberta MLA, former member of the Canadian Senate, Board Member of the Sheldon Chumir Foundation for Ethics in Leadership

Robert Kagan
author of *Of Paradise and Power: America and Europe in the New World Order* (2003) and Senior Associate of the Carnegie Endowment for International Peace

Sheldon M. Chumir

Sheldon Chumir was, by anyone's standards, an outstanding human being. Born in Calgary on December 3rd, 1940, he excelled at virtually every endeavour he undertook. As a Rhodes scholar, tax lawyer, rock concert promoter, politician, civil libertarian, public interest advocate, hockey player, businessman and many other things, Sheldon worked and played with passionate intensity. His life was characterized by intelligence, humour, hard work, decency, and fairness. As a student, Sheldon achieved excellence in sports, academic pursuits, and student activities. After completing a law degree at the University of Alberta as his class's gold medallist in 1963, Sheldon was awarded a Rhodes scholarship to study at Oxford. When he returned to Canada in 1965 he pursued careers in the law, business and politics.

These accomplishments were impressive, but Sheldon wished to help those whose civil rights had been infringed and so he left his practice as a tax lawyer in 1976 and set up his own firm to defend the rights of the powerless. His commitment to civil liberties was unmatched; typically, he worked *pro bono* for causes that he felt were important. He also taught civil liberties at the University of Calgary Law School.

Sheldon loved to debate issues, recognizing that principled and respectful disagreement was vital to the democratic process. His approach to issues was characterized by careful reflection and independence of mind. His educational and legal experiences turned him into a vigorous supporter of public education, civil rights and individual freedoms. Whatever the issue, Sheldon could always be found acting for the underdog – for the person or group he felt needed his help.

As a politician Sheldon was convinced that voters wanted political leaders to strive for fairness and honesty in all of their dealings. He rejected the notion that politics was a blood sport where only the ruthless could survive. His political instincts helped him to get elected in 1986 – the first Liberal elected in Calgary in over fifteen years – as a Member of Alberta's Legislative Assembly for the riding of Calgary-Buffalo. He was re-elected in 1989.

In addition to his unique personality, Sheldon also had a unique perspective in that he was familiar with the internal dynamics of both the public and private sectors. He was, therefore, able to conceptualize and to criticize the strengths and weaknesses of both systems.

Sheldon sensed that our society suffers from a crisis of leadership. Both in government and in business, he perceived that people had lost faith in the capacity of established institutions to meet the needs of those they served. The first sign of this loss of faith was the public's increasing reluctance to spend time reflecting on issues relating to the public good.

When he died at the age of just fifty-one in January of 1992 following a brief illness, there was an enormous outpouring of respect and admiration not only from his many friends, but from people from all walks of life who felt how keenly they would miss his integrity, his dedication to humanitarian causes, his gentle humour and sense of fun, and his genuine warmth toward people from every corner of the community. Following his death, Sheldon was recognized by the Law Society of Alberta and posthumously awarded the Distinguished Service Award for Service to the Community. The inscription on the award reads in part:

Founder of the Alberta Civil Liberties Association, he was a tireless champion in pro bono work for various unpopular causes and wrongs to be set right. His spirit lives on through the Sheldon Chumir Foundation for Ethics in Leadership, created as his last wish as a legacy for Canada.